TOTAL ENGAGEMENT

Using Games and Virtual Worlds to Change the
Way People Work and Businesses Compete

Byron Reeves

J. Leighton Read

Harvard Business Press
Boston, Massachusetts

No part of this publication may be reproduced, stored in or introduced into a retrieval system, or transmitted, in any form, or by any means (electronic, mechanical, photocopying, recording, or otherwise), without the prior permission of the publisher. Requests for permission should be directed to permissions@hbsp.harvard.edu, or mailed to Permissions, Harvard Business School Publishing, 60 Harvard Way, Boston, Massachusetts 02163.

ISBN : 978-1-4221-4657-6

Library-of-Congress cataloging information available

The paper used in this publication meets the requirements of the American National Standard for Permanence of Paper for Publications and Documents in Libraries and Archives Z39.48-1992.

Contents

Acknowledgments

This book is about a new idea—incorporating the power of multiplayer games in the redesign of work, making work more engaging and making workers more productive. The proposals that follow originated in exciting new research about how games work, and business literature about important new challenges as work is redefined in an electronic age of global competition and an uncertain economy.

The most important source of the ideas, however, emerged in conversations we have enjoyed between ourselves and many others over the past 6 years. There was no specific literature, intellectual property, professional association, company, or university program to look to for detailed guidance on this thesis. Consequently, the conversations mentioned here are our most important acknowledgments. You'll learn in the book that sophisticated computer games aren't for soloists. Advancement requires coordinated action among a group of players in which each individual plays a unique role. That is, you have to belong to a *guild*. Fortunately, we did.

The games and work conversations started in 2003, initially between the two of us on pool decks watching daughters who swam on the same team. So thanks first to Katie and Haley, whose dedicated efforts provided our first conversational venue and topical interest. Poolside discussions quickly led to exciting brainstorming sessions with colleagues we cajoled into helping. Eventually, a small group hatched a first project—a conference about games and work that we planned with Alpheus Bingham and Aaron Schacht of Eli Lilly. Alph deserves special recognition for his encouragement and creative input early on, ranging from product ideas to game math.

At our first group effort, we divided into teams (students, professors, businesspeople, and investors) to compete on generating best ideas. The players, motivated by the promise of an iPod for the winners, created amazing plans, and we've drawn from those experiences over the years. The players included (in addition to the planners) Rene Patnode, Andre Marquis,

Aaron Thibault, Aaron Schact, Nick Yee, and Carmi Weinzweig. Two great judges gave us excellent early success criteria and watch-outs as we pursued the thesis; they were Channing Robertson from Stanford University and John Shoch from Alloy Ventures.

As we continued assembling ideas and slides to share with others, we were fortunate to receive an invitation from David Krakauer to make a presentation at a Santa Fe Institute Business Network workshop on innovation in June 2004. We received wonderful encouragement and thoughtful feedback from people in a dozen industries as well as from SFI scientists and board members, including Esther Dyson.

That experience, along with encouragement from Dan Rubin, a partner at Alloy Ventures, led to the founding of Seriosity, Inc., in 2004. Dan contributed his network of relevant industry leaders and participated regularly in the conversations, offering creative product ideas and business use cases, as well as critical insights about how to grow a business from a thesis. We thank him and the other Alloy partners for listening, critiquing, and giving this project more leash than it may have deserved.

The start-up began with the ambitious goal of using "the power of game technology to transform information work wherever mediated by computers." It was two years before we settled on a first product. We spent that time learning about the games and studying work by meeting with executives and technologists from dozens of large enterprises across a wide range of industries. For our study of games we are greatly indebted to Helen Cheng and David Abecassis, then recent Stanford graduates who became our first employees, and Nick Yee, who knew more about games than anyone we'd met. These were our first expert gamers, our jungle guides. Several others also contributed to early thoughts, including Andrew Lev and Danny Taing. Seriosity has continued a tradition of engaging student game experts, and projects described in this book have benefited from the thinking of Thomas Cadwell, Macy Abbey, James Scarborough, Marc Doucette, Matt Paden, and Preet Anand.

Simon Roy has been our colleague at Seriosity for almost four years, serving at various times as general manager, CEO, and board member providing ideas, advice, organization, and patient management of the students (and us). He helped sharpen the thesis, contributed continuously to Seriosity product designs, coauthored articles about our product tests, and led a technology team building the first products to come from the game inspirations.

Early on, we knew we'd need to find out more than we knew about the future of work and the science behind the games. Three Seriosity advisors, each the reigning expert in his area, deserve the highest recognition for extended, thoughtful, and influential conversations. We put Thomas Malone first on this list as our intellectual futurist on enterprise work, a valued coauthor on research projects (much of the chapter on leadership comes from work we did together), and a steady and wise advisor and board member. Edward Castronova, in addition to writing the two books about synthetic worlds that influenced us the most, has been our in-house game economist (mentioned extensively in the chapter on virtual money), offsite game designer, and one of the most creative conversationalists about games that we've encountered. John Beck helped us understand the new gamer generation, and his book with Thomas Davenport about attention helped inspire our first software product. We also thank Rev. Timothy Read for early thoughts on religion and play, and Stuart Brand and Peter Schwartz for early pointers to game literature and stories from their own work and play.

We continued playing games as we studied games, determined that all offsite meetings with advisors should also be a game. In addition to the Seriosity team, we invited business and game stars on those weekends and benefited from their contributions. Special guests, who each won a prized white hat in one of the games, included Philip Rosedale (founder of Linden Lab) and Daniel James (cofounder of Three Rings Entertainment). We also continued playing games at conferences, patterned after our first experiment, and we had several distinguished players and judges, each of whom contributed to the growth of the thesis. Some of the notables include Ellen Levy, Andrew Dahlem, Vanessa Vogel, Timothy Chou, Daniel Leemon, James Rutt, and Elizabeth Evans.

Virtual worlds and multiplayer games are active areas of research for a radically interdisciplinary group of faculty and students at Stanford. For three years, there has been an influential weekly meeting of a lab group of faculty and graduate students participating in a National Science Foundation–funded project that is part of the H-STAR (Human Sciences and Technologies Advance Research) Institute at Stanford. Those conversations have been the best of interdisciplinary collaboration (social scientists from departments studying learning, neuroscience, and media) and included Dan Schwartz (Stanford School of Education), Jeremy Bailenson (Stanford Department of Communication), Anthony Wagner (Stanford Department of Psychology), and Roy Pea (Stanford School of Education). Graduate students who worked on related research, all of it reported in this book, were Kevin Wise, Sohye Lim, and Vanessa Vega. The research funded by the National Science Foundation was part of the LIFE project (Learning in Informal and Formal

Environments), a Science of Learning Center at Stanford University, the University of Washington, and SRI.

From the beginning, we were committed not only to a thesis but also to its *application*. That meant we had to talk to people who were building technology as well as those who owned the business problems that the technology might solve. We've had extensive conversations with people in business and have used their stories, protecting when appropriate the exact sources. Our best memories include Jim Spohrer and David Boloker (IBM), Tony O'Driscoll (formerly at IBM and now at Duke University), Franz Dill and Larry Huston (Procter & Gamble), Christian Reynaud (Cisco Systems), Rick Holman and Daniel Roesch (General Motors), Alan Koenning and Robert Burman (UPS), Max Christophe (Morgan Stanley), Michael Heinrich (SAP), Tobin van Pelt and Jim Greenwood (Lockheed), and, especially, Ross Smith (Microsoft). The Media X Program at Stanford, an industry–university partners program, also generated significant interest in games and work among industry partners, including influential conversations with Chuck House (Executive Director of Media X) and Martha Russell, and with partners from Sun Microsystems, Time Warner, DNP, Philips, Intel, BP, Visa, Motorola, Qwaq Forums, Sesame Workshop, and Konica Minolta.

Penny Nelson, our agent at Manus & Associates, was an early champion and an experienced guide to publishing. Jacqueline Murphy, our publisher and now editorial director of Harvard Business Press, quickly recognized the potential for games at work and was a valued advisor through reviews and revisions. Her editorial colleague, Kathleen Carr, has also been an excellent resource. We thank our copy editor, Cindy Kogut for an eagle eye and good judgment.

We have to note the advantages that come from living in Silicon Valley. In addition to those already mentioned, people here who have shown a genuine interest and kept us honest include Gordon Eubanks, Mark Thompson, Ken Ross, Reuben Steiger, David Kelley, Steve Jurvetson, and Pierre Omidyar.

And, best of all, we are lucky to share this environment with our families: Roxanne and Katie with Byron, and Carol, Haley, and Travis with Leighton. In our case, they knew each other well enough to know which author was ahead or behind in writing commitments but in all cases they provided much-appreciated encouragement to pursue something we think is a ton of fun.

—Byron Reeves
J. Leighton Read

Chapter One

Introduction

MEET JENNIFER (TAKE 1)

Jennifer quit her job at a catalog call center after only nine months and applied to Circle Cruise Lines for a small pay increase. She was also looking for more on-the-job engagement, better social experiences with coworkers, and a greater sense of belonging.

Jennifer has a tough but typical information job. She talks a lot (and listens) while staring at a computer screen. She gets an average of seventy-five calls each day and thirty-seven calls on light days when the center is not "on queue." From her open carrel on the call center floor, she and her managers can view the progress of the center on a huge lighted board that is all numbers: average handling time, number of calls waiting, projected versus actual call volume, abandoned calls, and other numbers Jennifer doesn't understand.

Many of Jennifer's calls are requests for itinerary changes, and some are from less-polite customers. No reciprocity on rudeness is allowed, however, because she never knows when QA (quality assurance) people will be listening to the call logs. And calls are not the only part of work that's closely supervised. When it's time for lunch (not a minute before noon), Jennifer keys in a lunch logout code so her team leader can record the start of her break. She risks a suspension if she's late from lunch three times in one month.

Pressure comes from everywhere for Jennifer—from customers, team leaders, QA, and herself. She really wants to perform well because bonus cash and an occasional promotion are possible, although she's not quite sure what it takes to get them. She wishes the hours were more flexible, but the pay is OK for now, and she likes that her work requires a degree of social intelligence. The social scene at work, however, isn't much different from her previous job. She's met a few coworkers in the lounge during training or morning briefings, but personal connections, especially those that might extend beyond work, are few.

After three months at Circle, Jennifer thinks there's been minor improvement in her work life, but there's an even stronger sense of déjà vu. Month three seems a lot like month one. Work is lonely and repetitive, and in spite of quarterly reviews, she never seems to know if she's making progress in the right direction. Once again, she's monitoring online job postings from other companies.

MEET JENNIFER (TAKE 2)

Jennifer puts down the baby in her family room, sits down at her computer, and logs in. Gone are the standard forms, the lists, the big data board, and the carrels. The first thing she sees on the screen is her avatar, an appealing animated character she created to represent her in a themed virtual world. Jennifer has already personalized her avatar (choosing everything from its gender and age to personality and appearance), and she begins her workday by walking (virtually) to the place in the 3D world where her team is gathering. Her twenty-person team is scattered in three different time zones, some at an office but most in their homes. They're all together now in the virtual world.

The first thing Jennifer does is check on her team's progress. After the last shift, how do they rank on number of call resolutions, who in the group has "leveled up" (achieved a new status based on performance), and who needs encouragement? All of the once-familiar call center metrics are now cast as points, ranks, and virtual currency within a large and engaging multiplayer game complete with a compelling narrative, interesting 3D environment, dynamic marketplaces, leader boards, and chat channels. Most important, there are teams. Jennifer knows that her success is determined in part by how well her whole team performs, and she has a clear understanding of what she gets when they win.

Data about the team are available for all to see (just right-click a character to discover its experience level, wealth in gold pieces, availability for new assignments, or recent compliments from other team members). Jennifer checks her own personal page as a reminder of her progress over the last several months. She sees her ranking on calls completed, talk time, successful up-sells, and total call resolutions. She also sees how these metrics are connected to the overall performance of her business unit as a mission-critical component of a world-class company (her group is making a difference). Jennifer notices quickly that the previous shift really stepped up performance, but she's concerned about Mike. She rolls her cursor over his avatar (all the players actually appear as pirates, the theme in the current game narrative) and clicks on his Get Info button. Mike's rank on number of calls resolved is still at the Novice rating, so Jen clicks on the Speak button in a chat window and sends an encouraging note for delivery when he's back online.

She begins her work as incoming calls are routed to her screen—but the interface is still in-game. Information about incoming calls surrounds her avatar. The information updates continuously as points accumulate at each stage of a call—small but psychologically significant rewards for making a first connection, inputting data accurately, or completing an up-sell. The feedback is driven by systems that monitor telephony and computer inputs, but the latest version of the game is also giving her rich feedback based on real-time analysis of language and voice stress (from both ends of her connection). There are visuals indicating team status (the teams are represented as ships sailing in close formation), progress toward team goals (they're currently aiming for an island that rewards free holiday airline travel), and a shopping mall where she can buy virtual goods to decorate a character or team workspace.

Jennifer is engaged at work. She feels like she knows the rules and how to advance. She's evaluated objectively throughout the day (not just at a quarterly review), and everyone's data are available for all to see (there are no secret routes to the top). She's interested in the narrative and rich visuals. She's met new people, at first virtually, but eventually in real life as the groups matured. Jennifer feels like she's part of a team, learning from team captains and then teaching novices, all in the course of playing a game at work. And perhaps most important to her, her progress in the game enabled her, once she reached the appropriate level, to transfer from a customer service representative to her dream job within the game, an agent soliciting proposals for the company's charitable foundation.

The Basic Idea of Total Engagement

Games will change how Jennifer and all of us work; this book is the story, as yet untold, of how and why that will happen. One hundred million Americans, and many more around the world, played a computer or video game last week with levels of engagement and focus rarely seen at work.[1] Some of this play was simple shooting, racing, or turning cards, and much of it appealed to adolescent boys. But an increasingly large portion of play was complex, strategic, social, and gender balanced. The hours flew by for people immersed in sophisticated online interactions, stealing time from real-world relationships, television, and work, and providing alternative environments in which to meet people and learn new skills. For anyone convinced that *engagement* is a key ingredient of the future of work, games are the definitive model. We'll tell you about their most important implications for business productivity during economic times when engagement is especially important but even harder to achieve.

This story is about far more than having fun at work, although that's not a bad place to start. In good times and bad, business is now driven by complex, globally distributed collaboration among people working with information. It's about offering a sense of purpose and aspiration to information workers in the context of tasks that are often repetitive and dull. It's about providing timely feedback so people know how they're doing and where to improve. It's about innovation, which is best achieved when interactions are socially rich and occur over multiple scales of physical and temporal distance. It's about arrangements for teamwork that motivate people by defining what individuals get when the team wins. It's about leveling the playing field to allow new ideas to bubble up from workers with little access to senior leadership. And it's about achieving these goals in real-world organizations that have trouble moving quickly because they are legacy bound, risk averse, overloaded with information and worried about the future. Modern information work is tough.

Our major premise is that games can help—big time. We are not talking about gaining a better competitive spirit by learning how to shoot better or win at blackjack, and we are not talking about using video games as training tools. We believe that some people will soon do their jobs *inside* a game, and many more will thrive in information environments that have features borrowed from today's best games. In other words, we think people should benefit from game ideas *while they are making money for shareholders*, not just while they are getting ready to make money for shareholders during training or school. Our thesis is inspired by sophisticated online multiplayer games that require extraordinary teamwork, elaborate data analysis and strategy, the recruitment, evaluation, and retention of top players in multiperson "guilds," the cooperation of people who have complementary roles that require coordinated action, player innovations that come from everyone, and decision making and leadership behavior that happens quickly and with transparent consequences.

We'll tell you a lot about such games in this book, but for now, be assured that the best ones differ from traditional video games as much as universities do from one-room schoolhouses. (If you can't wait to check out the most sophisticated of the offerings, you can start with the websites listed in the second endnote for this chapter to get a feel for their complexity and attraction.)[2] The games are sprawling online communities where players collaborate with and compete against one another in real time within visually rich three-dimensional virtual worlds, ones that persist and evolve even while a player is away. And in spite of all the serious work that's required in the games, people *pay* to play. One title collects $15 a month and has twelve million subscribers.[3] This is a big business that's applicable to big business.

Complex online games are played by millions of people worldwide. The youngest of the players constitute a new generation that will demand different attractions and technology when they join the workforce. Millions more players have their own kids, mortgages and yard work, and they are as likely to be in their thirties, forties, or fifties as in their teens. Most are *already* working—some almost surely in *your* company. We know they think about their game experiences when they make decisions that affect your company (they've told us so, and we'll tell you what they said), and we know they'd very much like to have their real-world job better parallel the richer experiences they've come to expect at home. Computing at home—the machines, software, and interfaces that deliver compelling entertainment—has not only caught up to the office; it's far, far better. Our aim is to help move those experiences, led by consumer sensibilities and attractive entertainment, into the workplace.

Gamers already perform every category of information work imaginable, from grind-it-out drudgery to sophisticated analysis and team building, all in the course of digital play. We found evidence of every category of serious work we examined, even though the gamers were doing the work merely because they thought it was fun. Gamers organize, categorize, analyze, evaluate, diagnose, invent, buy, sell, lead, and follow. We found gamers who were manufacturing pharmaceuticals to sell to doctors who healed warriors, role-playing CEOs who were negotiating financing packages for spaceship leases, guild officers conducting performance reviews for probationary players seeking admission to top teams, and hundreds of people performing jobs that were far less glamorous—casting a fishing pole in a lake hoping to catch (by mere random chance) a prize worth a few gold pieces, searching for hidden animals in virtual terrain, and assembling all sorts of gadgets for sale in virtual marketplaces. We'll tell you about their work and how it links to contemporary business. But so we don't bury the lead, our proposal is this: let's give the gamers a real job.

We are sure that game sensibilities will revolutionize work, but we are more confident that the games will change work than we are that they'll change work for the better. The appearance of game sensibilities and technology at work seems inevitable. Games are too much fun and too similar to work that's currently being done in challenging real-world contexts not to have an influence. And as the history of links between entertainment and the enterprise show (we'll review some of that soon), media innovations eventually make their way to the office. The critical challenge is to apply what is powerful well, which is our aim in this guide.

Games are certainly engaging, but the psychological tools we are talking about here are so powerful they are also dangerous. Game design offers an unprecedented tool for workflow engineering, but bad stuff can (and probably will) happen. Exquisitely paced feedback delivered perfectly by algorithm could drive unhealthy behavior, resulting in everything from repetitive stress syndromes to aggressive behavior. If game design principles are not applied with due regard for workers, we could see the digital equivalent of the degrading and dangerous work that characterized the early industrial era.

Two Trends

Two trends—one concerning the future of work and one concerning the current state of digital play—are converging to make game technology a valuable business platform and an inevitable presence in the future of work. Regardless of whether we are on the way into or out of an economic downturn, the future of work is about engaging workers more than commanding them.[4] This is certainly true in tough economic times, when innovation and collaboration are jeopardized by employees who are fearful or disappointed. People want to be engaged in work with a purpose, and they want insight into how their work is linked to larger organizational and societal goals. They want to know where they fit in. Competing in an upturn also demands a highly engaged workforce.

When workers are engaged by rewards that are intrinsic to their task rather than controlled by bosses, organizations can better decentralize, allowing people to live where they want but play in the same game. Well-designed game environments can define work via loose hierarchies, where self-organizing behavior by player-workers is productive. Work can be democratized, allowing people to choose the tasks they take on and to have influence on how and when the work is completed. Work can have a more compelling purpose, allowing people to be continuously reminded how their efforts contribute to something worthwhile and larger than themselves. Teams will convene, often on their own initiative, across organizational levels, departments, and cultures. Internal motivation will become more important than external persuasion, encouraging people's best efforts.

The second trend is part historical (digital play is already engaging) and part a look forward (it will only get better). New multiplayer games represent a high level of compelling interactivity with great prospects for continued refinement. Game play has light-speed pacing, constant feedback, transparent levels and reputations, compelling narratives, and interesting methods for self-representation in the action. And all play depends substantially on team cooperation.

Digital games, and entertainment in general, have long influenced work, but current games raise the bar substantially. Games are seriously fun, as we'll review, and they offer a template for reengineering the entire human/computer interface. This is very attractive stuff, and as has been true for many communication innovations, there is money to be made betting on the power of entertainment to eventually spread to serious media. Entertainment values have influenced advertising, news, and political communication, even when the first uses of each were often deadly serious, information-only, monotone messages. More explicit examples of entertainment influences on business software include high-end visuals and audio, devices that mimic game hardware (for example, the mobility of the Game Boy showing up in PDAs five years later), and the excitement about social networking tools replacing bland corporate directories and collaboration software.

Alignment of Personal and Organizational Goals

Who benefits when work meets games? This match may create an ideal alignment of individual and organizational goals. For business, productivity and job satisfaction are key metrics, and games could help. Information work of all kinds—ranging from repetitive jobs in call centers to difficult collaboration in distributed groups—could benefit from technology that transforms work into compelling and entertaining play.

Some work is too easy: productivity can't be maintained because people become bored or tired by prolonged and tedious attention to detail. Turnover is high in these jobs. By embedding easy work into story lines and quests that are part of an extended multilevel game, workers will be more engaged, leading to increased productivity and enthusiasm for the job. Games can create aspirations that are concrete, observable, and transferable to others.

Some work is too hard: productivity suffers because goals are in conflict or difficult to define. Sometimes it's hard because the learning curve is too steep, or success takes a long time to achieve, or it's not easy to measure and thus celebrate intermediate steps. Sometimes work is too hard because of interruptions and information overload. Sometimes work is too hard because other people make it that way. Good game design can fix poor work design and bring new life to well-designed jobs that are still too difficult to be satisfying. In these situations, game designs will offer new tools to clarify objectives that adapt to external challenges and will give immediate and *inter*mediate reinforcement for progress accompanied by intrinsic training to ensure personal growth. These design principles are all mainstays of successful interactive games.

What Gamers Want

Should real work ever be as much fun as a game? It may need to be. The best young people entering the workforce will be engaged by experiences that allow their serious interactions to parallel playful ones. Gamers expect quick feedback (good or bad) and opportunities for trial and error. Risk is familiar, failure part of the game, and competition expected and governed by known rules. The new gamer generation is already in the workplace, but the work that awaits them shares little with the engaging computer experiences that shaped their youth.

Successful businesses in the future will redesign work from the gamer's point of view. Businesses will create a workplace that accommodates employees ("players") who want to know the rules, advance frequently, partner quickly, and nurture reputations in a narrative that aligns their own objectives with those of the organization that pays their salary. Gamers also want to have fun—not necessarily a constant party, but engagement that facilitates success and exposes their contribution to the larger good. Even if the idea of mixing work and play seems uncomfortable, it is worth careful consideration because the incoming workforce will demand a different set of tools, and competitors know it.

To complete the story about games and work, we have to define tactics that can be used to rewire the enterprise. Not everyone in a company will be receptive to the idea of looking to games for insights into human nature, let alone stealing game elements to use in conducting serious work. Champions for change will need arguments, evidence, cases, and stories. Here's what we've done to help prepare the way.

Gathering the Evidence

The ideas in this book began informally—a PhD academic doing laboratory experiments about physiological engagement with media talking with an MD life science investor and former CEO who wondered why work in his companies couldn't be more fun. The PhD had been studying media psychology for twenty-five years and had recently completed several experiments about psychological responses to game mechanics. Those experiments included not only observations and interviews but also psychophysiology (does a person's heart beat faster when interactions are real or virtual?) and even functional magnetic resonance imaging scans of a player's brain while interacting with virtual-world characters. The experiments were often complex, but the summary is simple: games are engaging.

The MD is a venture capitalist and serial entrepreneur with management experiences of his own in which worker motivation was a key to productivity but sometimes difficult to sustain. From his years in academic medicine, he carried memories of a successful software product he produced in the mid-1980s (the dawn of personal computer games) that used text dialogues with simulated personalities to engage people attempting difficult behavior change related to diet and exercise.[5] With an investment eye toward new trends, he wondered how these two worlds might usefully converge.

Our shortened summary for the convergence of these experiences is this: Work is hard enough already as globalization, technology, and the economy create new challenges and opportunities; games are the sandbox where compelling design principles are engaging millions of talented minds. Might a blending be in order? Imagine the value, we speculated with abandon, if online workers could chase surreal characters through a virtual forest with villains, spells, and dragons, all following a set of rules that if broken would result in pretend tragedy, and at the end of an evening's successful quest, the computer tracking this complex human/computer solution would output the design for a new computer circuit or a better routing plan for delivery trucks in Chicago. To complete the picture, you need to imagine a Rube Goldberg algorithm that maps human problem-solving behavior in the game to the real-world problem.

Stranger things have happened, but we are quick to admit that the mapping is yet to be done. If successful, this would be an astonishing alignment of personal motivations and business value. Work would be hopelessly confused with play, with the result a possible win-win for the players and for the businesses that sponsored them. There is a spectrum of possibilities that runs from "stealing work" from unsuspecting players to "renting work" when players are in on the deal and to what we call "buying work," where a game is sufficiently bad that you may have to pay people to play it (as epitomized by most jobs today).

If this sounds like science fiction, then you may know Orson Scott Card's Hugo Award–winning classic *Ender's Game*, in which a talented young boy is recruited to lead simulated interstellar war games. The story eventually reveals that his prowess in the simulation is being translated into actual epic battles with grave consequences for the human race and its enemies.[6] *The Last Starfighter*, a 1984 film, has a similar plot, in which video game play and actual war fighting are conflated by the game's designers.[7] In the 1983 film *War Games*, a young man finds a back door into a military computer and almost starts World War III by accident, thinking he is playing a computer game.[8] And if you think these scenarios are too far over the horizon, consider Luis von Ahn, an up-and-coming researcher at Carnegie Mellon University who is busy building games that "solve complex computational challenges through the medium of online entertainment."[9] This is serious computer science. Millions of data points have been collected in his games, and you can play them online now.[10]

Consider the experiments being conducted by an unlikely group of software testers at Microsoft. Ross Smith has created an environment in which a dozen of his colleagues are creating games for a larger group to make the job of testing operating system software more interesting.[11] They have focused on trust as a key requisite for embedding work in a game.

Home-run applications where games enable output that is otherwise impossible are a holy grail, but we are hopeful. There are plenty of equally intriguing variants, however, similar to the story about Jennifer's work at the cruise line call center, that are completely possible with today's technology. Even closer at hand is the possibility of learning from games and adjusting the work environment and its context by borrowing some of the best tools from games.

Our first step in documenting the possibilities was to look carefully at games, especially the complex multiplayer titles that have the best prospects for application in serious contexts where collaboration is key. We wanted to see what work was *already* being done in the games where people were paying to play rather than being paid for work. Armed with a formal taxonomy of work (reviewed in chapter 3, which covers the different types of work that can be helped by games), we scoured the top multiplayer titles, cataloging the best examples.

Knowing how people are already working in games is important, but the best way to actually observe their efforts isn't obvious. When you study movies, television, or websites, you cue up the digital file or domain name and start taking notes. For complex multiplayer games, it's best to have jungle guides. The reason? It can take five hundred hours to get to the highest level in the current best-selling title, and it's impossible to even get close to the best virtual places, challenges, and teams, let alone score an invitation to play with the teams with access to these challenges, without achieving high status in the game. This makes the study of games tricky, and it's a stumbling block that needs to be solved by anyone interested in being a champion for game applications in his or her organization.

Our game guides were Stanford students who responded to a campus ad that said "Get paid to play." The students sent in their game résumés attached to their academic ones. We wanted to know who had *actually seen* Silvermoon, the capital city of the Blood Elves, explored the Lich King's Dread Citadel Naxxramas, and defeated Illidan, the demon hunter lord of the Black Temple. The students we hired were experienced guild leaders, an officer in the Stanford Game Society, and other game experts who knew how to access the cool stuff—and they were all eager to write home to tell their parents that something assumed trivial or bad for them had finally paid off.

Playing Games to Learn About Games

Now we needed brainstorming about the work that could benefit from total engagement. Our first impulse, well rehearsed in our academic and business lives, was to convene a conference. We chose speakers, format, and a venue—but one problem lingered. The event we outlined was at risk of being as boring as the work we were trying to change. Our response was, "Why not play a game instead?"

The game format we created for the conference was simple and successful. Teams of five to six people signed up from several large enterprises (including Cisco Systems, Eli Lilly, Intel, GlaxoSmithKline, SAP, and a secretive government agency). Participants competed to formulate a business plan that used games to solve an important enterprise problem of their choosing. It's amazing what the prospect of winning an iPod (and having to make a team pitch to a distinguished panel) can do for intensity of competition. Executives and managers stayed up late and got up early to polish creative presentations made to a judging panel composed of venture capitalists, university professors, and corporate officers.

It may have also helped that our game was played in a hotel adjacent to the annual Game Developers Conference, providing a rich resource of gamers, programmers, and exhibitors to provide inspiration and consultation during the contest. The format was successful enough to encourage two encores in subsequent years, and several insights and stories in this book come from those contests.

University and Business Inspirations

Silicon Valley businesses and Stanford University academics have co-evolved, with significant influences in both directions, and we used that cross-fertilization for our study of games and work.

The prospect of using games in business has been on the research agenda at Stanford, and we've benefited greatly from work in one particular program. The Media X Partners Program at Stanford sponsors university and industry partnerships at the intersection of information technology and human sciences. Games and virtual environments, and their potential for learning, training, and productivity, are active areas. There are research programs about psychological responses to avatars, scalable computer architectures for virtual worlds, the pragmatics of conversations in games, and the legal regimes that develop in virtual communities. The Media X conferences and conversations between researchers and industry partners have been a rich source of practical information.

Another source of relevant experiences regarding games and work comes from our involvement with Seriosity, Inc., a venture-funded start-up company we cofounded in 2004. With our Seriosity colleagues, we have met with dozens of *Fortune* 500 companies to understand their management challenges. Seriosity consults for large companies about game strategies and builds business software inspired by game elements. Several of these projects are reviewed here, including a project for IBM about group leadership in large game guilds and its implications for real-world leadership and the use of gamelike virtual currencies at Intel to create a marketplace for the attention of busy people with overflowing inboxes.[12]

Who Should Think About Games and Work?

We think anyone interested in the evolution and design of work should consider how these ideas can be applied in good times and bad. Game psychology and technology are broadly relevant to business. There are new and important lessons for those whose work touches on recruitment, hiring, training, retention, leadership, teams, evaluation, collaboration, and innovation. The lessons are applicable across business functions—sales, marketing, research, development, production, and management. We'll make the links as we review business issues in each category.

We believe the highest use of games will be to redesign work so that it is more like a game and to allow work to be conducted within games. Even if games seem irrelevant to your business, they certainly aren't to people you're going to be hiring, and that's reason enough to find out about how they work. Business needs to motivate and engage workers who have very different expectations about communication based on extensive, new, and often intense media experiences. These workers will bring new expectations about user interfaces, communication tools, and, importantly, the pace of challenge and reward. We've already heard the words "I wish my job could be more like my game." Soon, we will hear "I quit that job because it wasn't enough like my game," and eventually "I'll take your job because my game experience tells me I can be successful here."

The book should also be relevant to those interested in games but skeptical about their value in any context other than entertainment. Do you marvel at the way games create an intense focus for friends, coworkers, and especially children and adolescents but have concerns about whether anything useful could ever come from the hundreds of hours spent online? Games have important social consequences, and new research helps define an appropriate level of concern. The summary is that stereotypes are often wrong, especially in relation to complex online games. Some people do play too much and to their disadvantage, but on average many players are physically healthier, work harder, make better grades, earn higher salaries, and are more socially connected than those who play less or not at all.[13]

What You Will Get from the Book

Most important, this book should enable you to evaluate the arguments for a new idea that has been discussed in academia and industry labs but that is only now poised to guide innovations and practices in the workplace. We think the timing is right. A global economic downturn creates enormous stress on management and workers, and opens the door to disruptive innovation of all kinds. Games give us a new lens through which we can examine cherished ideas about management and new tools—some simple and some radical—with which to experiment. We are just starting to see applications that execute this vision and will tell you about the best examples we have been able to find. We wish we had even more; maybe they will come from you and your colleagues. It's even possible that the early *misapplication* of these powerful techniques in the workplace could delay broader use until people are comfortable with checks and safeguards. To supplement stories from real companies, we'll describe some examples that we think will advance the field, and each chapter will begin with a story like Jennifer's that has either already happened or could happen in the very near future.

You'll also get information about games—revenues, audiences, narratives, demographics, interfaces, and typical play patterns—and where to look for more.[14] Never mind business applications—this phenomenon is a huge new direction for media, and we review the basics early in the story. Games are big. Details are in chapter 2, "The Game Tsunami: Who Plays, How Much, and Why."

We'll review what we and others think are the critical challenges facing business right now and in the next decade, with an eye toward linking them to what's going on in the games. The details are in chapter 3, titled, using the words of a young gamer: "'Work Sucks': Corporate Problems That Games Might Solve."

Why do games deliver so well? We've spent a great deal of time over the past four years with gamers and game designers to identify the ingredients used in the most successful recipes. Chapter 4, "Ten Ingredients of Great Games," presents our findings and some of the science that explains how these ingredients drive engagement and performance. The ingredients are an original checklist for overhauling business processes using affordances proven effective in entertainment.

We next detail the implications of four powerful game features—virtual people, money, teams, and leaders—and what they could mean for business. Chapters 5 through 8 discuss the differences between real and synthetic versions of each feature (e.g., exploring the difference between real money and a synthetic currency), highlighting the role that each can play as game pieces in business. The answers to the real-versus-synthetic question, based on new research and product tests, are surprising. The differences aren't as great as you might think.

The subsequent two chapters provide background about a larger intellectual framework that supports our thesis. The effective use of games will require serious analysis and persuasive evidence about the behaviors they encourage and the fundamental properties of the communication technologies that give them power. We've saved this discussion for the end, not because it's less important but because we didn't want to divert the first part of the story away from the games themselves, which is where the excitement is. But it's this bigger picture that may be necessary to sustain a revolution that redesigns work.

The chapters that provide this background are about play and media psychology. In chapter 9 we argue that play is *not* the opposite of work; rather, it's a catalyst for engagement. Play isn't frivolous, and it doesn't just mean parties and laughs. Play is an extremely serious concept that philosophers, educators, and psychologists agree is critical for everything from intellectual development to learning and to the creation of culture.

Chapter 10, "Caught Between Fact and Fiction," discusses the most important psychological responses that people have to media and describes how games use those properties to create environments that are far more real than a mere entertainment label would suggest. Media are not psychologically trivial ("Not to worry—it's only a picture"). Rather, games—and in general the media that enable them—offer powerful experiences that are processed much more as fact than fiction, in spite of media stereotypes and personal wishes to the contrary.

As we put our argument together, we knew we would also need an important chapter to discuss ethical issues related to games and work. There are some tough issues. The sources of the concerns are often personal because there are important psychological consequences at stake: addiction, gender bias, violence and aggression, and health. We review those issues in chapter 11, simply entitled "Danger." What can organizations do to mitigate the possible negative effects of game applications at work?

The finale in chapter 12 discusses tactics for change. Our guess is that your world has recently changed a lot already. In the sense that a crisis shouldn't be wasted, this thesis is presented at a time when conditions are ripe for disruptive innovation in products and processes. Here's where we offer a guide for a game strategy in your organization. We have suggestions about how to start applying game psychology to leadership, collaboration, and innovation. We suggest ways to meet the gamers in your company and those who'll be coming to your company soon. We help put the game revolution in the context of your own business.

We begin with a discussion about the games. But before that discussion, we'd like you to meet Nick. He makes pharmaceuticals and distributes them to doctors—in a game. For now.

Chapter Two

The Game Tsunami

Who Plays, How Much, and Why

MEET NICK

Nick is a twenty-eight-year-old computer professional who plays the online game *Star Wars Galaxies* (SWG). Based on the Lucas films of the same name, the game allows players to create Star Wars characters (Nick is a Wookie) that have special talents, appearances, and social styles. Nick plays about twenty-five hours a week, time more easily given now that enthusiasm for his real computer work is waning.

If you want to advance in SWG, it's critical that your character have a job and be able to contribute to the larger community by making products or offering services that other players purchase. Nick's character is a pharmaceutical manufacturer, and he's a good one. His success depends on his ability to create drugs that he sells to other players, mostly doctors, who in turn sell their services to warriors injured in battle.

Making the pharmaceuticals is no easy trick. Nick must find the best raw materials, strewn over galaxies, or he can make substitute synthetic materials himself. He has to find and experiment with the best catalysts to mix the materials. He has to make judgments about the pharmaceutical market based on his observation and analysis of what's happening with other players in the game. And in the end, he has to effectively market and advertise his products to those who will transfer a virtual currency to his account only when the goods are delivered.

This is pretty serious "work," albeit in the context of hugely engaging entertainment. About half of Nick's time in the game is spent on the hard tasks of learning how to make the drugs, gathering materials, and experimenting with manufacturing techniques. (Nick's character is well known for his invention of a harvester that gathers raw materials from outer galaxies—work carried out while the real Nick is logged off the game and asleep. It's possible to discover how to manufacture the drugs by trial and error, but that wastes time. Nick's character communicates, via an in-game messaging system, with other successful players, and he visits numerous game-related websites to learn new tricks.

Nick's biggest worry while playing is making sure, before he even thinks of going to bed, that there's enough product in the supply chain to meet the demand from his premier customers. They'll complain, and he'll suffer in the game, if there are logistical snags before his next logon.

Games Are Big

Our overall thesis—that games will change the nature of work—is based on two intersecting arcs. One is the popularity of games (Nick loves his), and the other is the future of work (that's not looking good for Nick). Games are an exciting revolution—innovations that are working in entertainment right now. Work has serious new problems, some imposed by broad economic challenges and some due to the dramatic rise of information work.

This chapter is about the excitement arc. Nick's story helps make the case, easily argued we think, that games are big. Staggeringly, stunningly big. Here are some details about the money they make, the people who play them, and the amount of time gamers spend on them and why.

Big Bucks

Nick is part of an entertainment revolution. Hundreds of millions of people worldwide have an avatar (a personalized character) in some type of online multiplayer game.[1] They play those characters on computers, game consoles, home theaters, mobile phones, and interactive cable systems. On screens big and small, they drive cars, fly fighter planes, sail pirate ships, create city plans, or act as hockey players, Kung Fu fighters, and medieval priests. They compete, cooperate, meet, join, quit, explore, laugh, cry and otherwise immerse themselves in social roles that pique imaginations and redefine self-concepts.

The industry responsible for these experiences has created a $10 billion market, one of the largest existing entertainment categories.[2] The major game consoles (including Xbox, PlayStation, and Nintendo) sold $1 billion worth of hardware in 2007. The 2008 version of the action-adventure game *Grand Theft Auto* sold 3.6 million units on day one and over $500 million in software in one week, surpassing by more than $100 million the best one-week movie launch ever. If you think it's all about violence, consider that only 15 percent of the games sold in 2007 were rated "Mature" and that the fastest-growing genre was "family entertainment." The growth continues. Since 2003, the game software industry has had an annual growth of 17 percent, with a 5 percent annual growth in employment. Electronic Arts, one of the largest game producers, with sixty-five titles for sale, employs about ten thousand people and had revenues of $4 billion in 2008.

At the high end of the multiplayer market, Blizzard Entertainment serves 12 million registered users with the most popular role-playing game ever, *World of Warcraft*. In the United States, people pay $15 per month to play; millions of others in Asia pay by the hour. The November 2008 release of the latest *World of Warcraft* expansion package sold 2.8 million copies in the first twenty-four hours.[3] Millions of other players, growing at 30 percent annually, pay similar fees for a hundred other titles published by the biggest entertainment companies (Sony, Disney, Vivendi) and the hottest start-ups in the entertainment industry.[4] Tens of millions more show up regularly or from time to time as customized characters, or avatars, in virtual worlds such as *Second Life*, where players create their own activities and trade a virtual currency for digital assets that include everything from land to buildings to behaviors (you can buy computer code that will make your character do just about anything—including that).

Game economics don't stop at subscription fees and software sales. There has been a $1.8 billion aftermarket for game characters and artifacts (you can sometimes sell the character, magic sword, or gold pieces that you acquired in the game on the Web for real money), evidence that digital assets are no less valued than so-called real ones.[5] All of the saleable artifacts can add up to significant real dollars. The size of the economy in one of the worlds, measured as per capita gross national product, ranked in the top one hundred economies in the real world, somewhere between Russia and Bulgaria. This kind of value attracts attention.[6] Until the publishers changed their enforcement policy, game sweatshops in China and Mexico were paying expert gamers a pauper's wage to create and train characters and acquire valuable assets, only to sell them for real currency at prices orders of magnitude higher than their cost of production.[7]

Big People

Nick's pharmaceutical manufacturing job is proof that online play is not just about fourteen-year-old adolescents, fast reaction times, and killing. And there's a lot of new data that agrees.

Nick's game is known as a massive multiplayer online role-playing game. Because the acronym for this genre, MMORPG, is a monster itself, people often simply call these games MMOs. We believe this is the game category that offers the most interesting prospects for business as well as the most counterstereotypical roster of players. Nielson doesn't yet count the number of people in different demographic categories who play MMOs (although it and others will soon—advertisers who'd like to buy space in these virtual worlds want to know who's there), but there are excellent new studies that report data from game companies. The new research relies on self-reporting of age and occupation, but you don't have to ask players to remember their playing time in a survey conducted outside of the games. Instead, Sony can say who plays (no names, of course) directly from the game logs. This section provides the latest summary, based on logs for seven thousand players in one of the most popular MMOs ever published.[8]

First, Nick, at twenty-eight, is actually younger than the average reported. The median age is thirty-three, which isn't too much younger than the median age for the general population (thirty-five). People in their thirties make up the largest concentration of players, six times larger than the number of teens who play and three times the number of college students aged eighteen to twenty-two. (Warning to researchers: studies of gamers done exclusively with convenience samples on college campuses—and there are a lot of them—will miss the main audience!) The statistics for the larger game market aren't different. Across all computer games (the simple and the sophisticated), the average age is thirty-five, and 26 percent of players are over fifty, an increase from 9 percent in 1999.[9]

The majority of MMO players work full time, many in jobs they say are similar to their virtual ones. A recent survey of executives and managers at IBM easily found a hundred guild members who were anxious to talk about how they've used lessons from games in their real jobs (and vice versa). We'll save details of the results for later (chapter 9), but suffice it to say now that most players were midcareer, and most volunteered that they'd learned valuable lessons.

The fact that Nick is male, however, does conform to stereotype and reality. About 80 percent of players in MMOs are male, although research on games more generally shows that over a third of gamers are female.[10] Newer virtual worlds increasingly appeal to both genders. Even though about 60 percent of registered users are men, about 60 percent of the most active users are women (or at least use female avatars).[11] There is some evidence, however, that the percentage of women in some venues might be declining.[12]

So far, most gender research in virtual worlds is not based on actual data from game logs. It's based on either observing the gender of the characters that inhabit the worlds (that is, actually looking at the characters on the screen) or talking with the players, usually via the chat channels where players write notes to each other. The methodology is important (and worrisome) because, as the classic cartoon noted, on the Internet (and in the games) no one knows you're really a dog.[13]

Other demographics bring us back to the counterstereotypical. Mean household income of players (these numbers also depend on self-reports) in one popular MMO was about $85,000; that's $25,000 more per year than the U.S. average.[14] That players even have an answer for a question about income shatters the stereotype about unemployed youth as the main audience. Similarly, education levels were also higher than average. Almost two-thirds of the players have some college education, compared with about 40 percent in the general population (only 8 percent of MMO gamers had less than a high school education, compared with 20 percent in the general population). A big difference between national and game statistics occurs for race: only 2 percent of players are African American, and 3 percent Hispanic. Those numbers are 10 percentage points less than the same racial categories in the general population.

Big Time

If time on task is a good measure of interest (and psychologists say it is), MMOs are *really* interesting. One sizeable cohort of players who are thirty-something, most with a full-time job and many with a family, play a lot—just over twenty-five hours per week.[15] That's compared with seven hours a week for video games (e.g., sports, racing, fighting on a game console). Clearly, there's an increment in engagement for the MMOs. We'll explore why when we talk about the game ingredients responsible for their success (chapter 4).

Who plays the most? Those whom you would think have the least time. In one title, the under-eighteen crowd plays the least (*only* twenty-two hours per week), with the numbers rising steadily as you get to those over forty (about thirty hours per week).[16] These new data have even surprised game developers, who generally tune the games for younger players. We'll probably see more attention given to older players, most likely in the choice of the narratives that organize the games, as awareness of age differences increases.

Another surprise: even though women are outnumbered more than two to one in the games, they play about five hours more per week than men.

They're also more likely to be involved in guild organizations as officers. There are no striking racial differences in the amount of time played, nor differences based on household income.

Where does all this time come from? Television mostly. MMO gamers spend ten hours per week *less* watching television (they watch about twenty-one hours per week) than does the general population. They also tend to read a little less but do catch up with news more on the Internet—the latter being easier because they're twice as likely as others to have a high-speed broadband connection in their homes.

Thus, multiplayer game demographics tilt mostly in the opposite direction from the stereotype of young players who are poorly educated and poor economically. The gamers in the MMO category are likely closer to middle age than high school, are mostly college educated, and make $25,000 per year above the national average. What's so cool about these games that attracts this audience?

What Do You Do in an MMO?

The answer to what one does in an MMO is a lot more than the game stereotypes suggest, if you haven't played one. We'll review details of the sophisticated play in chapters about specific features we think will be most critical in changing work, but an introduction to the larger genre is useful here. This section discusses how you get started and a bit about first experiences—all in a fictional world.[17]

Before You Start

Before playing, you first have to buy or download the basic software (average price around $50) and load it on your computer. (The need to load software on your computer will change in the near future as technology moves to Web-based games, but for now, it's a necessary first step.) The software on your computer communicates with the game publisher's server, where most of the game assets are stored. Also, it is best if your computer was purchased in the last year so that it has up-to-date graphics chips, video cards, and displays.

You then go to the game publisher's website (forget playing without broadband, by the way), knowing that you're in for a monthly subscription fee (around $15). You get to play as much as you like for that fee, and your character gets to die as often as necessary. (This is a subscription business—you can't kill off the customers permanently!)

You're now ready to log in, but don't think it's time to start slaying dragons. The first thing that happens is that the client software on your machine most likely needs to be updated. This is critical. These games are hugely complex, and there are constant updates, most related to new game features and software bugs. In either case, everyone in the game needs to be playing the same version. The update might take a while to download. Be patient.

Next, you need to do business. You fill in credit card information, agree to the End User Licensing Agreement, and then see an official-looking Code of Conduct document. Take this latter document seriously. Saying or doing bad things in the games (generally, bad things, both words and deeds, are defined in the same way as they are in real life) will not be tolerated. You'll be banned from the world. No questions. No refunds.

A million people might be playing your game at the same time; that is, you could conceivably run into any of them in the 3D world you hope to get to soon. But that's too many people to put on a single computer, so players need to be divided among several servers, each running the same copy of the game. The servers aren't always random divisions of players. You'll have an opportunity to request the same server that all your friends are on, and if you don't have any game friends yet, you can make your server decision based on style of play. One server might emphasize player-versus-player combat (frequent combat, without remorse, taking no prisoners). Another might emphasize more cooperative group action.

Getting in Character

Time to enter the 3D game world now? Nope. First you need a character. These are *role-playing* games. And the role you choose, as well as the complementary artifacts, powers, and duties, will shape how and whether you have fun. You'll see a default character on the screen, but the expectation is that you'll spend considerable time reshaping it. There are lots of decisions: man or woman, priest or warrior, facial hair or not, tall or short, intelligent or strong. And on and on, ending with a name, hopefully a cool one that hasn't been taken.

Next might appear what looks like the beginning of a movie trailer. This is usually a five-minute or so backstory about the world you'll soon enter. You'll see some of the places in the games, and some of the prominent villains. But most important, you'll be immersed in a *narrative*. The game world has a history, sometimes a long one, and many of the decisions you'll make about play will need to conform to that narrative. The story is likely a good one, crafted by professionals, many straight from the film industry. You're getting sucked in. "I wonder what will happen next in the world?"

Movie over. And now you're dropped into the world—finally. You're occupying space in a 3D representation of a real-looking place. There are buildings, trees, objects, weather, light (depending on time of day), and other avatars (or characters) operated by other players. Now some interface learning is required. What you see on your screen (analogous to where the camera is in a movie) is totally up to you. You can watch yourself in the world from above or you can put the camera in the eyes of your character (called the first-person view). The default and most popular position is to place the camera over your character's shoulder (you'll soon start saying "over *my* shoulder"). That way, you get to see yourself and everyone else in the scene at the same time.

Getting into the Game

The next interface tricks involve movement. You'll use a mouse to move your character left, right, backward, or forward or to run, take flight, or ride on a flying reptile. When you move your character, the scene changes around you just as it seems it should if you were actually there. There's a ton of information surrounding you, and there are other characters (that is, other real people represented in the game) in the center of your screen. We'll talk more later about the information that's available, but know now that it's an impressive dashboard of buttons, sliders, graphs, data tables, and visual icons that give you moment-by-moment information about your (and every-one else's) location, health, needs, expertise, and success.

Now you've crossed over. You're now *in* media, not just watching it. Tele-vision will never be the same. *You* get to determine where *you* go (you're no longer saying "your character"), how fast, and with whom. *You* are now free to do anything you want in the virtual world.

Here's where the fun starts. What are you going to do? The answer is almost always the same thing you'd do in real life. You'll never be teleported into a medieval forest in real life, but if you were, what would you do? Prob-ably walk around and look for signs of life. Is there anyone else here? You find a stone that's glowing. You press a button on the screen that gives you information about the stone. You next meet another character who tells you about objects that are needed in the village at the edge of the woods (he adds that they're willing to pay gold for them). Gold is good in the game, so you search the forest, find what might be a desired object, figure out the interface buttons you need to transfer the object to your personal inventory, and then deliver it to the village. Five gold pieces are yours when you get there. And you're no longer at level 1. You've moved up to level 2, and it says so in your character profile, which everyone can view. Cool.

Promotion to the highest level in the game can take another five hundred hours.[18] Along the way you'll participate in all of the following, and each will take substantially longer than your first walk about in the forest: you'll do combat, solve puzzles, auction and buy virtual goods (stuff you've found and stuff you need), open a bank account to store and trade gold, join a guild (you can't get to the higher levels without a lot of help from other characters), and go on raids (quests that require twenty-five or more participants). And you'll do all of this (and much more) while in character and in costume according to the details of an entertaining narrative.

The important point is that the games we've examined with business in mind are about more than shooting, fast cars, and sports. They're about developing characters and relationships in groups, strategies and tactics for collective action, sophisticated communication between players, and metrics and money that enable vibrant economies. The single most important comment about the games echoes the first reaction most people have when they enter a 3D game world—the boundary between real and virtual is not as precise as one thought it would be.

Popular Games

Our thesis is about a genre of games and a new generation of gamers, not about any particular game title that's popular today. That said, some specific recommendations are in order for those who may want to study up by looking at current products. Don't expect to take a quick look, however. The threshold for entrance into these worlds is pretty high: hundreds of hours to get to the top levels or to gain the best game artifacts that will be the keys to future play. And you'll need to be at the top level while possessing just the right gear before you get to see the coolest places, participate in the biggest adventures, or hang with the best players.

Here's a sampling of multiplayer online role-playing games that might help you and others in your organization get acquainted with games and their possibilities.

- *World of Warcraft* (Blizzard Entertainment). Gamers create their own characters by choosing among ten races (including dwarves, orcs, and humans) and nine roles (such as hunter, mage, and rogue). Players advance in the game by joining guilds and collaborating to explore new destinations and complete complex quests.

- *EVE Online* (CCP). Players participate in a hypercapitalistic competition among corporations that battle in outer space for galactic domination. Gamers progress by making money rather than killing monsters.

- *EverQuest* (Sony Online Entertainment). This medieval fantasy game involves three types of play: adventuring (gaining experience and loot), trading with other players, and social interaction. Gamers must cooperate with rather than hinder one another.

- *Lineage* (NCsoft). This game is based on a castle siege system, in which castle owners set tax rates in cities and collect taxes on items purchased in city stores. Victory in player-versus-player fighting is the route to success, but gamers are penalized for killing players who don't fight back.

- *Star Wars Galaxies* (Sony Online Entertainment). Based on the *Star Wars* characters and narrative, this game requires that players either train for professions that provide game services or make useful products—and then market those services or products on game planets. To advance, players must keep the supply chain filled and satisfy customer demand.

A search on any of these titles will return hundreds of websites with the most recent news, pictures, and even movies of current play (including last night's best raid). Have fun!

Games Versus Virtual Environments

When people talk about games, especially those where the play is in 3D worlds, they often confuse multiplayer games and virtual environments. We have a lot to say about the differences, but for now it's important to note that gamers (including the undergraduates who we employed to help show us the games) are adamant that these categories are different.

Visual three-dimensional online social worlds—such as *Second Life* for adults and *Club Penguin*, *Webkinz*, and *Habbo* for children—are becoming increasingly popular. Like MMOs, virtual environments are characterized by real-time interaction among avatars (the online personae that participants create), and they typically have virtual economies that allow people to buy and sell virtual goods (land, clothing, furniture, and more) using a synthetic currency.

Unlike MMOs, however, virtual social worlds lack structured, mission-oriented narratives, defined character roles, and explicit goals. Instead of collaborating to slay monsters in accordance with an intricate narrative, people simply do things together—go to a club with friends to listen to music or invite people over to a home they've decorated with items purchased from virtual stores. People in a social world *can* play games, many of which offer prizes or currency to buy even more virtual stuff, but the world itself isn't created around game objectives. You have to design and build the game yourself within the virtual world.

Chapter 4 describes our idea of the key ingredients in terrific games. We will say more there about the ingredients that differentiate virtual online worlds from games. Still, virtual social worlds offer significant opportunities for collaboration. In *Second Life*, for example, virtual residents can work together to build things or establish businesses that offer an array of virtual products and services. A common use of virtual worlds is to provide a place to meet, not unlike places in real life, but without the need for an airplane ride to get there. You could have a sales meeting, do leadership training, or set up a human resources booth. That's why real-world businesses of all kinds have set up shop in these worlds to experiment, and it's why there is significant investment in new technologies that will make these worlds industrial strength enough to support corporate computing.

Why Do People Play?

Why in the heck are Nick and friends willing to spend so much time in the games? Is there purpose to their experiences beyond a pleasurable way to pass time? It's tempting to say that everyone needs downtime or that it's just fun to play. The surprise, however, is that research has discovered there are diverse reasons to play, and substantial ones that parallel the motivations to do almost anything in life.[19] Most participants have several reasons to play, but any one reason could be enough to join the game.

A first division in categorizing motivations is personal versus social. Are you seeking play that involves other people, or can you find purpose on your own? The social motivations are competition and socializing; the personal ones are achievement, immersion, and exploration. We'll start with the personal.

Achievement

Gamers motivated to achieve are interested in personal rewards and in gaining power within the context of the game. They like to collect rare or special items in the game (and brag about them afterward), they like to see themselves at the top of leader boards, and they generally prefer the games that have lots of opportunity to advance and the potential for the largest possible difference between people at the bottom and top of the game hierarchy. They like clear goals and less ambiguity about what's needed to advance, and it's best if there's a lot of score keeping. They're hooked on game reinforcement and have a constant desire to become more powerful. Unlike most work experience, the yardsticks for achievement in games are pretty clear before and after one has done something. Recognition is dependable.

Immersion

MMOs require that you play within the role of your character and the skills you have acquired. This involves creativity to produce an immersive fantasy experience. Players motivated by immersion like trying out new characters with different personalities (many players have more than one character—"tonight I feel like playing the priest"). These players are good actors who enjoy being cast in dramatic roles that help elaborate the narrative that guides the game. They're escaping to a fantasy world. The game features they enjoy most are character customization, complicated plots, and emphasis on the filmlike features that surround the play—great soundtracks and aesthetically pleasing 3D surroundings. They like good metaphors in the game and emotionally appealing stories. The downside of this motivation, the research shows, is that it's often a response to real life, as in "I'm trying to avoid it."

Exploration

In real life, we frequently spend time with people driven by curiosity about how they and their environments work. The same is true for some gamers. The motivation to explore includes simply traveling around to interesting places. Much of the current 3D art in games is interesting and some stunningly so, especially if you're playing on a high-definition, large screen. Game designers call it "eye candy." You get to jump into the picture and walk around, a little like teleporting to a favorite vacation spot, but one that keeps adding acreage every time there's a software update. Exploration also includes more than 3D places. Players enjoy exploring game mechanics, finding out how the game works even if they don't plan to fully engage in the mechanics themselves.[20]

Competition

The most obvious social motivation is competition. It's clear to any game newbie that points, levels, badges, and rewards identify winners and losers. Many enjoy the competition, and their play is efficient and optimized for victory. Competition is social because it's often player versus player. Some competition is friendly and meant as an opportunity to optimize individual contributions by pitting one's talents against others. But it's also true that players with this motivation often have a desire to annoy, anger, manipulate, scam, and yes, kill the enemy. They're attracted to game metaphors about combat, and it's best if the combat gets bigger and nastier as the play unfolds.

Socializing

Finding friends is a second important social motivation. Because the games require cooperation, much of the action affords at least an opportunity to begin a social relationship. It's not often that spontaneous and intimate conversations happen, but they might, and many people play the games just for this reason. Achieving a higher game level for these people might be just a ticket to better conversations rather than an end in itself. The game features most important to satisfying this motivation are chat channels, integrated e-mail, guild membership, and service within the guild communities. These people also extensively track social relationships and are drawn, just like the myriad users of Facebook and MySpace, to any game features that allow them to list, order, and map social networks and to expose that information for others to see and use.

Gamer Sensibilities

Do gamers think differently? We initially referred to this section as "The Gamer Generation," after a good book about new attitudes that young players have about collaboration and play that have been influenced by their in-game experiences.[21] There is also a wonderful new treatment of how the millennial generation is shaking up the workplace.[22] We think it's now the case, however, that this is *more* than a generational issue. It's tempting to believe that the gamer sensibilities described in this section are somehow bestowed on youth as a result of deep and enduring experiences they've had with digital technology, starting almost at birth. But the truth is that people of all ages can acquire these same sensibilities, and often easily, as a result of sophisticated game play. Recall that thirty-somethings are more likely to play the sophisticated games than teens, college students, and other twenty-somethings. And it's the older folks, those in their forties, fifties, and sixties, who are putting in the most hours per week. Consequently, we review here the sensibilities that *any* gamer can be expected to develop with extended play.

Regardless of age, gamers will have different ideas about collaboration, learning, and the best ways to use technology at work. Nick's experience— long hours with trusted friends accomplishing difficult tasks—creates major expectations about how technology should be used to guide group activity. These expectations are more important than the game demographics of age, gender, and time. (How many of the following gamer generation traits are well considered in business, even at companies spending millions per year on collaboration technology?)

First, many gamers are extremely social, especially online. Game inter- faces facilitate social interaction, even if emphasizing the quantity of relation- ships over their quality. Game environments feel more social than a typical workplace. All aspects of planning, action, rehearsal, and evaluation—and plenty of goofing around time in between—involve *conversations*. Gamers expect and are comfortable with discussion, group action, and, importantly, group conflict. In this aspect, games only accentuate what is true of all con- temporary media: social information is ubiquitous, quickly disseminated in short bursts, updated constantly, and really interesting.

Second, competition is fun and familiar to gamers, and losing isn't such a big deal. True, the wins and losses don't involve real dollars or jobs, but it's also true that real egos, reputations, and feelings are on the line. Research shows that psychological responses to games are almost equally sensitive to real and virtual consequences, much more than may seem appropriate. You win and lose often in games, and you get used to both, dampening the extremes.

Third, the speed of the games encourages trial and error as a reasonable, and for many the best, way to learn. Go ahead and experiment: if it doesn't work, we'll try something else, and usually right away. A trial-and-error strategy redefines risk, an important ingredient for innovation in business. Gamers learn to expect that plans will often fail. What's important is to make the effort, register the feedback, and keep going.

Finally, the games promote a meritocracy. Any player who performs well (and remember, the computer is keeping track and displaying results for all to see) has a chance to advance. There are no secret paths to the top. Leader- ship is bestowed on those who are doing well now, and it's not predeter- mined (as it often is in business) by a résumé of past accomplishments. Supervision is less important than mentoring, in part because the environ- ments in which leadership happens contain so much useful information about how things are going. Not all of these features are going to translate literally into the workplace, but each receives further examination in the coming chapters.

These sensibilities can usefully guide the construction of game-inspired software that will fundamentally change how work is accomplished. But it's also true that these sensibilities are important beyond a business appetite to "gamify" work. Some scholars think that games have become a powerful influence on *all* expectations about everyday life, not just work. McKenzie Wark, in his book *Gamer Theory*, says that games, as the new dominant forms of media, have become the *only* place in life where utopian promises (including those of meritocracy and a free market) are truly kept.[23] The ubiquity of games makes them a primary lens for evaluating real life, and as experiences with games grow, the comparison looks increasingly bad for real life. The real world becomes an inescapable series of less and less perfect games—unless, of course, the real world can be redesigned to meet the games halfway.

The Game Revolution in the Context of Media History

Like similar media revolutions over the last century, the role of games at work will be controversial. How can a collaborative raid on a famous dragon and his protectors be a blueprint for serious work that will affect a company's bottom line?

A common reaction, especially when people think about how colleagues might respond, is doubt—at least doubt projected on those who are in control. "I might really enjoy the games," some say, "but I'm pretty sure my boss would never allow it." This sentiment is particularly true as the level of the work considered becomes more serious. "Well, maybe call center workers would work more effectively in a game, but certainly not the scientists in my lab."

There are lessons from history, however, that might help persuade those who doubt the power of entertainment. The history is about the original purposes envisaged for new media by the organizations that introduced them, how people have greeted new media inventions, and especially about how they've greeted media originally designed to be serious when they've come to emphasize fun.

The eventual, if gradual, fusion of what is serious and fun has been a theme in the last century of media innovation. Traditional media, when they were first proposed and launched, often promised benefits that were serious, and most of the early research about their effects concentrated on serious outcomes such as learning.[24] Telephones, radio, film, and television were heralded for their potential to inform, facilitate democracy, or help during emergencies. New media have often invited utopian dreams—universal wealth, enhanced freedom, revitalized politics, vibrant communities, and personal fulfillment.

Pure entertainment—gossip on the phone, music on the radio, situation comedies on television—was not often anticipated to be the popular use of media technology and certainly not the mainstay of the media business. The history of media has precious few promises that "this is going to be a lot of fun!" Fun was more a sideshow, and it described primarily novelty uses.

The history of modern media, however, shows that it's rarely wise to bet against fun; entertainment dominates modern media, even when the first uses are serious. Some of the influence is easy to see, but much of the influence is subtle. For example, product advertising changed from thoughtful teaching about how products work (the doctor in a lab coat discussing a new drug) to emotional appeals that engage attention (the person next door talking about a changed life because of a new drug). Television news changed from "just the facts" to compelling narratives that highlight the struggles and accomplishments of people with whom audiences can identify.

Computers, the newest medium onto which the utopian promise was projected, were to be standard bearers of all that is efficient, fast, and powerful. Only recently (and slowly) has computing succeeded, at least partially, in fulfilling this promise by using connections, interface simplicity, advanced displays, and processing intelligence as much to make interactions engaging as efficient. It may be a stretch to say that computers are fun, but it's certainly correct to say that computing experiences are moving toward more compelling interactivty.

The commonality in all of these examples is that entertainment eventually makes its way into media experiences, either in a pure form or as an important overlay that energizes serious topics. It's reasonable to worry that this evolution describes the triumph of commercial appeal over substance. Catering to entertainment patronizes primitive instincts and may limit the potential of media to nurture the best of human communication. But that concern ignores what is human about *social* connections. Humans are built to interact in a complex fashion that hopelessly confuses the emotional and rational, including what is fun and serious. We think this is a primary reason why games will eventually find a reception in serious places.

People think and work hard when they're excited. As media make possible increasingly rich exchanges (more ways to communicate emotion, excitement, and enthusiasm), engagement will determine how information influences and facilitates work. When people talk about fusing what is serious and fun, they typically refer to traditional content such as news, advertising, and public affairs. There is little mention of office technology, and we think that's wrong. Increasingly, social, emotional, and engaging interactions will make their way into the office, and in fact, the migration is well under way. What we advocate is making the transition more explicit. It's one thing to benefit from small doses of engagement, as might be the case, for example, when groups use visually rich (and even fun) social networking software to facilitate office collaboration. It's quite another, however, to immerse the full range of work activities in the narrative of a comprehensive game. Both could have a positive influence, but it's the latter that may be required to truly change the nature of work.

What specific business problems might the engagement of games solve? That's next. To start, let's eavesdrop on Henry, Sang Yap, Deepak, and Alice. They're talking about how work is going in their company.

Chapter Three

"Work Sucks"

Corporate Problems That Games Might Solve

The waiter has just delivered the second round of beers (and a cosmopolitan) to Sang Yap, Henry, Deepak, and Alice at the front table of their favorite watering hole. Alice is riffing on why she said that her work sucks. "First of all, it's not really clear if our project is going to make a difference. I keep getting conflicting signals. And the stuff they have me working on is not really in my power alley, especially since Bill and half of his department were laid off. The timelines are totally unrealistic, especially given how often I have to stop and answer e-mail—my inbox is killing me!"

"No kidding, Alice," says Deepak, "I know we're trying to make the numbers for this quarter but this stuff doesn't seem to have anything to do with the big picture." Sang Yap interrupts, "Not me: I know I'm working on the right problem, but I'm frustrated because I can't tell if I'm approaching it the right way and probably won't find out till the end." Henry finally speaks up and says, without even a hint of irony, "It's a good thing the boss cares about loyalty because that seems to be all that really matters here."

Seeking Engagement

When the youngest members of the workforce gather after hours, it's no surprise when rude descriptions are heard partway through happy hour. If for no other reason, these young adults are coming to terms with real-world roles and responsibilities in the narrow slice of the business cycle that represents their brief worklife. But they also know that there's a vast gulf between the deeply satisfying, purposeful, and engaging work that people truly yearn to do and the reality of today's enterprise "user experience." Our story is about how the user experience available to gamers *outside* of work will drive expectations about what the experience should look like at work.

In addition to the rites of passage that younger workers endure, they bring the sensibilities and expectations of their millennial cohort into institutions struggling to come to terms with titanic shifts in the flow of information among global collaborators and competitors. New school meets old school just as the old school is facing unprecedented challenges.

That said, we find it a bit hard to take seriously people who argue that the corporation per se is in crisis. It's good for selling books, but the real story is one of accelerating change that requires *all* institutions to evolve and adapt faster every year. This is a disaster in slow motion that requires attention. If economic turmoil isn't motivation enough, companies should take responsibility for driving change because demographic tides will force the issue of productivity.

Demographic Imperatives for Productivity Gains

The number of workers in relation to dependents is going down in developed countries. The number of elderly nonworkers per one hundred U.S. workers will increase from twenty-two today to almost forty in 2040.[1] Meanwhile, the number of workers is being replenished more slowly, because the number of children per one hundred workers is expected to decline from over seventy in the 1960s to about fifty in the next thirty years. Thus, the ratio of workers to dependents is declining dramatically, from five to one going toward two to one in the middle of this century.

Unless productivity improvements keep pace, we can expect the standard of living to decline. A U.S. Federal Reserve Board forecast has real per capita consumption down almost 27 percent by 2040 unless worker participation or productivity changes for the better.[2] Based on the productivity gains seen in the last few decades, growth will have to come from information technology combined with new ways to organize work. People sitting in front of computers (or wearing them or walking around inside them or some such) will be part of the equation for a long time to come.

As we've said, a big part of our argument is that the user experience *outside* work will drive expectations about what the experience should look like *at* work. It's not so hard to see how popular forms of the latest social media, such as blogs, wikis, personal Web pages, and social networks, can support enterprise collaboration and teamwork. Indeed, these ideas are being deployed or at least studied at every company we know. We are pushing further, to explore how the full immersive user interface of multiplayer online games, with all of the related affordances, could shape expectations at work and eventually the entire workplace.

Analyzing Work

It may be useful here to further describe our own journey as we examined the portion of our argument that's about the workplace. Neither of the authors has a reputation as a management guru, but we have read many books by them. We have both run organizations of middling scale and have been part of high-performance teams in large organizations. As we have developed this thesis, we have immersed ourselves in some of the business literature on management and organization in order to look for parallels with the games we are studying. This was a deliberate attempt to map across these domains looking for useful similarities, differences, and metaphors. And then we have listened hard in hundreds of meetings with enterprise workers and their leaders. We've surely missed some important insights and trust our readers to add them.

We have alternated between examining the details of the work and the context in which work takes place. By *details*, we take note of the difference between transformational, transactional, and tacit work, as described in writings by McKinsey & Company.[3] By *context*, we find it useful to consider the large drivers of human performance: purpose, meaning, and consequence.

What appealed to us in these ideas is the attention to improving the productivity of tacit workers, the category McKinsey & Company believes will be most important in the future.[4] If you've missed the argument, it goes like this: old-school work, such as extracting raw materials or converting them into finished goods, is *transformational work* and accounts for a declining 15 percent of the U.S. workforce. The second category, *transactional work*, includes people interacting with people but in fairly routine ways according to rules that may eventually be automated. Mechanization and offshoring can improve productivity for the first category (but not without consequences), and automation will sometimes improve productivity in the second. It is not so obvious how to improve productivity in the third category, *tacit work*, which defines tasks that are ambiguous and require tacit or experiential knowledge. The report concluded that because machines can't replace tacit workers, we need to complement and extend their capabilities and activities. Strategies include using machines to get the transactional part of tacit workers' jobs out of the way so they can concentrate on the thoughtful stuff.

The rise of interest in tacit work is coupled to the increasing importance of intangible assets that are shared between the firm and the individual. Although companies own intellectual property, it is people who possess knowledge. Firms may own networks, but it is people who have relationships. A company can own a brand, but individuals own their own reputation.[5] The implication is that a lot of value can walk out the door unless the conditions are in place to create loyalty, and a lot of assets are wasted unless the conditions are in place to allow talent to be unleashed. Put another way, you can't *command* the things you want from tacit knowledge workers; you have to create the conditions in which they want to give you innovation, collaboration, and insight. Furthermore, traditional performance management metrics that are derived from a world focused on *efficiency* aren't going to work when what we need from tacit workers is *effectiveness*.

In *Good Business*, Mihaly Csikszentmihalyi brings the discussion of "flow" into the workplace.[6] We'll have more to say about flow in chapter 9, but relevant here is that he warns of the consequences when organizational purpose is not clear and inspiring, when individual goals are uncertain, when feedback is missing or confusing, when there is a mismatch between skills and challenges, and when people don't have sufficient control over their work, especially with respect to time. The warning comes through: the most important changes may be to stop doing harm to people so they can flourish. The dependency between employer and employee is shifting in favor of the worker who brings informal tacit knowledge to the job.

Our own simple scheme overlays these useful categories. Some work is too hard and some work is too easy, but in both cases, quality work experiences are hard to find.

Work That's Too Easy

Information workers like Jennifer, whose story introduces chapter 1, are plentiful. Most of them are sitting in front of a computer. They dominate the U.S. economy in numbers (in 2003, 55 percent of all U.S. workers used a computer at work) and in financial importance.[7] The growth trend for information work has been steady over the last century, increasing 12 percent per decade as jobs move out of factories and agriculture. This shift, however, is finite. Increased value will have to come from increased productivity within jobs that are already well defined.

Jennifer's evaluation of her job defines an impediment to growth in the information economy: the work is often boring and tedious. This is especially true for workers whose *task is their job*. Mechanical automation will continue to rescue workers from some boringly easy and dreary jobs in the category of transformational work, and computer automation and artificial intelligence will help avoid the same for some people doing transactional work. But much transactional work may yield slowly to computer automation because there are still pattern recognition tasks (and relationships with other human beings) for which the human brain has evolved special advantages. For example, we are thinking about the millions performing jobs in call centers or carrying out video surveillance, and those who process forms for a living. This may not describe you, but consider for a moment how many people in your finance, sales, compliance, production, quality, and shipping departments do pretty much the same thing all day long. Important jobs that would be easy if they weren't so tedious will remain part of the economy for some time to come, and humans will need to do them, either because such jobs are too hard for machines or because some form of personalized involvement is required.

When inefficiencies are extracted from information work, an obvious risk is that jobs will become even more boring, tedious, or stressful. Going faster, communicating at a higher clock rate, or forcing attention to greater detail could make things worse. Consequently, productivity gains may come at the risk of quality of work life, and by extension may eventually circle back to depress productivity. Decreased quality of work life has its own costs: job churn, absenteeism, and stress and its related health consequences. Games have a lot to offer people like Jennifer by introducing satisfying levels of complexity and aspiration over longer time scales that may not be intrinsic to the original job (more on this later in our discussions on feedback, levels, and teams). Games are also powerful enough to make things worse if badly implemented. Productivity must increase, but without jeopardizing the quality of life—and preferably enhancing it.

Work That's Too Hard

For another large class of information workers, many of whom must summon tacit knowledge to get through the day, work is too hard. As we said earlier, sometimes work is too hard because goals are in conflict or difficult to define. This guarantees confusion and stress. Sometimes it's because the learning curve for the task is too steep or because success takes a very long time to achieve. Few people can sustain real effort over time without seeing signs of intermediate success that allow moments of celebration.

Sometimes work is too hard because of interruptions and information overload. This is no small problem. Our most important workers are getting hundreds of e-mails a day, many of which are of low importance but must be processed.[8] When information workers are interrupted by a colleague, ringing phone, or an alert from their computer, the cost is not only the time spent handling the interruption but also the surprising amount of time it takes to get back to the original task.[9] Workers typically turn to two other tasks before returning, and some studies have documented an average lapse of twenty-five minutes before returning to the original task.[10] After only a few minutes of interrupted performance, workers reported significantly higher stress, frustration, workload, effort, and pressure.[11]

There has been a substantial effort to structure and filter information for tacit workers so they can be more productive, but the results are mixed. Think of the strategies your company has offered to help manage e-mail, for example. Collaboration tools and richer forms of communication are seen as part of the answer for helping tacit workers make their greatest contributions to the enterprise. Our conclusion is that this work is on the right track, but it hasn't gone nearly far enough.

And finally, sometimes work is too hard because other people make it that way on purpose.

In our study of games, we see design principles that can address all of these reasons that work is too hard. The first point is that games *are designed* and not just left to happen, as is the case for many jobs. A design discipline makes it easier to insure that goals are clear and not in conflict, for example. Successful games excel at providing intrinsic learning at just the right pace so that players don't drop out in frustration. Instead, players get feedback all along the way signaling their progress and personal growth. The best game user interfaces are a blend of the designer's vision and modifications (the gamers call them *mods*): software add-ons selected by users to customize how they see the state of play and the communication channels they want to use. Games don't encourage players to spam each other or interrupt key tasks. Games also give users avenues to avoid player-versus-player conflict if that is not their style. There are many paths to get ahead that don't require engaging in office politics.

If, right now, you are finding it easier to envision a call center worker going to work in a game than harvesting the benefits of game technology for work that's too hard, we hope you will hang in for the rest of the argument. It's built on the extraordinary importance of engagement, the exploitation of flow, the redeployment of feedback, and the use of graded challenge against compelling aspiration.

Mapping Games to Work

A key question involving our thesis is whether the activities going on in games have anything to do with the real world of work. A systematic look at this question yielded astonishing parallels.

We have already described the Stanford students we recruited, based on their gaming résumés, to help us explore the intersection of games and work. We launched our collegiate gamers into this project by giving them a quest: find taxonomies of information work that could serve as a template for mapping games to work. There are obviously a lot of ways to slice and dice the world of work, and a few rather serious attempts to make sense of the various lists.[12] What the students found most useful was a list, not limited to information work per se, from a project called O*NET. The Occupational Information Network is a large-scale collaborative project hosted at the North Carolina Employment Security Commission and sponsored by the U.S. Department of Labor.[13] It publishes and maintains a list of over eight hundred different occupations and provides tools to help employers with job design and to help prospective workers match their skills to defined jobs.[14] We think that even the most complex and sophisticated senior management jobs can be encompassed by choosing an ensemble of activities from this list.

The next step was for the gamer guides to dive into the games and look for examples of work guided by the O*NET categories of "generalized work activities." We thought the exercise would yield a lot of good examples. The findings surpassed that expectation. Keeping in mind that the taxonomy was intended to cover *all* the key building blocks of modern jobs, it was interesting to find that *every skill in the list* was represented in multiple instances of gamer experience. The student gamers could most often provide multiple examples within a single game title for each job category as well as examples from multiple games. This conclusion, of course, equates the manipulation of virtual objects in a graphical 3D world with physical tasks in the real world. We'll develop the argument in favor of that comparison later, but for now we'll say that there's good evidence that the equation is justified: work is work, virtual or real.

In the next section, we list forty of the O*NET work categories (in italics) accompanied by game descriptions from the gamers that can be linked with each category. This sample is clearly biased by our attention to a few titles, especially *World of Warcraft* (WoW), but other work suggests that most of the modern, collaborative online games would yield similar findings.

You don't have to study the entire list to get the main point. People are paying game publishers to do work just like the kind of work that companies pay workers to do! One might argue that different or better taxonomies could be used to perform this analysis, and it might be possible to find *some* real-world tasks that aren't yet well represented in the games we've studied, but we find it difficult to reach any conclusion other than that the real world of work is beautifully and deeply represented in games right now.

We've included references to websites and defined game language in brackets. You can peruse these examples and absorb game details in the words of our student gamers.

1. *Getting information: observing, receiving, and otherwise obtaining information from all relevant sources.*

    In order to shape their own army in *Company of Heroes*, players scout the opposing party using a swift squad of infantry to see which units the opponent is upgrading.[15]

    On the first raid attempt against a new boss [a game-generated monster that needs to be conquered] in *WoW*, each guild member is expected to know the boss's attacks, the nuances of the encounter, and the role he or she is expected to play in the raid's planned strategy. To do this, everyone needs to check a site such as WoWWiki [www.wowwiki.com/Portal:Main], a collaborative Web game guide that also contains extensive details on quests, items, and even the game's backstory. From a boss's page here, players learn about the strategies used by other successful guilds. Often, there will be links to multiple YouTube videos providing a visual guide to an encounter.

2. *Monitoring processes, materials, or surroundings: monitoring and reviewing information from materials, events, or the environment to detect or assess problems.*

    In *Diablo II: Lord of Destruction*, players must be mindful of their surroundings as they travel, careful not to set off any traps planted for them.[16]

    Healers in a *WoW* raid must play close attention to their raiding party's health, being alert to send a heal [a spell that restores health] whenever someone is too low.

    In *WoW*, people who play a "tank" class [players that draw fire during raids] must monitor the constantly changing threat of the other twenty-four players in the raid and react accordingly by either changing their actions or asking their teammates to change theirs.

3. *Identifying objects, actions, and events: identifying information by categorizing, estimating, recognizing differences or similarities, and detecting changes in circumstances or events.*

    In *Guild Wars*, players identify spells cast by other players by their signature visual effects so as to avoid being poisoned by passing through an enchanted area.[17]

    Players in *WoW* must constantly analyze the environment around their avatars, including identifying what type of hostile mobs [dangerous nonplayer characters] are in the area and what they are doing. This information is critical in allowing a player to either progress through an area safely or engage an opponent effectively.

4. *Inspecting equipment, structures, or material: inspecting equipment, structures, or materials to identify the cause of errors or other problems or defects.*

    In *Age of Empires III*, players must inspect and repair the defenses of their towns.[18] If they don't recognize the early signs of decay in the walls, they are more vulnerable to an attack.

    Raid leaders in *WoW* use special tools to ensure that their entire party has recently repaired their equipment prior to starting a raid, as well as ensuring they have brought the required "consumables" with them to the raid.

5. *Estimating the quantifiable characteristics of products, events, or infor-mation: estimating sizes, distances, and quantities or determining time, costs, resources, or materials needed to perform a work activity.*

    When a boss is successfully conquered in *Guild Wars*, players decide whether the virtual items dropped [or left] by the com-puter-generated monster should be retained to improve their character or used for financial gain.

    In a given set of *WoW* raid dungeons, there might be several items that drop [prizes for success that confer special powers]. Deciding which item to choose is a trade-off between subtleties. One item might improve a player's chance of hitting a raid boss [the main target of raids] with his or her spells by 1 percent, and another might improve the damage that those spells cause by a factor of 37. Deciding between the items requires trade-offs between options that will cause different types of damage during a boss fight. Players have created sets upon sets of complex spreadsheets to evaluate relevant game statistics that help with decisions. The analyses require players to enter their characters' personal statistics in order to model and compare quantitatively the benefits of different decisions.

Before stepping into any instance in *WoW*, group members must decide which other anonymous player characters to take with them based on abstract information. This information may include a player's in-game statistics, gear, talent specialization, or in-game reputation for skill and personality.

6. *Judging the qualities of things, services, or people: assessing the value, importance, or quality of things or people.*

Captains in *Counter-Strike* use practice sessions to judge players' reflexes, abilities, and teamwork on tactics before they assemble the most capable team for difficult matches.[19]

When a raid leader in *WoW* decides who to use on a given night, he or she needs to keep in mind the intricacies of the boss encounters that are planned. If the raid is up against a strictly timed boss like Brutallus in the Sunwell Plateau, he or she will want to bring as much raw firepower as possible. If the raid is up against the black dragon Onyxia, whose fight at some points requires slow and steady damage, he or she needs to know fellow guild members well enough to be able to choose gamers mature enough to hold back.

One successful character in *WoW* made his in-game fortune by tanking [fighting as a player specialized in taking damage] in raids well below his level of ability to maximize collaboration with players at a lower progression level in the game. Other players were willing to pay substantial amounts of hard-earned gold for his services, because they knew he was fast. This behavior appears to have been unanticipated by the game designers.

7. *Processing information: compiling, coding, categorizing, calculating, tabulating, auditing, or verifying information or data.*

Captains continuously evaluate their opponent's troop deployment over the sixteen rounds that make up a match in *Counter-Strike* in order to adjust their own plan of battle.

When fighting Gruul the Dragonkiller, the Gronn overlord of the ogres of *WoW*'s Outland, players must be highly conscious of the location of their fellow raiders on the battlefield. One of Gruul's attacks freezes the raid for several seconds before causing each player to deal massive damage to any nearby ally. Just as in the game of soccer—spread out or lose!

During encounters in *WoW*, players must be able to adapt to random events in an encounter and be able to quickly coordinate twenty-five people to respond to incoming information.

8. *Evaluating information to determine compliance with standards: using relevant information and individual judgment to determine whether events or processes comply with laws, regulations, or standards.*

Traders in *Diablo II* barter for goods based on careful consideration of the worth of virtual objects in game marketplaces.

When a *WoW* raid leader recruits players, he or she needs to determine whether a player's items are powerful enough to contribute effectively in raids. For example, it is generally thought that a warlock ought to have about 900 bonus shadow spell damage (a metric for player protection during a raid) before entering the haunted mansion Karazhan. But it's not just a numbers game. If the character has an especially high critical-strike chance, this might make up for a low bonus damage statistic; likewise, unusually low health might make the leader think twice before letting the raider join the group. Additionally, the raid leader needs to judge when the assembled talents as a whole are powerful and experienced enough to advance to more difficult dungeons.

Miners in *Star Wars Galaxies* must constantly reevaluate survey results from different places among the galaxies to determine the quality of materials being harvested.[20] Materials below a certain standard will make them hard-pressed to return a profit relative to time and money invested in their mining machinery, whereas materials of better than average quality will turn a much higher profit.

9. *Analyzing data or information: identifying the underlying principles, reasons, or facts of information by breaking down information or data into separate parts.*

To avoid having one of their five players picked off by an opposing team, *Counter-Strike* captains must decide whether to abandon a strategy, reposition, or stick it out based on the evolving game action.

During a *WoW* raid performance evaluation, the leader looks at a number of recorded statistics specific to each class, as well as anecdotal evidence supplied in chat channels from fellow raid members.

WoW players may compare their in-battle statistics against other players in identical situations to determine their performance level.

10. *Making decisions and solving problems: analyzing information and evaluating results to choose the best solution and solve problems.*

Once a *WoW* raid reaches a certain size, it's inevitable that certain members won't get along. Guild leaders must help resolve conflicts over personality, performance, and loot in the interest of keeping the guild an effective team.

Working through progression raids [a series of ever more difficult encounters], *WoW* guilds often struggle to learn new, complicated encounters. Players must identify the problem areas in the fight that are causing failure. It could be a boss ability, a player's skill, a group composition problem, or even a misunderstanding or bad assignment of responsibilities among the players. Leaders must be able to decide on the best changes, even if that means something as difficult as replacing somebody from the group, or maybe something as simple as changing a healing assignment.

11. *Thinking creatively: developing, designing, or creating new applications, ideas, relationships, systems, or products, including artistic contributions.*

Fallshrimfager was an infantry unit that was invincible until the makers of *Company of Heroes* introduced a patch that allowed players to discover eventually that it could be defeated by two units working together.

Every *WoW* raid is different. Guilds may have more (or just plain better) tanks, damage per second, or healers, and this may vary from night to night. Raid members must jointly develop alternate or entirely new strategies in order to bring bosses down.

Players in *WoW* have been able to tweak and expand player abilities and actions far beyond the intention of the game designers. This has led to an in-game terminology, "working as intended," to ironically describe an ability that is overpowered and that works counter to what the developers intended.

12. *Updating and using relevant knowledge: keeping up-to-date technically and applying new knowledge to your job.*

Patches for games are at least a monthly occurrence. New places are added and there are changes to the abilities of characters, making it impossible to stay up-to-date without consulting the lively Web communities that monitor the games. Recently, a *WoW* talent called Cheat Death was significantly rebalanced (that is, it didn't work the same way as before), and if you didn't know that the change increased vulnerability at low health, it could easily lead to death on the battlefield.

Database websites for *WoW* are extensive resources for players. They are updated daily, if not hourly, recording even minute changes in game information. Players must sort through and reference vast amounts of information relative to their needs.

13. *Developing objectives and strategies: establishing long-range objectives and specifying the strategies and actions to achieve them.*

Warcraft III players often choose to cripple the economy of opponents by attacking infrastructure prior to attacking armed forces so that they'll have an advantage rebuilding after battles.[21]

Raid leaders have timetables for expectations about when to move onto more advanced bosses and more difficult dungeons. Every so often, guilds discuss progress against the plan and analyze success or failure relative to the goals.

When a publisher updates a game by introducing new bosses, players must go on a crash course to explore the new content. Often, solutions will include highly organized actions among twenty-five people that involve specialized talents of several classes and players in the game. Open-mindedness is a must when attempting to explore the possible methods to overcome obstacles in an encounter.

14. *Scheduling work and activities: scheduling events, programs, and activities, as well as the work of others.*

Competitive *Counter-Strike* teams often practice four hours a night in anticipation of a tournament or match. To accommodate availability of computer servers and players, this often means playing from 11 p.m. to 3 a.m.

Guild members often organize practice sessions to introduce newer members to the game. Because many members are casual players, it is very important that the leader pick a time that will not interfere too much with offline obligations.

EVE Online has players from around the world who are engaged in the largest ongoing online battle in all of multiplayer gaming.[22] This takes place between the large corporations BoB and LV [their abbreviations in the game]. Battles may include over one thousand players, who must log on at all times of day depending on what part of the world they inhabit. After logging on, careful coordination must take place to organize the thousands of players in an effective battle strategy.

15. *Organizing, planning, and prioritizing work: developing specific goals and plans to prioritize, organize, and accomplish your work.*

Groups in *Guild Wars* plan voice-server meetings using e-mail and text messages so that they can develop battle strategies and decide whether investment in armor or weapons would more likely yield success.

When a guild prepares for a new encounter, raid officers must research the details of the fight and decide what members need to know, how to tell them, and what special preparation should be organized. In *WoW*, for example, Ragnaros the Firelord in the Molten Core was famous for requiring players to collect a special set of fire-resistant gear in order to survive his attacks.

WoW has vast amounts of content, and groups must decide not only when to play together but also how to most efficiently spend their time together. There are several options, some easier and with more certainty of a payout—but it's the more risky and difficult options that yield a better reward when completed.

16. *Performing general physical activities: performing physical activities that require considerable use of your arms and legs and moving your whole body, such as climbing, lifting, balancing, walking, stooping, and handling of materials.*

Players train to get stronger for contests in *Mount & Blade* by virtual horseback riding, including training with weapons such as a swinging rock or bow.[23]

Transport from village to village in *WoW*'s Azeroth is largely accomplished by riding on flying gryphons, bats, or even fire-breathing dragonhawks. The only problem is that to fly somewhere you must have traveled there on foot first. Part of starting any new character is walking around to different settlements and collecting these "flight points" for convenient travel later in the game.

Player progression in *WoW* includes leveling up the individual skills of your character. Do you want to get better at using swords? Pick one up and start practicing. Over time and repetitions, skills improve.

17. *Handling and moving objects: using hands and arms in handling, installing, positioning, and moving materials, and manipulating things.*

    Much of the challenge in *Diablo II* is embodied in quests where players must retrieve an object from a difficult game location.

    Many guilds have a bank officer in charge of keeping hundreds of items that the guild owns and giving easy access to guild members when they need them. Similarly, many characters have their own "mules" or "bank alts," characters whose sole purpose is to store items for a player's other characters.

    It is often necessary in *WoW* to travel the world, mining ore or gathering herbs before transporting them back to town for processing by blacksmiths or alchemists.

18. *Controlling machines and processes: using either control mechanisms or direct physical activity to operate machines or processes (not including computers or vehicles).*

    Some quests require you to assume a form other than your character. For example, the chess fight in *WoW*'s Karazhan involves each player taking control of a "chess piece" that is really a powerful soldier with unfamiliar abilities that the player must learn to operate in order to destroy the opponent pieces.

    Players in *EVE Online* control drone ships using a set of special commands. Advanced players may be simultaneously controlling dozens of these robots at the same time as they perform different tasks. Individual drones may need new instructions at any time, depending on changing circumstances.

19. *Operating vehicles, mechanized devices, or equipment: running, maneuvering, navigating, or driving vehicles or mechanized equipment, such as forklifts, passenger vehicles, aircraft, or watercraft.*

    Action in the single-player game *Grand Theft Auto 4* involves driving a vehicle to accomplish missions. Players can avoid arousing police suspicion by making smooth turns, stopping at traffic signals, and staying within the speed limit.

When a *WoW* player first gets a flying mount [an easier method to travel in the world], it takes some adjustment to get used to the altered control scheme of liftoff and three-dimensional travel.

Players in *EVE Online* spend their entire in-game lives in the cockpit of a space ship. The controls and functions require a special set of skills to control objects in a zero-gravity environment.

20. *Interacting with computers: using computers and computer systems (including hardware and software) to program, write software, set up functions, enter data, or process information.*

In *EVE Online*, players in space stations can use the station's computer to view complicated data regarding the regional or galactic market for goods and services. The market information includes in-depth price history of items and materials, current buy and sell orders, market basket analysis, and more.

21. *Drafting, laying out, and specifying technical devices, parts, and equipment: providing documentation, detailed instructions, drawings, or specifications to tell others about how devices, parts, equipment, or structures are to be fabricated, constructed, assembled, modified, maintained, or used.*

Most MMOs have a complex professional system in which players must learn the materials and processes involved in creating items needed for different jobs. In *WoW*, blacksmithing is famous for its recursive item creation; for example, in order to make the powerful two-handed mace Stormherald, you must have previously made the other two-handed mace, Deep Thunder, whose creation in turn uses a weapon called Thunder.

In *Star Wars Galaxies*, creating an item includes several stages of development. Special resources can be involved in each stage that will change the outcome of the final product. An in-depth understanding of the crafting process coupled with careful tweaking of materials is necessary to be a successful craftsman.

22. *Repairing and maintaining mechanical equipment: servicing, repairing, adjusting, and testing machines, devices, moving parts, and equipment that operate primarily on the basis of mechanical (not electronic) principles.*

Machines in *Star Wars Galaxies* wear down, requiring owners to produce or buy new parts or materials to replace old ones before putting machines back to work. Downtime can be harmful to players expecting continuous in-game income.

23. *Documenting/recording information: entering, transcribing, recording, storing, or maintaining information in written or electronic/magnetic form.*

    During a raid, the leader may reward or punish members by adding or removing points from their DKP balance (DKP is a guild-specific currency for the distribution of loot and is discussed extensively in chapter 7). Someone is usually assigned to keep track of DKP transactions, most often using a spreadsheet available for all members to see.

    In *WoW*, a common advanced activity is called combat log parsing. Players must record information from their combat logs into a readable form so that later on they will be able to analyze the information to improve future performance.

24. *Interpreting the meaning of information for others: translating or explaining what information means and how it can be used.*

    Not every boss action will affect all players in a fight. For example, a powerful melee attack will be relevant to healers (who must mitigate the damage to the tank) but not to players who are primarily concerned with making the bosses' health go to zero as fast as possible. Strategy must take into account who needs to pay attention to what in order to maximize each raid member's ability to focus on a task.

    Guild and raid leaders in *WoW* simply do not have time to break down the individual statistics for each of the fifty-plus members of a guild. Leaders will often appoint class leaders to analyze the performance of other people sharing their particular job in any given encounter. Class leaders must break down the combat histories, determine who is performing well (or underperforming), and inform guild leaders.

25. *Communicating with supervisors, peers, or subordinates: providing information to supervisors, coworkers, and subordinates by telephone, in written form, e-mail, or in person.*

    Preparing to fight a battle in *Guild Wars*, experienced players are in brainstorming mode. Their suggestions are important, but the team leader must make a decision about what will happen. The newest members mostly listen.

Many guilds have a complex officer system in which responsibilities (such as taking care of the bank, maintaining the website, or introducing new recruits to guild rules) are assigned to specific people. Other responsibilities (for example, picking new officers) might be more of a collective decision. Guild officers must use the organizational hierarchy to keep the guild running smoothly.

Players must understand that in groups, some sort of leadership must be assumed or the raid pace will be too slow. Players have to be prepared to give orders or receive them, depending on the situation. Eventually, the most established and skilled leaders take on a permanent role, sometimes lasting for years.

26. *Communicating with persons outside the organization: communicating with people outside the organization, representing the organization to customers, the public, government, and other external sources. This information can be exchanged in person, in writing, or by telephone or e-mail.*

    Guilds and raids will often have people in charge of recruiting. Their job is to use communication channels both inside and outside the game in order to find players qualified to fill a needed role in the group.

    In *EVE Online*, conflicting schedules or activities with other corporations can lead to costly battle engagements or unnecessary wars. Special positions within each corporation have the sole responsibility of communicating with outside corporations.

27. *Establishing and maintaining interpersonal relationships: developing constructive and cooperative working relationships with others, and maintaining them over time.*

    The amount of time and effort involved in progressive raiding in *WoW* more often than not leads to close relationships among members. As players become comfortable and better trust their guild mates, the guilds become a safe haven for discussion of personal issues and concerns. One couple we know in the guild Dawn of Victory eventually married after meeting in *WoW*.

28. *Assisting and caring for others: providing personal assistance, medical attention, emotional support, or other personal care to others such as coworkers, customers, or patients.*

Although healing classes love epic goodies [rewards from successfully defeating the boss], most bosses could rip through a priest's flimsy armor and kill him or her in a single swipe. Even the more durable classes might survive a swing or two, but certainly not long enough to do meaningful damage. Classes need to cooperate; the healers must keep the tough class (tanks) alive long enough to down the boss.

The sole responsibility of resto shamans in the *WoW* dungeon, Sunwell Plateau, is to use their Chain Heal ability to heal several thousand points of damage to multiple team members, all at a single point in time. Players may heal teammates hundreds of times in an encounter, allowing teammates to continue with other jobs.

29. *Selling or influencing others: convincing others to buy merchandise/goods or to otherwise change their minds or actions.*

To acquire the best players in *Counter-Strike*, captains must convince them they are a good fit with the team, that the team they're joining has the best chances of success, and that players have better options for advancement.

Over the course of the game, players come across (or become proficient in creating) many items that they do not have a use for but that may be great upgrades for other players. Although you can always sell them in the auction house, the rarest items may be so hard to price (or have so small a market) that it becomes more effective to spend your time advertising them in a chat channel or tell individual players about them.

Joining a guild in *WoW* is a complicated process. Players must make a résumé containing information about their current gear, statistics, past experience, ability to learn, and ability to mesh personalities with the rest of the guild.

30. *Resolving conflicts and negotiating with others: handling complaints, settling disputes, and resolving grievances and conflicts or otherwise negotiating with others.*

As *Counter-Strike* captains develop their rosters, they must convince players from the bench to participate as well as starters, and sometimes must also help a team get comfortable with new recruits.

Raid leaders are often faced with conflicts between members competing for the same loot. The raid can only progress if the members are motivated to cooperate, and this represents a significant roadblock unless the leader can resolve all issues.

In *EVE Online*, loyalty and trust are paramount. Suspicion lasts for months regarding new players entering the ranks of established corporations for fear a newbie might be a spy reporting economic or military plans back to rivals. Leaders, however, must be prepared to spend the majority of their time in diplomatic relations with other corporations and the hundreds of rival corporations spread throughout the game.

31. *Performing for or working directly with the public: performing for people or dealing directly with the public. This includes serving customers in restaurants and stores, and receiving clients or guests.*

Many guilds and players have made their names by accomplishing unusual feats such as defeating formidable bosses with laughably small groups or performing roles very unusual for their class (for example, a traditional healing class acting as tanks). They then publicize the accomplishments on sites such as YouTube.

Each guild in *WoW* takes pride in its public website. This is the place to post new accomplishments or to ask new recruits to apply. Needless to say, appearance is everything and can mean the difference between recruiting a successful team or floundering.

32. *Coordinating the work and activities of others: getting members of a group to work together to accomplish tasks.*

No strategy is successful in *Counter-Strike* without coordination of player movements, as in the 3/2 split, where two players simulate an attack on one side of the map while the other three try to split the defending team coming to the rescue.

Much of the challenge in the fight against the naga Lady Vashj (*WoW*) is a result of the unpredictability. In addition to damaging the boss's minions, players must also play virtual hot potato with an item called Tainted Core to shut off the generators powering the boss's protective shield. Holding a Tainted Core paralyzes a character, but the character is able to toss it to someone closer to the generator. In order to minimize the total time, health, and mana that the raid wastes fighting minions (called "adds") while the boss's shield is up, players need to use voice chat tools such as Ventrilo [a trademark of Flagship Industries, Inc.] to alert the recipient of the core that they have it and need to use it.

Riven's "2,3,4,5" arena teams in *WoW* occasionally rely on coordinated "burst" damage [a lot of damage in a short period of time]. This requires the simultaneous action of everyone on the team when attempting to defeat an enemy player, and success varies in direct proportion to the level of coordination.

33. *Developing and building teams: encouraging and building mutual trust, respect, and cooperation among team members.*

Forming a new raid group and keeping it healthy can be a challenging undertaking. This often involves learning to work with and trust people that you're meeting for the first time, and adapting strategies and rules to their personalities and play styles.

When creating a "2,3,4,5" Arena team in *WoW*, Riven the warrior already knew that he wanted an MS warrior, frost mage, elemental shaman, disc priest, and a holy paladin. The question was, of the hundreds of characters to choose from, how should he form his team? Riven used personal references as well as player profiles to determine what types of player personalities and abilities he wanted. Some of the best players were too arrogant, and some of the most personable players simply didn't have adequate gear or natural ability. After considering several possible choices for each player slot on the team, Riven finally found a solid group of five players. Later in the season, however, Riven was forced to acknowledge he'd made a bad decision choosing Annihelea as his frost mage and was forced to replace him with Icefoxx.

34. *Training and teaching others: identifying the educational needs of others, developing formal educational or training programs or classes, teaching or instructing others.*

When preparing the team for a *Counter-Strike* match, a strategist may walk them through practice sessions in an empty server to rehearse the necessary actions, such as throwing a grenade just right so it bounces off a wall and lands in a particular nook.

Often, when a raid group is performing a new encounter, members with similar experience have the responsibility to teach others how the fight works and about strategies that have proven effective in the past.

Solia's job as the most experienced raider in her *WoW* guild, Burning Sensations, is to explain to the rest of the raid the abilities of each boss they encounter before they attempt them, as well as to walk each person through what his or her job will be during the encounter. There is always room for improvement, even on farm content [easy raids that guilds carry out to acquire resources] that has bosses the guild has been able to defeat several times in a row.

35. *Guiding, directing, and motivating subordinates: providing guidance and direction to subordinates, including setting performance standards and monitoring performance.*

    Before a big *Counter-Strike* match, captains often give pep talks extolling the team's might and pointing out weaknesses in the other side that can be exploited.

    Some guilds have a "mentor" or "class lead" system, in which individuals are chosen from each class in order to help less experienced players learn about their roles and how to optimize cooperation and performance in a raid.

    Solia's job in *WoW* didn't end after giving directions. Her guild, Burning Sensations, had a trial by fire against the boss M'uru in the Sunwell Plateau. M'uru punishes players hard for any mistake during an encounter. After spending over thirty hours and thousands of gold pieces per player learning about this quest, the guild still wasn't successful. Solia had to keep her guild mates motivated and optimistic, even though progress was not readily apparent.

36. *Coaching and developing others: identifying the developmental needs of others and coaching, mentoring, or otherwise helping others to improve their knowledge or skills.*

    Raid leaders often need to give quick summaries of previously discussed boss strategies before every action. It's important to analyze the opportunities for failure so that the raid group knows what to avoid.

    Vantes has been playing his holy paladin character for well over two years and has extensive knowledge and experience in the *WoW* world. He has recently started his own guild, One Button Heroes, on the Korgath server with the sole purpose to train new players. The guild has spent hundreds of hours learning old content under the instruction of the more experienced veteran.

37. *Providing consultation and advice to others: providing guidance and expert advice to management or other groups on technical, systems-related, or process-related topics.*

Some *Counter-Strike* teams recruit players from other teams and then observe them during practice, pointing out weaknesses. They then advise them on weapon use, communication, and teamwork. Paid strategists help elite teams in major competitions.

In *WoW*, performance evaluations are common. Players need to understand that giving, receiving, and incorporating feedback is vital to the success of a team.

When Solia had run out of ideas to defeat M'uru, she turned to the Raid and Dungeon Forums. These forums [on Worldofwarcraft.com] have extensive archives of players helping players. Advice and consultation is given and received on a minute-by-minute basis between thousands of players.

38. *Performing administrative activities: performing day-to-day administrative tasks such as maintaining information files and processing paperwork.*

Members of competitive *Counter-Strike* teams build websites, organize servers for matches, and sometimes write letters seeking corporate sponsorship.

Formally inviting a new member to a guild usually requires officer privileges, and often people are assigned to these specific tasks in order to keep the guild running.

Guild banks in *WoW* hold the combined wealth of all the members of the guild. Many items and resources take the effort of twenty-five or more people to achieve, and they belong to no one in particular but rather to the guild itself. Someone must manage these resources in the guild bank, and specific leadership positions are often assigned for this task.

39. *Staffing organizational units: recruiting, interviewing, selecting, hiring, and promoting employees in an organization.*

The *WoW* class lead system was put in place to ensure cooperation among members of a particular class. If two players are choosing between an ability that helps warlocks (e.g., Curse of Shadow) and an ability that helps mages (e.g., Curse of the Elements), the team needs to ensure that there aren't wasteful overlapping buffs [abilities that protect players]. This is assigned by the class lead.

In *EVE Online*, the Alliance Band of Brothers consists of thousands of players in hundreds of groups. Such a large force would be impossible for a single person to manage or maintain. Vacancies in the Alliance are filled through a complex system requiring résumés, background checks, and other case-by-case necessities.

40. *Monitoring and controlling resources: monitoring and controlling resources and overseeing the spending of money.*

To be able to expand or replace forces, players in *Company of Heroes* must simultaneously wage war on supply lines, units, and bases while managing their own diversified economy.

It is often the responsibility of the guild bank officer to make sure that a raid has enough potions and crafting materials to maximize member performance every night. If, for example, the raid runs out of an enchanting material when a powerful new item drops from a boss, performance would be severely diminished until the supply was replenished, essentially putting on hold all progress in the raid.

Everything in *EVE Online* starts from the limited raw materials available in asteroid fields. Big money comes from controlling these fields, protecting the transport ships, and maintaining processing and production facilities.

What Is the Difference Between Real and Virtual?

Our primary conclusion from the O*NET exercise was that work and play (at least play as defined in this new world of complex multiplayer strategy games) are quite similar. The next task is to understand the differences. Why do people pay to do work in one setting and have to be paid to work in another? In the next chapter, we discuss some of the characteristics of *flow*, a mental groove where time disappears during a fully absorbing activity. Here we want to consider the context in which enterprise work is carried out.

Recently, one of us participated in an extraordinary meeting of forty management experts, including business school professors, management consultants, venture capitalists and CEOs of path-breaking companies, convened by The Management Lab and chaired by business writer and professor Gary Hamel. The meeting's purpose was to brainstorm and debate radical remedies for the great management challenges of the day. Naturally, everyone was expected to have a point of view about the flaws that need addressing. The resulting homework assignments and group deliberations provided a feast of problems. Although the organizers have provided their own synthesis of the meeting, we heard the comments as falling into three important thematic categories: purpose, structure, and behaviors.[24]

These experts largely shared the view that the most important ingredient frequently missing from management is a compelling *sense of purpose*. Either the imperatives that follow from quarterly accountability to Wall Street aren't inspiring or a company that has a deeper purpose isn't communicating it in a way that people can believe and use to guide their behavior. This fine idea had already been around for quite a while when it was featured in the mid 1990s as the core theme in the acclaimed book *Built to Last* and its sequels.[25] As with many of the credos reviewed in these books, the attendees also pointed out the importance of serving multiple stakeholders in a common dedication to purpose (certainly beyond only *share*holders—in addition to employees and customers, even vendors made the list). In the case of games, the overriding purpose is to entertain, of course. But inside the game, hundreds of hours of individual player time are structured along a vector of aspiration and accomplishment that is part of a larger narrative that ties the pieces together. There is much that the modern enterprise can learn from this.

Beyond the need for meaningful purpose in individual and corporate lives, the Management Lab conference attendees agreed about common *structural* impediments to getting work right. Alternatives or modifications of the typical hierarchical organization chart and the imperial CEO were roundly preferred. Of course, silos were out of favor, but a more subtle critique regarding structure dealt with the disconnectedness of people working inside large functional organizations that permit more than two degrees of separation between a worker and actual customers. For many, looser hierarchies, wherein "release" is emphasized over "control," held attraction. Given the amount of attention in other fields to complex adaptive systems as a model for solving challenging problems (for example, in engineering, computing, and economics), it was surprising that only a few of these business thinkers had spent time pondering how biological models of emergent structure could be relevant to the enterprise. The example of plasticity in brain development was offered by Steve Jurvetson, whereby neurons connect and reconnect and even die off in order to provide the correct organization for function, memory, and skills. Game designs that have left room for complex evolving networks of player behavior may be just the kind of examples needed to design new ways to manage.

As for *behaviors* that need remediation, everyone had a favorite suggestion: short-termism in setting goals for self and others, hoarding and filtering information as a source of power, restrictions on free speech, measuring and rewarding the wrong things, micromanagement, and best of all, burnout from too many corporate change initiatives. You will not be surprised to note that these are not the personal strategies that lead to success in today's multiplayer games.

The collective advice from the Management Lab meeting was more than to do the opposite of these bad behaviors. Perhaps it is as simple as nailing an inspiring purpose for the enterprise, communicating it with conviction, and then loosening up the hierarchy so that better systems, structures, and behaviors can evolve to serve a clear and compelling mission. If that is a good start, it helps to have a smorgasbord of good practices to consider as this process takes place. In addition to getting the purpose right, people need clear and compelling goals that offer important challenges for which their skills are a good match. They must get feedback that is relevant and timely, and they should have an appropriate sense of control over their world. They must experience the satisfaction of meaningful learning.

Is it possible that games do a better job than sophisticated corporations of creating a purposeful environment where action is imbued with meaning as part of a valued goal? If so, it will be because of some of the ingredients of great games that we explore in the next chapter. First, meet Helen. She's personally experienced all of the ingredients as an officer in the Whitelist Guild.

Chapter Four

Ten Ingredients of Great Games

ANATOMY OF A RAID

Helen is a product designer at a successful software company. She's three years out of Stanford, a wiz at software requirement documents, and already a young business star. Helen is out of the house at 7 a.m., her day packed with meetings, writing, software testing, and plenty of the unexpected. But at 5:20 p.m. on Tuesday, she's out the office door not a minute late to catch the last possible train that will get her in front of her home computer by 7 p.m. sharp. That's the time when twenty-five fellow members of the Whitelist Guild will meet online to attempt victory over the big bad boss of the Serpentshrine Cavern.

Helen plays an online role-playing game twenty hours a week with sixty friends from three U.S. time zones and two foreign countries. She knows five of the members in real life but has never met the others. About ten are women (she knows for sure only because game play involves voice interactions as well as on-screen ones), but she knows remarkably little about other demographics of the group. The guild is a network of networks, patching her California friends with groups from Texas, New York, Florida—and Australia. Although she couldn't tell you the age of more than a few in the group, she could tell you a ton about their personalities, aversion to risk, demeanor in a conflict, ability to negotiate, and commitment to the group.

There are certainly things to do in the game that involve solo play, but the big rewards and major fun come when Helen is online with her team. She doesn't win (more gold, higher status, cool new game pieces) unless her team wins.

Helen signed up for the raid this Tuesday two weeks ago on the Whitelist Guild website that was created and is maintained by the guild outside of the game. In addition to scheduling, there are pages on the site for recruiting, player profiles, calendars, polls, and a gallery of in-world and real-life pictures. Helen grabs enough snacks to last through the three-hour event, and logs into the game right on time at 7 p.m.

Helen's first decision is which of her eight different avatars to play tonight (there are sixty people in her guild but twice that many characters). The choice tonight is her main avatar, a level 70 priest. Helen is the lead healer in the guild and one of its top officers. That means it's her responsibility to coordinate players during raids (in this case, other priests, paladins, shamans, and druids) whose job it is to keep the warriors healthy during battle. Tonight she'll be in charge of fifteen other healers who are each critical to team success.

After the last raid, Helen parked her character in one of the main cities so she'd have a head start on preraid tasks, and that's where she finds her character tonight. Only in one of the game cities can she check mail and bank accounts (the currency of the realm is gold pieces), and, important for tonight's action, that's where she'll stock up on potions (used to heal the warriors), repair armor damaged in the last battle (if it's weak you jeopardize the team), and purchase reagents that will allow her to buff (or protect) other players. There's a vibrant ongoing auction or marketplace for all these items.

There's a message on Helen's screen inviting her to teleport to the summoning stone at the dungeon entrance where the team is gathering. At 7:20 p.m., all are present (the guild is working hard to increase promptness), and they zone into (enter) the dungeon for a preraid strategy review. All the players take their potions and buffs while they gather inside.

Tonight's raid leader starts making assignments. He's not the same person as the guild leader (the political head who mostly arbitrates disputes) but rather the logistical wizard who coordinates action— quickly. He assigns tanks (warriors) to take out trash mobs (guards) so that the team can get to the boss (the head monster) who drops loot (prizes and rewards) that the team will share. The sharing is based on participation: show up more often and on time and you'll receive more DKP (dragon kill points), which is useful to bid for single items that more than one team member might like to own.

Helen's participation in the raid is enabled by one of the most complex and successful interfaces for collaboration ever created. On her screen she can see all of the avatars in the action and, important for her particular job, quantitative information displayed with dazzling graphics about the health of her charges. At the bottom of the screen are data about her potions and spells, chat windows for text communication, maps of the area, inventories of gold pieces and armor, and buttons that open third-party mods, or software add-ons, that do everything from enabling digital voice communication to keeping track of trades to assessing the healing per second accomplished by each of the priests.

The boss finally succumbs to the Whitelist team, although not on the first try. There were two wipe outs (failures where everyone dies) that required each player to go through a resurrection routine and meet back at the dungeon entrance for another go. After the victory (at about 10 p.m. that night), the guild leader submitted the results of their raid to a tracker, and the victory was posted on a guild leader board. Not only can Helen brag to her friends about being level 70 or owning a new magic sword, but also there's now public acknowledgment that she's in the guild that defeated the boss in the Serpentshrine Cavern—no small feat.

Ten Game Features to Guide Real Work

There are lots of recipes for great games. A bad cook, or just an unlucky one, could spoil any of them, but by and large, the successful multiplayer titles work their magic using variations on the ten ingredients described here. Helen experienced them all during her raid, as we'll point out. These are the same ingredients that we think will help solve the business problems mentioned in the last chapter. New research shows why these features work, and Helen's story helps illustrate the powerful psychology behind how they work in the games. The invitation, of course, is to consider what it would be like to experience each *while at work*.

One note ahead of the tour: it's not necessary that these ingredients be experienced as a package as was true for Helen. Games that weave together all of these tools are huge undertakings. The best ones cost tens of millions of dollars to produce. We strongly believe that the ingredients can be quite useful in smaller batches and even one at a time. Some can make huge improvements in work with only small adjustments to current practice and technology. You don't have to build an entire game to use games at work. We'll say more about how that might play out in subsequent chapters.

Here are the ten ingredients.

1. Self-Representation with Avatars

The central feature on Helen's screen is her avatar, and those belonging to other players, friend and foe. Like a puppeteer, Helen controls a personalized character that's her stand-in within the game—her "mini-me." The ability to represent oneself *within* media, and exert precise control over that representation, fundamentally changes the psychology of using technology. Helen isn't stuck on her side of the glass. She's in the scene, she can speak to and touch (at least virtually) other players, and her presence alters what happens next. She's part of the story, with a character to mark her presence. She's not just a recipient of a story someone else authors. Engagement is the result. Here's why.

Avatars Are Easy to Use

Avatars are engaging because they're easy to use, once you have figured out which buttons to press to make them move, jump, and speak. (There is a bit of a learning curve on the motor skills.) What makes them easy is that they represent *people*. Avatars tap into primitive abilities, evolved over hundreds of thousands of years, to communicate with other humans. In real life, there's much in a face-to-face encounter that's critical but doesn't need to be said. Gender, race, age, dress, and emotional expression are available visually and instantly; there is no complicated language to parse or instructions to read about how to give or receive important signals. Avatars take advantage of highly evolved talents of humans—processing faces, gestures, and movement by observing other social actors.

Avatars Mark Expertise

Avatars can help identify and keep track of important social information such as expertise and the potential for relationships. Helen can determine players' expertise just by looking at them (orcs look different from dwarfs, and they have quite different talents). The same is true in real life. When something is wrong with my computer, I could search for a paragraph about the fix in a manual, or just go down the hall and ask Jack, the computer expert. Jack's expertise, as well as much else that might be useful to know about him, is all part of the same *body*. Consequently, the difference between bodies becomes a very useful categorization scheme. Remembering specific faces and bodies, and the ability to attribute knowledge and likely behavior to them, is a strong determinant of mental organization. Much of our memory is parsed by how we remember people's attributes.[1]

Avatars Increase Engagement

There is no real-life counterpart to an avatar, with the possible exception of the primitive devotion a parent might show a child. Although the psychology of self-representation is new, there is good evidence that the engagement people have with avatars is substantial, even if unconscious. Avatars can dramatically change how people experience media. Consider this result from an experiment in our Stanford University lab.

Imagine that you've been asked to select an avatar and spend some time personalizing its appearance, making it your own. You choose its size, gender, facial features, dress, and the role it will perform in a game. Then you're asked to play. In an online game, you cooperate with a teammate to collect game artifacts, and then practice some fighting moves with virtual swords. Different people are asked to participate in the same game activities as you did, but instead of being allowed to personalize an avatar, they are assigned one and have no opportunity to customize its appearance or role.

What's the difference in how players engage in the game? The answer is ten heartbeats per minute. That is, when playing the exciting parts of the game with your customized avatar, your heartbeat accelerates more than those of people playing an off-the-shelf avatar.[2] Heart rate is a good measure of physiological arousal. People have a primitive and unconscious response to their avatars. When an avatar is involved in action, so is the person who creates and controls it. Importantly, an accelerating heart rate is more than some reptilian response of old brains to new media. Arousal is consequential for a broad range of thoughtful reactions, including how interested you are in the experience, how much you remember about the experience, and how long you're willing to participate.[3]

Social Trumps Efficiency

It's true that Helen could probably help her guild without paying much attention to her avatar, and she might even be able to do it in less time without the distraction of a character. But efficiency isn't the sole criterion by which virtual interactions should be evaluated. Although Helen's standing in her guild is based on performance, she's also got a very cool character in the game, and she's as much known for her interaction skills, magic robes, and virtual dance moves as her position on the leader board. Translated into appropriate work motifs, these social and emotional cues could be useful in business. These are the social and emotional features of interactions that often drive brainstorming and innovation, qualities absent from many current collaboration tools.[4]

Businesses tell us that a primary interest in exploring the use of avatars is the facilitation of collaboration in distributed groups. Virtual environments including avatars could be useful as the challenges of travel and distributed work increase. A counterpoint is often made, however, that it's not worth the extra effort to create, manage, and communicate with an avatar when all a worker wants to do is communicate quickly, share important facts, and make work more efficient. There is valuable social interaction that goes on as teams form up or address a new environment, but there is also a cost to learning new tools. In 2004, when we first started using a virtual environment—ten of us trying to work together in a start-up—our meeting times doubled as we fumbled with the 3D interface or spent time chatting and having our avatars do cool but organizationally useless gymnastics. It was like doing a ropes course off-site together. After several meetings, we reverted to more familiar meeting ground in the office. The virtual-world interfaces are getting better, and avatar familiarization time may be worth the overhead when combined with other core building blocks of collaboration.

Many jobs could benefit from the engagement that avatars offer, which is why we pay a lot of attention to them in chapter 5.

2. Three-Dimensional Environments

Helen's priest lives in a visually rich three-dimensional world. This makes the game interesting not only because her presence in the world is embodied via her avatar, but also because she navigates in a game space that parallels physical properties of the real world. This is created through the rendering of 3D graphical models onto a two-dimensional screen much like the way that perspective drawings on a page simulate depth. In today's games this effect is extremely powerful without virtual reality goggles or wrap-around screens. This is an important ingredient because it allows virtual space to be understood in the same way people negotiate the real world.

Virtual Space Works Like Real Space—No Instruction Necessary

People know what to do in the real physical world. The human brain is wonderfully evolved to negotiate space, and virtual space is close enough to the real thing to be easily understood. Helen may be in a fantasy castle room, but it has walls, doors, and furniture like a real room, and the physics of time, distance, and gravity are plenty familiar. Avatars walk from one place to another. Standing close has meaning. Big avatars are more imposing than small ones. People get a sense of playful immersion as they move characters through spaces that parallel the real world.

Places also have meaning, just like they do in real life. Physical places, represented in rich 3D visuals, are more than metaphors. They convince the senses into thinking they are exactly like the real places they represent, even if people can thoughtfully describe the differences.[5] For example, Helen started her game play in a particular city, she walked to the mail center to retrieve a note, and she visited a vendor in the marketplace to replenish her potions. Each of those places is identified by a function just like similar places in real life. No instruction necessary.

Three-Dimensional Space Helps You Remember Where Stuff Is

James Gee, a respected game researcher and learning scientist, describes his own play experience while traversing the vast virtual environment of *World of Warcraft*: "Every place I pass by again reminds me of a person [avatar] I spoke to here, a challenge I met, a reward received."[6] James Wallis has estimated the surface area of *WoW* as of mid 2008 as 113 square kilometers.[7] That's a lot of virtual real estate and potentially a lot of memories.

While a macro sense of place helps people understand and remember the purpose for places in a 3D world (cities, regions, galaxies), there is also an important advantage for 3D representations of *micro* spaces. Everyone uses physical space to organize personal environments (desks, offices, and living rooms) so they can remember the location of objects and even people, and virtual space works just as well. When information and objects are stored in or associated with a physical space, they're often far easier to locate. Even if you can't recall exactly where a desired item is, once in the environment, it's usually easy to navigate right to it using cues in the space. With a quick scan of a room you've customized, whether it's real or virtual, most people can tell if even the smallest item is out of place.

Special Properties of Virtual Space

It's often said that the worst thing to do with a virtual place is make it look exactly like a real one. What a waste. Computers allow you to do things otherwise impossible in the real world, so why not partake? Although the virtual and real are similar perceptually, there's much Helen can accomplish in a computer-controlled physical space that would otherwise be impossible.

For example, a simple interface allows her to quickly change visual perspectives. With the press of a key she can view the world from the eyes of her character or put the "camera" anywhere she pleases, such as looking down from above or from over the shoulder of her character so she can see her position in space. And she's not limited to just walking: flying, teleporting, or catching a ride on a dragon are also options. None of these are real-world possibilities, but it's also true that all are easy to understand because they incorporate familiar features of reality.

Opportunities to Explore

Browsing a virtual space is more like taking a walk than perusing a directory, and for many, that's in and of itself a reason to play. Some people just like to explore in virtual spaces, and they can't wait for the designers to add more virtual acreage, as they often do to keep games interesting. People are naturally curious, and no less so virtually (where it may be safer). They like finding out what's around the corner, a primitive motivation that keeps them in the game.

The Use of Three-Dimensional Space Can Organize and Inspire Work

Think of the evolution in graphical user interfaces for desktop computing. What began as a blinking green cursor has evolved into panes and windows and folders and trash cans that take on increased dimensionality with each software update. Now consider how physical spaces in the real world can influence how people think and feel at home, school, and at work. This includes appropriate uses of everything from lighting to walls to art on the walls. Most of the literature about how space influences productivity has to do with the physical co-location of workers, the impact of open carrels versus office doors, and an occasional reference to the value of windows.[8] In virtual space these advantages are not only easier to produce but also can be infinitely more varied because they involve only digital construction—but with real psychological results. *If* bigger windows or colorful walls are more engaging (or increase productivity), it's easy to go wild.

3. Narrative Context

Good games have good backstories—galaxies at war, people who need rescue, or places that may soon be destroyed. Such narratives guide action and organize character roles, rewards, and group action. The information Helen sees about her character and team is drawn from a particular game narrative and is constantly reinforced ("Four years have passed since the Reign of Chaos, and a great tension now smolders throughout the ravaged world of Azeroth . . .").[9] Stories have several important psychological advantages that help keep people engaged.

Stories Are a Human Specialty

First, stories are primitively important to thinking, emotional experience, and social expertise. Great stories make for great politics, advertising, entertainment, sales, and sermons.[10] We love to hear and tell stories. Good speeches and books are good stories. Business case studies work best as stories. The most engaging journalism tells a story. You can't just give the facts. You need to place them in the context of events sequenced with a beginning, middle, and end, some tension about how things will resolve, and detail about the people involved that will engage audiences in something that becomes real because they can imagine themselves in the same narrative space.

Great games also have great stories—epic stories. There isn't a quest, raid, or guild assignment in Helen's game that isn't well placed in a larger narrative. Players know their role relative to those of others. They know where their current activity fits in the larger picture. They know how pieces of the story—each linked to their actions in the game—are linked, making it easy to understand *why* they're doing something now, as well as making people eager to find out how what they do will affect what happens next.

Narratives Tell Players What to Do

Game narratives give players hints, and sometimes strong ones, about what to do, and that helps with execution and tactics applied to larger goals. If you know the story of Lord Nefarian's dungeon, you know that he has qualities and behavior that are vestiges of battles past. Keep that story in mind, and you'll know why you need to attack from the rear. And unlike stories experienced via print media or conventional video or film, game stories are designed as unfinished frameworks where players complete the narrative by living it.[11]

Narratives make play easier. In game challenges that have strong narratives, grand strategizing is often *less* necessary than it may be in titles (or real life) with weaker narrative organization. Some games basically tell you what to do, and the main action then becomes tactical, even for the leaders. The story strongly suggests the strategy; now you simply recruit the players and execute.

Notably, strong narratives are not part of all games. Some place an emphasis on players supplying their own narratives. For example, one popular space game (*EVE Online*) requires that players make up their own economic goals in a game heavily driven by a massive synthetic economy. And stories, at least those supplied by the publisher, are similarly absent from virtual environments. For example, *Second Life* only offers the infrastructure for interaction. You need to supply your own story (and certainly many do).

Narrative Increases Excitement and Attention

Psychological responses to stories are primitive. The uncertainty that all good stories have ("What a dire situation . . . how will this get resolved?") creates excitement and tension that sustains player involvement, and it focuses players on resolution and release. People stick with stories until conflict is resolved, keeping them tuned in even in the face of competition for attention from elsewhere.[12]

The uncertainty that goes with stories is arousing physically as well as mentally. Hearts beat faster, skin becomes moist, and brain centers that regulate emotion show increased activation, especially during those times when uncertainty about outcomes in highest.[13] People have a natural response to excitement that is critical to the engagement of stories: they attempt to reduce excitement, especially if its source is conflict, by searching (and searching) for resolution. The engagement people find in an ending is driven by the excitement that comes with uncertainty. Helen wouldn't have enjoyed the eventual positive outcome of her raid nearly as much if she had been certain about how things would end. Psychologists say that excitation is *resolved* (that is, it feels good when it stops hurting).[14]

Narrative and Memory

Stories also influence memory; that is, it's easier to remember information when it's presented in a narrative format than when it's merely stacked, one fact on another, in random order or even bunched by similarity.[15] Better memory gives gamers a sense of control over the information environment. Here's how.

Psychologists divide memory into semantic versus episodic storage and retrieval.[16] When people process semantic information, they are storing and accessing information based on *meaning*, usually in relation to other things that have similar meaning. For example, information about the people we work with is stored together, and thinking about one person at work might increase the probability that we'll think about others in the group. Another form of memory, one often easier to build and use, stores information in *episodes* that define the story of how events transpired. When experience unfolds as a story (eventually also true for work that embraces a narrative), people can more easily know where they are in the story. That's especially useful if you come and go from the story, as would be the case for games at work. More important, people can make useful and important guesses about the episodes, even if they haven't experienced the specifics, because it's easy to imagine how parts of a story could be bridged.[17]

Narrative Already Guides Business

The use of narrative in business planning and management is familiar.[18] Stories are mostly used for training, however. It's rare to find extended work immersed in stories to the same extent as online game play. Most often, a narrative merely guides a single training session or a motivational pitch by an executive. Imagining a more complete alignment of game and business narratives offers intriguing possibilities to increase involvement in work by making explicit the *story* of how people should participate in work. The story will be primitively engaging and will help solve one of the important problems discussed in the preceding chapter—namely, allowing people to see how they fit into the larger picture.

4. Feedback

It's impossible to imagine Helen's group spending a single minute on a raid without some indication of how things are going—both for the individual players and for her team as a whole. Game interfaces set a new bar for feedback. At any one time, Helen sees progress bars, zooming numbers, and status gauges, all in a well-organized dashboard that lets players know how things are going, good or bad. Numbers indicate the health of players, the time left before an attack, the amount of gold accumulated so far, the bids from other players for scarce resources, or the reduction in a competitor's powers. All of this quantitative feedback increases engagement in the action. Here are some principles of psychological reinforcement very much at play in the games.

Feedback Changes Behavior (And That Makes the Game Fun)

One of the simplest and most enduring principles of psychology is that feedback changes behavior.[19] We often think of this effect in terms of control: a boss, teacher, or parent can influence performance by issuing the right type of positive or negative feedback at the right times. Those on the receiving end are most often viewed as passive participants; they don't know they're being controlled, and if they did, they might be resentful. In the games, however, feedback is actively sought and highly valued by anyone who wants to advance. Gamers certainly seek positive reinforcement—as much as they can get and mostly because it feels good—but they're equally receptive to negative feedback because that's just as likely, and often more likely, to be information that will get them to their goals more quickly.

The Long and Short of Reinforcement

Some of the feedback in games signals progress over the course of days and months—for example, the level of a character or progress through difficult levels of play over the course of multiple sessions. But importantly, much of the feedback is about what is happening *this minute* and even *this second*. Knowing how things are going moment by moment calibrates action and is a tremendous advantage for learning as well.

Gamers want to know how things are progressing continuously, and the games accommodate. Quick feedback creates immediacy and contingency in the interactions. When you make a new move, you know quickly whether the action was right or wrong. The close connection between behavior and feedback (it's usually obvious which reinforcement applies to which behaviors) increases the likelihood that the reinforcement will be effective.

We are impressed by the fact that great games not only give relevant feedback over long and short time scales but also deliver feedback at every scale in between. There is feedback on the scale of seconds, minutes, hours, days, weeks, and months.

Breaking Down Behaviors into Smaller Pieces

Reinforcement in the games is layered. Play is facilitated when complex tasks are broken into more manageable units. The effect is remarkable. There are games within games within games, like Russian babushka dolls. Larger accomplishments are recognized as smaller ones accumulate. Helen's raid group was involved in a complex action in which success was ultimately measured by the completion of a five-hour task. The bulk of the feedback, however, was targeted at micro behaviors. You can't vanquish Lord Nefarian without accomplishing hundreds of milestones along the way.

Extrinsic Versus Intrinsic Rewards

Helen's feedback during the raid came from two sources—one obvious and another less so but more important. Most obviously, Helen received praise, encouragement, and critique from other players. Much of the reinforcement came from real people via their avatars, for example, from the raid leader or fellow priests signaling encouragement as the action unfolded. Other reinforcement came from computer-controlled characters in the games (called nonplayer characters, or NPCs), who gave feedback that was programmed but influential nonetheless. In both cases, the feedback was *extrinsic*; it came from another social actor.

Less obvious to someone watching Helen play were the *intrinsic* rewards. These are the feelings of accomplishment and gratification that come from within. Intrinsic rewards are primitive, unconscious, and can have physical consequences. For example, even a small game success (you've been turning over rocks in hopes of finding a prized sword and you finally looked in the right place) can cause a dopamine release in the brain that acts like a powerful stimulant and increases the probability of similar action.[20] Intrinsic rewards, unlike words from others that can be forgotten quickly, are important for sustained long-term behavior change.[21] Game designers use their tools very effectively to trigger these intrinsic rewards.

Vicarious Reinforcement and Self-Efficacy

When Helen's raid began, no one knew for sure if it would end in success. Often, raid groups "wipe" (everyone dies) on the first try. But the possibility of failure doesn't interfere with the certainty players feel that *eventually* they'll get it right. Gamers believe that they have the capacity to succeed. They believe in their *self-efficacy*.

The essence of self-efficacy is belief regarding the source of your destiny. Those who have high self-efficacy believe that they control situations rather than the reverse.[22] A high level of self-efficacy is a catalyst to behavior change. That sounds good, but how do you acquire self-efficacy? One method is experience. Nothing breeds success like success. The more you are in situations with successful outcomes, the more you believe you can succeed. Games certainly help here, providing numerous experiences that cause people to conclude they can be successful and that their success is attributable to them.

But there's an even more powerful set of experiences that may increase the power of reinforcement in games. Self-efficacy is created almost as easily by *watching* as by doing. If someone else can do it, then so can I. When we observe success, we think we're more capable of similar results (and the opposite for failure). Reinforcement doesn't need to be direct; it can be vicarious. And vicarious reinforcement is most powerful when people think that they have something in common with the person (or model) they're observing. This is likely true when watching fellow guild members in the game, and it's especially true when watching your own avatar.

Primary and Secondary Reinforcers: Games Deal with the Basics

A lot of reinforcement comes from arbitrary signals in the environment that we learn to associate with positive or negative outcomes. This was the case, for example, for the celebrated dogs in Pavlov's lab.[23] They had to learn that a bell was associated with food; the bell wasn't in and of itself the reinforcement. The same is true for money. A hundred dollar bill is a *secondary* reinforcer relative to the *primary* reinforcers it can purchase (such as sleep, food, shelter, and water).

The games have plenty of learned secondary reinforcers, to be sure. Helen wouldn't know, absent experiences in the game, that a flowing white robe made especially for priests represented the highest achievement for her avatar class. But importantly, many game reinforcers are not arbitrary (like the robe) but are in fact primary reinforcers: no experience is necessary to determine their value. Characters (and their players) live and die in the game, have enough to eat or not, find companions or not, and live well or poorly as primary reinforcement linked to the quality of their play. Of course, these reinforcers are only virtually primary; that is, it's only a picture that signals better health or needed shelter, but as we'll soon review, that's often enough to trigger the same primitive responses that occur with their real-life counterparts. Games reinforce the basics, and that increases engagement.

Feedback for All the Senses

You can't watch a gamer in a raid without realizing that feedback comes in multiple time scales, as well as via multiple senses and signals. The bandwidth for reinforcement in games is large. The most obvious and familiar feedback acknowledged in work groups is text and spoken language—if we're lucky via crisp and unambiguous sentences matched with the behavior that triggered the response. But for Helen, the feedback is not only constant, but also visual and auditory. Fancy graphics update as her health increases and decreases, and there are sounds associated with the smallest game moves. You don't have to play long to know which sounds mean "keep doing that" and which mean "you're on the wrong track."

Games Suggest Opportunities for Feedback at Work

New ways of designing real work will benefit from the feedback and reinforcement that are commonplace elements of games. Managers know three things about current opportunities for reinforcement on the job: they're effective, they happen all too infrequently, and they're really hard to do. Games provide the possibility to automate feedback, especially in short and intermediate time domains between formal performance reviews. They teach us how to create contingency—an obvious link between behavior and corrective or positive responses—that fills the senses and makes explicit the most valuable changes in behavior.

5. Reputations, Ranks, and Levels

If someone asked Helen what character she played in the game, she wouldn't just say a priest—she'd say a *level 70* priest, and she might also throw in any number of other markers, most quantitative, that describe her reputation. Gamers, like power-sellers on eBay, have ranks and ratings that are available for all to see and are hard to spoof. Reputation information not only identifies their place in the game hierarchy but also makes apparent competencies, talents, and special experiences that others can use to make choices about other players.

Digital reputations (sellers on eBay, hotels in Hawaii, or books on Amazon) are increasingly easy to compile and are clearly influential in online commerce.[24] This is equally true in the games, at least with respect to their ability to create an easy-to-use and engaging social scene. The very point of the games is often to augment reputations (that's one reason Helen wanted to get to level 70) and then broadcast accomplishments widely. If players didn't care about their reputations, most multiplayer games wouldn't work. What fun would it be to bring down the Gates of Az Koran if there were no way to possess—and, more important, no way to display—evidence of the accomplishment? Here's how reputations help make games work.

Reputations Are Persistent and Transparent

Helen's reputation in the game is always accurate, up-to-date, and obvious. Her level, performance on raids, and inventory of prized artifacts can travel with her at all times. It's a complete and public package of competency, prowess, and experience. And it's the transparency of the information— relevant data made prominent throughout the interface—that makes it more true in the game than in real life that what you see is what you get.

Game designers have figured out how to let players wear their résumés on their sleeves without forcing them to be braggarts. To complete the picture, guilds compile metadata on players using special interfaces to the game and third-party software called add-ons. The games make the use of reputational information a natural part of play. Virtual life is far more transparent than real life both because the interfaces and game designs emphasize that information and because the players themselves are convinced of the value it has for promoting group success and for having fun.

Reputational Markers Are Important

Reputations are not just arbitrary markers of status. You wouldn't get far with a new fancy sword won at random or just because you stumbled on it. Instead, reputational markers often communicate capabilities that are integral to game success. For Helen, the choice of a role for her character locked in reputational information that was critical for teammates to know (priests are healers, and that's just part of the game). But Helen also had a chance, through her own talents and achievements, to personally author large parts of her reputation. When other players become aware of her reputation, they know exactly how she should fit into the group. And it's obvious, but worth saying explicitly, that it's hard to collaborate or lead, in the games or in real life, when you can't identify which people are capable of doing the tasks that need to be done.

Reputational information is socially relevant for many decisions about collaboration and leadership. Players can quickly use this information to find other players, contact them in the game, begin negotiations and trades, and know their current status in a quest or raid. Guild leaders can quickly scan these indicators and know how and what to say.

Reputational Updates Are Continuous

During Helen's raid, reputations can update moment to moment. Some games are able to output performance updates every second. Imagine a spreadsheet that has players in the rows and in the columns metrics such as damage or healing *per second* listed for each player. With the exception of high-velocity stock trading and air traffic control, this is orders of magnitude more and faster information than is typically captured in most real work. Players enter a different mind-set about reputation: it's not only something that's developed and repaired over a career, it's something that's important (and could change) in the next minute.

A good example of how players use reputational data can be found by eavesdropping (as we've done with some of the biggest guilds) on the performance reviews that occur after game action. There is detailed information and conversation about player contributions. The discussions seem natural but they're also extraordinary given the detailed quantitative performance information available. The evaluations, and the changes in reputation that follow, would not be possible without the help of a computer to keep track and a good interface to prominently display the results. Without this information, par for the course in most real-world collaborations, evaluations would also be more impressionistic than empirical, and often wrong.

Reputational Information Is Trusted (Because It's Hard to Cheat)

Players trust reputations, and are comfortable with more transparency, in part because it's difficult to cheat. In the bigger games, there are game police who work for the publishers and are present as avatars. Some work behind the scenes looking for mischief (or worse). They're looking for cheaters and "griefers" trying to get ahead unfairly. As a result, players are relatively confident about the use of reputational information for important evaluations. Also, unlike real life, there are no easy social routes up the leader boards; that is, you can't advance merely because the leader likes you or owes you. You advance because you perform well, and recognition for good play is communicated directly from your computer and not from other players.

There's a caveat about reputation worth noting, however. There is one way to cheat big time. As we describe in chapter 6 on virtual money, it's actually possible to purchase a reputation by buying (for real dollars) game artifacts or even an entire character at one of several auction sites. That means it's technically possible that people you meet in the game really didn't earn the magical sword they're now wielding but rather purchased it. (There are plenty of groups who "farm" game pieces and characters explicitly for the purpose of selling them for profit.)[25] Many players, guilds, and publishers, however, are on to this trick. You might have just purchased a level 70 orc, and that might get you an interview with one of the better guilds, but you still have to perform once you're there. This particular form of cheating is likely to be manageable for applications of games in enterprises that do a good job of assessing identity before allowing access to corporate systems and data.

Reputations Accelerate Social Interaction

Psychologists know that basic knowledge about the people we communicate with is necessary to establish common ground in a conversation. People may not say much of interest until they determine the basics, which is often what the first several turns in a conversation are about. The most necessary pieces of common ground in real life are exactly what the games help with the most—things such as race, gender, expertise, wealth, and status in the group.[26] A player's game persona is available in an instant.

The ease of establishing a reputation accelerates play and social familiarity. A great hesitancy in any interpersonal encounter is the hassle of introductions. Gamers can get to the point quickly (which they need to do if they want to win), which makes social interaction easier, and for those who fear small talk, less awkward.

The Explicitness of Reputation

In business, there are pins, plaques, and subtle differences in office size that indicate important differences and reputations. But those markers can be unreliable and imprecisely linked to information about expertise, project successes, and special talents. In business, these insignia typically show up days, weeks, or years after the accomplishments that might have merited their award. When work happens in a game, timely reputational information will travel with you, and the symbols that mark the expertise have shared definitions.

In business, there's often not enough information about capabilities and talents to put together the right set of complementary skills quickly, let alone an opportunity to reconfigure a team once an action is under way. Games give us clues about how persistent, transparent reputations could solve this problem.

6. Marketplaces and Economies

An important feature of all multiplayer games is a synthetic currency and the marketplaces it enables. Every title we know of has such a currency in one form or another. Currency systems allow players to make trades efficiently and to quantity all manner of value. In real life, economic scoring might include savings, revenue, profit, and especially salary (in dollars, of course). For Helen, the currency is gold pieces, the synthetic currency in her game. She knows the value of her character, her share of loot from raids, and the price of artifacts she's accumulated (for example, she rides a rare white horse) in pieces of gold. She has a bank account for the gold, and she can trade currency for items at any time during play. Much of the trading is for game-relevant objects and services, but she could send gold to anyone for any reason—including just for fun.

Virtual Currencies in Games Work Like Real Money—But They're Not

Synthetic currencies enable real economies; that is, they facilitate decision making under conditions of scarcity, but without the consequences that accompany transactions with government-recognized money (problems such as taxes, withholding, and salary disputes). But just because the currency is synthetic doesn't mean that tried and true economic principles don't apply and that people don't take it seriously. The price of game artifacts affects the likelihood of purchase (it's more likely as the price declines) regardless of the fact that the currency used for the trades is artificial.[27] This is a simple but startling result: the scarcity of a synthetic currency used in an entertaining game can create the same economic behavior as the currency of the realm in real life.

Multiplayer games have replicated the historical shifts from barter to currencies and markets—but they did it in a couple of years rather than centuries. Synthetic currencies create the efficiencies and precision of a marketplace and allow their benefits to extend to all aspects of play. The currency may be synthetic, but it's a real economy because people are making choice under scarcity. Translated to business, this has tremendous implications for future communication and management within work groups. A synthetic currency may allow workers to trade information, tag ideas, or auction scarce resources in a real market instead of using cumbersome and inefficient barter.

Social Micropayments

Psychologically, trading a synthetic currency activates the same brain centers as real money.[28] Some of the uses, however, are unique. One interesting use is for micropayments that are purely social ("Nice new armor; here's a copper piece!"). The economies in online games provide the motivational benefits of real money, but they can be used more broadly to price things not easily traded in a marketplace. A reward with a synthetic currency is like a *social* micropayment—it's not consequential by ordinary financial standards (worth only pennies if you were willing to take the time to trade it), but it's a precise, quantitative marker that is informative and even fun. (We review the application of synthetic currencies in business in chapter 6.)

Game Economies Enable Scorekeeping

Incentive systems, real or virtual, require a method to keep score, and games are at their best when scores are useful. People want to know precisely how they will benefit (that is, how many points or how much currency) from selling virtual goods or cooperating with other players. It's important that the records in the economy are quantitative. There can be impatience with promises tied to social relationships but trust in systems that record deals with numbers.

Economies Facilitate Meritocracies

Gamers often comment that action during complicated raids such as Helen's is less organized by social relationships compared with similar action in real life. This may happen because the data relevant to judgments about the quality of play, data often pegged to game currencies, is so precise. A game economy facilitates a meritocracy. Achievement is economically recognizable, and when the only thing a player needs to do to "win" is play well, motivation to excel increases. An economy helps makes that possible.

Game Economies Help Align Personal and Group Goals

It's hard to collaborate and lead if players don't have incentives to do things that are in the interest of the group, and it's much easier to lead when players are individually motivated to do what helps the group. Effective incentives are both compelling and task relevant. By compelling, we mean that people actually want them. By task relevant, we mean that the incentives are leading people to do the things that need to be done. The opportunity to closely align personal and group goals is a central promise of games in the real world. More on how games accomplish this can be found in chapter 7 about virtual teams.

For now, it's important to emphasize that without the economies that synthetic currencies create, other ingredients in the game recipe would be less effective. The economy acts like a psychological operating system, tying together other elements. Feedback would be less precise, reputations would be more qualitative, and teams could not easily divide common loot.

7. Competition Under Rules That Are Explicit and Enforced

Most gamers play to win. There's substantial variance between them in the intensity of competitive urges, but by and large, it's good to win. We discuss in chapter 9 why the explicitness of competition is a fundamental and underrated aspect of play that can help business. For now, however, it's important to note an ingredient that allows competition to work: rules.

Helen and her guild are intimately familiar with the rules of play, as much because they're trying to stretch them as to follow them. Rules allow games to work, but it's important to note that the discovery of those rules can itself be part of the fun. Where else can you transgress with impunity as the preferred method to find out what's really possible?

Once discovered, however, rules allow players to trust the game. Players value the level playing field created by rules when they're evenly and impersonally applied (after all, it's the computer that most often enforces them). Rules that are well known and enforced establish a sense of fairness that pervades play.

What Does It Mean to Win?

Guilds know precisely what it takes to win. Players know the rules about leveling up, defeating dangerous dungeon bosses, auctioning digital assets, building spaces, or creating materials. They also know that everyone else knows the rules—or will soon if they're new.

Explicit knowledge about the rules has a major psychological advantage in play: it establishes confidence that everyone has the same information.[29] It's uncomfortable, and perhaps the epitome of social discomfort, to think that you alone are unaware of what everyone else knows. When people think a situation is unfair, they are more likely to react strongly to events, whether they bolster or violate their own worldviews. Knowledge that the rules apply evenly mitigates that uncertainty.

Game Rules Help Develop an Internal Sense of Control

It's fun to think that you're in charge, and games encourage that feeling, even if you're not personally inclined toward an internal sense of control. When something happens in the game (and in real life), people can have two different thoughts about why. Some people tend to believe that their actions are caused by their own personal decisions; that is, they are *internally* oriented. Others have a belief that their behavior is guided more by fate, luck, or other *external* circumstances.[30]

In general, it's psychologically healthy to believe that you have internal control over how things will turn out, and it's certainly an advantage on the job (who wants to think that in spite of their best efforts, others will determine whether they succeed?). Psychologists have tried to determine whether internal versus external attributions about success are a part of personality, wired into who we are, or whether they are a response to circumstances. There may be a natural inclination, one way or another, that we're born with, but there's also good evidence that an internal orientation can be taught, and games are a good candidate to do the teaching.[31] The knowledge that rules apply to everyone helps create a sense of internal control. Gamers think that "I can do this" and that decreases the worry that "success depends on who you know." Ambiguous rules create distrust, often a cause of failure in business collaboration as well as poor game play.

Player-Generated Rules

Game rules apply most obviously to those invented by game designers—the ones that are hard coded into play. Players themselves, however, construct some of the most interesting rules within the games. These additional rules are discussed in guild meetings or during play, published on guild websites, and incorporated into add-on third-party software that appears in the main game window. These are sometimes the most intimate rules because players themselves are the authors; they directly affect a sense of personal control and ownership of one's fate in the game.

Any guild leader will also mention, however, that a majority of their job involves *applying* the rules, regardless of their origin, and arbitrating disagreements. We'd say the game rules are *relatively* explicit but they're not a guarantee that disputes won't occur. Gamers will quit if treated unfairly (that happens a lot) or they may try to influence guild recruiting with public posts about what they believe are transgressions that shouldn't be forgiven.

8. Teams

There has been a sea change in the popularity of solo games compared with those that involve multiple players. Group games, whether played at a computer, a console, or even casually on a phone, are winning. The commercial era of multiplayer games started modestly, with LAN (local area network) parties where players could hook their game consoles together to allow four or eight individuals to compete. Very good small team experiences can be had in successors to these early LAN games, for example, *Quake*, *Half-Life*, and the *Counter-Strike* and *Call of Duty* series cited in chapter 3.

With ubiquitous and affordable broadband now available for many people, most top-selling titles now permit multiple players to engage with and against each other over the internet, although it is the more sophisticated role-playing games that are optimized for complex group play over extended sessions.[32]

The social relationships that form in games, and the attraction of players to those relationships, are one of the more studied aspects of the MMO genre.[33] It is clear that games afford interaction opportunities that are every bit as engaging as those in real life, even if not as numerous. Fellow players yell and scream, reveal personalities, and disclose personal experiences in the course of organizing and collaborating to reach team goals. The close connection to other players causes one's social-emotional engine to run continuously, and that charges interactions.

Team Identification Is Primitive

Players don't have to learn that team play is engaging—people are built that way, and in this sense, games play on what is primitively true about humans. People are evolved to thrive in groups. Survival (in the games as well as during human evolution) depends on social affiliations and the ability to recognize those who can help with food, shelter, health, or offspring. A significant portion of our social brain is specialized for these purposes—for example, facial recognition and emotion detection.

It's amazing how easy it is to create team allegiance. A social psychology study had people separate at random into a blue and red team (just like at camp, people count off, and 1's are the blue team and 2's are the red team).[34] Participants interacted briefly as a team and then answered questions about their evaluation of the two groups. The result: if a person was assigned, at random, to the red team, he or she thought the reds were smarter, better organized, and more likeable. The same happens in the games.

I Win When We Win

For many, the stereotype of a fun game is a solo player competing against the computer or some character or group that's controlled by the computer. Sure enough, there are things to do by yourself in most games, even in the role-playing ones, but the MMO genre *requires* group play to advance, and in many cases, just to start playing. For those games, *I'm* not having fun unless *we're* having fun.

Helen was highly motivated to look after players in her guild during the raid. She diligently tracked the health status for the entire raiding party, and before the raid started, she did a substantial amount of preparation by acquiring potions and raw materials for her use during play. And she did all that knowing that even if her work were executed flawlessly, the team could still lose—easily. So in addition to fulfilling her special role in the raid, she also thought it was important to encourage the group to keep up the good work.

Gamers are not attracted to group play because someone's commanding them to collaborate but rather because they find it engaging, at least over the long haul, to be involved in a team effort. And that engagement is something they *pay* for rather than the other way around.

Social Relationships Extend Beyond the Game

There's no way Helen would run for the 5:20 p.m. train if she didn't think her teammates were counting on her. Her relationships are not only enjoyable;

they are socially important. She doesn't want to let her teammates down. Teams are focused on game experiences, but they also create environments for a broad range of other conversations—about work, parents, children, disease, politics—anything. Many gamers get to conversations beyond the game mechanics more quickly than might be the case in real life. In chapter 8, we hear from a guild leader who ended up counseling a member who had been diagnosed with breast cancer. This type of engagement isn't necessarily enjoyable, but it does create social bonds difficult to come by otherwise, and ones that keep people engaged with each other.

Virtual Interactions but with Real People

It's worth noting that Helen's feeling of responsibility to her teammates is directed toward characters or avatars rendered in artificial light on a computer screen. Can mere representations of people create the social and emotional ties necessary to foster team cohesion? The answer from research is that they create even *more* affiliation with others.[35] When people believe that real human beings control characters, their reactions to them, and their desire to affiliate with them, increase substantially. This is so fundamental to the success of games and virtual worlds that we've devoted the entire next chapter to discussing how this ingredient engages and how it can be used to build teams—in both games and business.

Encouraging Community

The intriguing promise of games is that the challenges for teams are similar to ones in business: What is the problem we are solving? How do we make resources available and apply them to a problem? How are roles assigned? Who is responsible for what, and who is in charge? Do we have the correct information? Does the assembled team have relevant expertise? How do we solve disagreements among team members? What are the risks and benefits to a given solution? All of these issues have to be resolved, and if done successfully, they will result in group *and* individual success. Chapter 7 about virtual teams gives some principles for ensuring that happens.

9. Parallel Communication Systems That Can Be Easily Reconfigured

The visuals in games get much of the attention, but it's the written and spoken communication that enables much of the social engagement. Helen can chat with any team member she chooses, either by voice or text, merely by clicking buttons. She can summon all the priests, just guild members in a specific location, or only fellow officers. It's fun to talk, and the games make this easy in the same way that the television remote changes TV programs. A small amount of technology, already available to enterprise information technology departments, creates an easily configurable communication experience matched to player style and the task at hand. That is, it's easy to change channels.

Communication Options Are Numerous

In traditional business communication, the choice of communication channels (for example, calling, face-to-face, or e-mail) substantially determines the nature of a conversation, including the number of people who can participate. There are options for some control (for example, muting, pointing cameras, and the use of cc and bcc), but most configurations are determined or at least constrained by the initial choice of modality. In the games, options are numerous, can be reconfigured quickly, and can occur simultaneously.

In Helen's raiding group, there were several different conversations layered in the action, and all were interesting and useful. Most obviously, her group was connected via a digital phone line coordinated with the game interface using a third-party plug-in. The voice conversations could be changed instantly from broadcasts to an entire group to selected commands to individuals. In Helen's group, the guild channel was used to broadcast instructions, a group channel to narrowcast comments to a few characters with similar roles, and a one-on-one channel to microcast to a single player who needed encouragement or special instruction. In addition to the voice channel, there was a continuous text chat channel that had a color-coded system for the same micro to narrow to broadcast selections. Still other communication was possible via e-mail from within the game, and of course there were occasional phone calls or even visits to a guild member's screen when he or she played in the same room or down the hall.

A Voice Channel Combined with Visuals and Text

The use of voice-over tools is a relatively new and game-changing technology. Even though instant messaging tools are widely available, players increasingly use headsets and voice-over-IP technology provided by third parties. The most obvious advantage is efficiency compared with typing. During Helen's raid, the voice-over chat was intimately linked to action on the scene—for example, when the leader signaled that all players should move to a specific location (right now!) to avoid damage to the raiding party. There may be limited times in business practice when group activity requires the synchrony of action that these techniques support, but in cases where tight coordination over group process is required, game techniques will work well. The military is obviously interested in this type of control, but precision coordination could usefully augment work in jobs ranging from financial services to factory production to routing delivery trucks.

The biggest use of voice-over communication is for quick instruction about the details of action. The same technology, however, is also used for what amounts to voice-only deliberations in performance reviews, strategy sessions, or discussions of guild policy. For example, critiques of play are accomplished with voice-over chat that uses privacy settings that are easily configurable to allow just the right subset of the group to participate.

Parallel Public and Private Conversations

Multiple conversations are interesting when one is public and another private. It can feel like gossiping about people in real time. This is a common practice in business when audio conference participants (who often feel like they're getting away with something) send text messages privately during multiperson conference calls ("How can we get this guy to stop talking?"). But in business you have to operate two different message systems that are uncoordinated. In the games, private comments about public activities are an expected occurrence, and the interface facilitates switching.

Mistakes (or "mistells") do happen. This mostly occurs when a message or comment is made outside of the narrow channel intended, revealing sensitive information. Gamers tolerate the mistakes because they value the flexibility that sometimes causes them. This may be a counterpoint to the generally accepted value of transparency in games: ranks, levels, and rewards are public, but communication can and should be private on occasion, made possible by game controls that can be quickly and easily reconfigured.

The private communication is not all gossip. It's also a chance to give an evaluation or ask a question without having to interrupt a public conversation. A raid leader might give private encouragement to a player who is falling behind. A warrior might ask a question, one that he should know the answer to, without having to interrupt the group. That makes it possible to ask dumb questions and give or receive a pointed critique without public embarrassment. And that makes it more fun to play.

Games Allow for Proximity-Based Control of Communication

In the physical world, it is easier to communicate with people who are nearby than those who are far away—regardless of conferencing system developments. Proximity-based control of communication has many useful (and some not-so-useful) consequences in ordinary communication. We move to places (such as meeting rooms) to be near those with whom we want to talk and isolated from those we'd rather avoid. We also sometimes benefit from conversations with people encountered by chance (for example, at the water cooler or coffee pot).

Games and their three-dimensional worlds bring back "water cooler conferencing" and the fun associated with serendipitous meetings. Helen had an appointed time to meet her raiding party on Tuesday night, but there were also plenty of occasions when she'd merely go to the guild hang-out spots to see who was around, never quite knowing what would happen next.

Communication favors those who are in your physical space, but it's also possible to use space to avoid people. Players not only go to the places in the games where there are people they want to engage but also stay away from places where they're likely to see characters they want to avoid. It's also worth noting that players don't have to take the time to literally walk to virtual spaces; generally, it's quite easy to travel from place to place using some means of instant transport. In business, one traditional view of effective leadership is called "management by walking around."[36] The usefulness of doing this may be no less in a virtual world, but the ease of doing it is greatly increased.

In Games You Can Easily Communicate with People You Don't Know

Games fall easily within the Web stereotype of easy (and to many, too easy) relationships. Because games depend on group action, it needs to be easy for people meet. To help, there are lots of fun tools within the games that facilitate social discovery; for example, Helen was able to find a group originally by using guild search options in the game, and also by posting what amounts to personal ads within and outside of the game.

It's possible, however, that the informality that players bring to games, learned over time using a broad range of social networking tools (chat, texting, social websites) is even more important. There's some learning involved if you're new to games, but most people catch on quickly. There is an expectation that saying "hello" is a much lighter social venture than it is in real life. You're *supposed* to communicate with people you don't know, and you're not supposed to think too much about the exact right way to express yourself. This attitude is almost a requirement. Too much social fastidiousness will mean you're not meeting enough people. This makes the games particularly fun for people who are otherwise shy and overly concerned about the intricacies of social introductions ("What should I talk about?"). Gamers are supposed to get to the point quickly, so there's no foul if that's in fact what you do.

Businesses are starting to find out what the gamer communication environment feels like through an evolving technology known as *unified communications*. The thrust of these products is to integrate telephony, voice mail, e-mail, instant messaging, Web meetings, and video so that business users can switch channels seamlessly.[37] If unified communication vendors want to show customers what that world will feel like, they should just have their customers spend an hour looking over the shoulder of a level 70 player on a raid in *World of Warcraft*.

10. Time Pressure

A good definition of a multiplayer game is collaborative achievement under uncertain winning conditions.[38] The uncertainty comes from two sources. One is simple expertise: "Do I know enough?" and "Am I good enough to do the right things?" The other is time: "Will I be able to do them in the time allotted?" For gamers, it's fun to be on the clock.

Clocks Create Excitement

Clocks are a big part of game interfaces. Raids have a time limit, spells disappear, and auctions close. To someone unfamiliar with the games and the speed at which players make decisions, meet people, coordinate tasks, and plan action, the pace of play makes a huge first impression. To players, the uncertainty about completing a task in the allotted time is a source of excitement ("I think we can, but I'm not sure").

Single-player games, and especially game consoles, have always used the clock as a way to generate excitement, and explicit time demands are increasingly more common in the complex role-playing games that are the better models for real work. A popular and extreme example is battleground action, part of many of the popular MMO titles. These encounters involve pick-up team competitions, often between groups of players not in the same guild. These are ten- to fifteen-minute games between two groups of about ten players, and they're often based on real-world games such as capture the flag. The players line up behind the gates and divide into groups based on their place in line, and then a one-minute clock starts counting down. That's the time available to decide on different roles, size up the opposing team, and determine the first moves. Even as an observer, you sense the heightened arousal as the clock counts down to the time when the gates rise.

Games Offer Chances for Quick Changes in Strategy

Although the clock creates pressure and excitement, it's also true that it can be reset with ease and frequently. There's no game clock that controls overall play like the ones in sporting events that determine the course of play. More typically, the clocks are localized to action that happens within minutes, and once they run down, they can be restarted again immediately.

This creates an opportunity for players to change strategy quickly, a game feature that keeps players engaged while increasing their willingness to take a risk. You don't have to wait until next Saturday to try again. Players get comfortable with a high probability of failure, and there's even an expectation that the group *needs* to fail once or twice before they'll really know what to do.

We have more to say about the ingredient of time pressure in games in chapter 6, where we further explore the concept of choice under scarcity.

The Value of an Ingredient List

These ten ideas describe important ingredients of good games, and we think they're the same concepts that can help reshape work. Whether used individually as a spice for a current business practice that solves a specific pain point or blended in a more comprehensive recipe, they offer a checklist for applying the engagement of games to the future of work. Some ingredients may be more relevant than others, however, and in the next section, we single out four for in-depth treatment.

In the literature about new media, the word *virtual* can be added to just about anything. Take something in the real world, pair its name with the adjective *virtual*, and you accent the threshold between its media version and real life. From the ingredient list we chose four "virtuals"—people, money, teams, and leaders—to delve into a little deeper. We're convinced of their importance for interactive play and their powerful roles in creating good *and* bad effects in games as well as virtual environments, and most important, we're convinced they will enable games to influence serious work. A central theme in each is the meaning of *virtual*. What is added and what is taken away when people, money, teams, and leaders are elements in an electronic game?

We start with the virtual people—the avatars that you control during play. As we've mentioned, hundreds of millions of people already have at least one in their lives. And it's likely you'll be assigned one in your work life quite soon. Until then, meet Mike. He just got assigned an avatar on the first day of his new job.

Chapter Five

Virtual People

FIRST DAY OF WORK: 2010

It's Mike's first day at his first job, his recent undergraduate business degree a fading memory. He'll eventually get his desk assignment in the downtown office, but for orientation tomorrow he's been asked to log into a virtual world using his home computer. The company doesn't expect to do a lot of hand-holding on this task—they've asked him to just jump into the world, create a personal avatar, and teleport to http://slurl.com/secondlife/Campus/150/100.

Fortunately, Mike's had plenty of newbie experiences in virtual worlds (he plays at least a dozen different avatars in various games). When he reads the assignment from his new employer, his first thoughts are "I can do this," "My new company is cool (avatars!)," "I made a great job choice," "I can't wait to get to orientation"—and "This is really a surprise." He never thought he'd be asked to show up for work in-world. (Note to parents: all that time wasn't wasted!)

The first thing Mike has to do before orientation is the first thing everyone has to do in games: create and personalize an avatar. "Been there, done that; this should take fifteen minutes," Mike thinks as he recalls his stable of regulars. His twelve avatars all get at least some action in a month, but three are his mainstay representatives in the games. He has a wizened male fire mage who's balding and frail with dark skin and eyes; a well-proportioned, young, and muscular female warlock with an arrogant personality; and an undead necromancer with rotting flesh, gregarious demeanor, and uncertain gender.

When he's playing games, the decision about which character to play is similar to thinking about who he would like to see socially on a particular evening—what's the mood, task, scene, and role that suits the moment? Plus, there are added benefits of being known in-world only by your avatar and not your actual face. You can decide not to be someone familiar if the mood or current events favor invisibility (that other avatar was the one who screwed up the last raid—not me). Or you can take a spin in-world as someone of a different age, personal appearance, race, or gender. This could be useful at work, Mike thinks.

Wait a minute. All of a sudden, the avatar decisions that were really fun in the games seem a bit puzzling and troubling—even scary! The avatar Mike's creating for orientation will be used for real work—collaboration on teams, negotiations with the boss, company presentations—and all with Mike's reputation on the line. This avatar is Mike's future!

The whole situation prompts Mike to ask, "Hey, are there rules at this company for how I'm supposed to create this thing?"

Why Use Avatars at Work?

No, there aren't rules regarding the creation of business avatars—at least not yet. But there probably should be. Avatars are powerful, maybe *the* most psychologically potent feature of new media. Avatars are ideal for channeling player passion into the games and the virtual worlds they inhabit. How avatars are created, personalized, and used matters a lot, corporately and personally.

But before the rules, first some background. Why would a company ask Mike to create an avatar? There are two responses: one about efficiency and the other about psychology. We think it's psychology that will fuel the sustained used of avatars, but its efficiency that's getting them first looks.

Indeed, avatars are getting looks. One analyst estimate of future avatar use in the enterprise predicts that 80 percent of information workers will have an avatar at home or work by 2011.[1] At IBM, thousands of employees meet weekly, using their avatars, in a virtual space to talk about business (dubbed the company "intraverse"). Large technology companies and a score of well-supported start-ups have teams building virtual-world infrastructure that will support avatars or are working on pieces of avatar technology separately.[2] A majority of the *Fortune* 100 companies we've spoken to in the last three years have at least one virtual-world prototype that makes use of avatars.

Here is what's driving the interest in avatars at work.

Not Everyone's Here Today

Getting people together in distributed global organizations is really hard, and for familiar reasons. People need to be and want to be out of the office. Several large companies estimate that only 50 percent of their workforce is in the office on any given day.[3] Although that's high relative to some more traditional companies, the trend is certainly in this direction. Add in declining travel budgets, infectious disease, different time zones, cultures, and even the prospect of a rainy walk across a company campus, and there's a lot of motivation to find ways to stay in touch without being physically present. Everyone agrees that face-to-face trumps other modalities, but it's less and less often a practical requirement. And for some companies—for example, virtual call centers—the impracticality of face-to-face is the very reason they're in business.

There's of course a huge industry and strong supporting cast of researchers trying to create collaborative technology that eases the pains of a distributed workforce. Much of today's collaboration software is useful and works well, and some could charitably be described as hard to use. But in either case, a major concern, quite beyond connection speeds and interface confusion, is *engagement*. Emotional and social compromises must be made when using collaborative technology. Many don't offer any visual social presence—facial expressions, gestures, posture, proximity—and those that do cost an arm and a leg and often need dedicated facilities and a talented support team. Even when there is a good amount of social bandwidth in a collaborative tool, there remains the fact that the conversations that are enabled might still be as dull as many face-to-face business meetings.

Emotional and Social Presence

There's a strong intuition that avatars can create emotional and social connections for those not physically in the office. The research we'll review confirms the intuition about engagement, but the business bet goes much further. The most important meetings in an organization are those where *innovation* happens: conversations where ideas are first cooked up and debated, passions are exposed, and people win, lose, or accommodate via personal conversations. These are exactly the conversations where the force of an idea depends substantially on the *social* information that's always hopelessly and wonderfully confused with the facts and figures. Did you see how passionately she presented that new product design? She must really think this one's got a chance!

The promise is that avatars will not only be fun to use but also will deliver channels of information missing in other business collaboration tools. In their current forms, crude compared with futurists' predictions of what's coming soon, avatars are at least good placeholders for the expressiveness that will come when facial features are more distinct, movements more life-like, and user controls more richly intuitive.

It's essential to note that the expressiveness avatars enable is *two-way*. I get to see how other avatars look and react, filling in social information where before there was little or none, *and* I get to see, for the first time in media, my own avatar and control how it reacts to others. I get to watch *me* communicating with *you*. That's a lot of social presence. (There's more about the media concept of presence in chapter 10.)

Have you ever wished you could see yourself the way others see you? This is your chance. Do you have a colleague who doesn't understand why people react unexpectedly to his or her behavior? Perhaps all that's needed is for that person to spend a little time using the over-the-shoulder view of his or her avatar.

Avatars in Games Versus Avatars in Virtual Environments

Mike's avatar problem at his new job (what should his look like?) could have been worse. He was merely being asked to show up for a meeting in a virtual world. As an experienced gamer, he was aware of the differences between virtual worlds and multiplayer games. We've been describing those differences, and they are nowhere more applicable than when considering avatars.

Virtual worlds offer the infrastructure for players to create and personal-ize avatars and build the environments in which they live. Players have to write their own game (or not). The particular role an avatar has in a virtual world is totally up to users and is not defined by the world itself, as it is in the games. Games often ask more of avatars. In the games, an avatar indicates your role in the narrative, and your identification and status within groups. This ups the ante considerably for the importance of avatar choices.

What's So Interesting About Avatars?

The original avatars descended from gods. The Sanskrit word *avatara* refers to the incarnation of a divine being on planet Earth, specifically, a god's descent from heaven into the lower realms of earthly existence.[4] Gods are allowed to configure their representations any way they want, depending on purpose and place. That's exactly what people can now do digitally, albeit for a descent that's merely from the real world to a virtual one.

Here's background that helps explain why avatars might be important at work.

Shape Your Own Existence

The ability to shape your own representation and then ship the result, with all the controls available to avatar owners, into a virtual space may be *the* most important new feature of interactive technology. You're no longer stuck with your real-world body, appearance, or personality. There's now a palette for each that goes far beyond the relatively small advantages available to mere humans—better makeup, a new suit, counseling sessions, or workouts at the gym. With avatars, you can make some serious changes fast.

Games and virtual worlds give workers an opportunity to optimize a self-representation. Players can build characters that have an appearance, personality, gestures, and behavior that may have some basis in reality, but characters can also project a *desired* self. Shy people can be socially competent and powerful. A poor self-image can be turned into physical attractiveness: you choose the height, weight, proportions, and musculature you want. You can buy computer code that will make you (at least virtually) a tremendous dancer, acrobat, singer, or lover. You can, much to our pleasure, easily have a full head of hair.

Who Is That on the Screen?

Usually, the field of psychology influences what researchers think about media. Psychologists know about thinking and feeling in the real world, and generally those principles transfer well to the virtual world. Once in a while, the influence works in the other direction when there's a new feature of media that causes psychologists to rethink their own ideas about real people. That's the case with avatars. There is no exact counterpart to avatars in the real world, so psychology will have to catch up.

Who is that person on the screen? I know him or her (or it) as *my* character, but exactly what does that mean? The possible models vary substantially.[5] The most psychologically heavy model is that the character on the screen really *is* me, or at least a "mini-me." It's the equivalent of looking in the mirror, only the character in the mirror has a lot more freedom to do things you can't do yourself.

On the lighter side, controlling an avatar is a bit like puppeteering. There are digital strings that give the performer control over movement and location, and there's an increased investment in the puppet if it's yours. At present, game avatars don't allow words that are spoken or written by a player to be replayed via the character, lip synched to make it appear the character is directly connected to the player. That's coming and will make this model even stronger. Sock puppets beware!

A really wild metaphor is that of avatars as biological offspring. When you watch your child on the stage or in the pool, there's a feeling of investment in their behavior and success that's extraordinary. You really want things to go well. Much of that affiliation is thoughtful ("This would be a good developmental experience for my kid"), but a portion of the reaction is also primitive and unconscious. More than one gamer in our conversations (and often the older ones) have referred to their avatar as their child.

The important feature that all of these models have in common is that avatars are compelling. Even if they're not an exact replicate of me, I'm invested.

Mirror Neurons, Imitation, and Learning

People at work depend on imitation to get through the day. This isn't just a business book admonition or a new-age influence technique—it's a fact about how humans learn. If personal experiences were required to learn about the world, we'd never keep up. Imitation is useful, and our brains are exquisitely built to watch others, record, and make adjustments accordingly; direct participation is unnecessary.

The brain process by which imitation happens involves mirror neurons.[6] These are neurons that fire when we perform an action (that is, when we actually move our bodies to accomplish some task) *and* also fire when that same action is performed by someone else, and we just watch. Mirror neurons allow us to simulate other people's experiences to better understand how to perform the action, with a secondary result being that we better understand the people and actions we're watching. This is the neural counterpart of being in someone else's shoes.

What's interesting is that mirror neurons don't just fire when we watch other real people. They work just fine with pictures as the stimulus. If you see a picture of a garden shear about to cut a finger, for example, you get activation in the same pain warning centers that would fire if the experience were real.[7] Thus mirror neurons are part of the mental machinery that enables imitation even when you're just looking at pictures or watching television or a film.

Now consider avatars. I'm invested in the strategies, plans, and actions that I've channeled into the character that I control. Something happens to my avatar (he or she is rewarded, insulted, pushed, or exploded), the result of which is displayed in 3D splendor right in front of me. The mirror neurons are firing in relation to the activities of my character on the screen. If another character cuts my (virtual) arm, at some level I feel the pain; if my character steps on a sharp (virtual) object on the road to Ironforge, the pain moves to my foot; and if I'm insulted by a character from an opposing team, the pain moves to brain centers active during social insults.[8]

Avatars may be more important in activating mirror neurons than other characters on the screen. The attachment that people have to *their* characters (pick any of the explanations we mentioned) increases engagement with the action on the screen. Important new research shows that the activation of mirror neurons is significantly affected by the *motivation* of the observer.[9] When motivation is high, mirror neuron activity increases substantially, with important implications for a sense of involvement in the activity and a better memory for the presentation as well. So learning from *my* avatar may be easier than learning from yours—a good argument for investing in avatars at work.

Watching and Participating at the Same Time

In games, players get to decide where the camera goes. What appears on the screen is under your total control. Press a button and the view changes. You're like the director of live television, only you're producing your (virtual) life. You can decide to observe from the top down (it looks like you're watching the action from an airplane, and you control the altitude) or you can view from a near or distant point; your avatar and all the others look small or larger as you zoom in and out to gain visibility of the surrounding environment.

Compare these choices with real life. Without technology, we're stuck with the "camera" in one place—our eyes. This is the first-person view, and it's not without disadvantages. It's certainly personal, but it makes it hard to know what's going on behind you, to see where everyone else is, and perhaps most important, to see what you look like when you're active in the world.

Multiplayer games do offer a first-person view. Just click a button and the camera becomes the eyes of your avatar. You can't see your avatar's face (just as you can't see your own), but you can look down and see its feet. One of our recent studies shows that playing games, especially violent ones, from the first-person view is significantly more exciting (increased heart rate and more skin moisture) than when the same play is experienced third person, with the camera positioned just behind and over the shoulder of your avatar.[10]

This result agrees nicely with the excitement players report in shooting games, which are almost all first person. A good prediction would be that players from all games would position the camera from the eyes of their avatar because that's the most exciting perspective. Wrong. Our observation is that almost all gamers in multiplayer titles use a third-person camera position, usually putting the camera close to their avatar but zoomed out enough to be able to see other characters and objects in the scene. Why? One reason is that it's a gaming advantage. You get a better angle on threats (watch out behind!). But you also get to see how cool you look running into battle.

The narcissistic explanation is interesting. Wouldn't we all love the flexibility of different camera angles in real life? It turns out that's true, as shown by experiments about human memory.[11] Question: Imagine the last time you gave a talk in front of a group. Now freeze on your image of the room. Where's the camera? For many people, memories are *third* person. We like the advantage of taking in the larger scene enough to rotate our memory from first to third person. And it's also the case that third-person personal memories are more likely than first-person ones to lead to behavior change (I can actually watch myself performing behaviors), making it all the more interesting that games allow substantial practice in self-observation.[12] With avatars, the interest and subsequent behavior change may even be greater because it is easier to construct third-person memories given that the third person was the format of the original action. Without an avatar to observe, there's some mental rotation involved.

Are Avatars Good or Bad?

The answer is yes. The danger theme applies well here. Avatars are indeed interesting, but more in the sense of interesting and disruptive than interesting and good, as the evidence presented earlier suggests. What can we expect as good and bad outcomes of avatars at work? Here's a review. Note: Most of these points are positive *and* negative. There's no easy list of pros and cons.

Allocating Time

How much will avatars be used at work? It's too early to tell for sure, but we do know that people spend time with things that are interesting. When the virtual experiences are mere entertainment, the average amount of game play (also "avatar time") is often over twenty hours per week (see chapter 2 for details about time spent in the games). If hanging around can be linked to organizational goals, avatars will help. For example, think of service or surveillance jobs, where avatars might extend time on task to an advantage.

Avatars can do amazing things, many of them purposeless but *really* fun to watch. Pre-raid strategy meetings, when avatars are milling about with most of the action in the chat or voice channels, are prime times to display the latest macros (computer code one builds, buys, or downloads). During such a conference, you could see a back flip, hot dance moves, or a new saber thrust. It's hard not to watch, which is probably both good and bad for work.

Avatar Infrastructure Can Be Hard

There's one extra time demand of avatars, and unfortunately, it's a mandatory and often tedious requirement before entering virtual worlds and games. It's about setup. It can be quite fun, but it is often time-consuming. The problems apply to more than just avatars, but because the creation of a character is one of the first things you do, the problems often get pinned here initially.

There's infrastructure with avatars. First, you have to gain entrance to the worlds where they live. This requires all the usual issues with new software (accounts, passwords, computer brands) but also some new ones. Any world that supports 3D depictions of people and places is at the upper end of demand on computers, and the bar keeps going up. You'll need the right processor, amount of memory, graphics chip, video card, screen resolution, and connection speed.

There will be a friendly invitation in most 3D worlds that will reassure you that you'll be fine with any computer purchased in the last year, and that's mostly true. But obviously not everyone is buying new machines at that pace. Your avatar might not work, or it may just move slowly in fits and starts, and it may take time for it to fully render in each new place it roams. The complexity of virtual world technology is increasing, and that's given rise to questions about their basic architectures.

Beware Your First Avatar Experiences

OK. You've downloaded the software and, like Mike, you're anxious to get to the first meeting. But unlike Mike, you're new to virtual worlds. Don't expect to start the meeting on time if you've only allotted fifteen minutes prep time.

The authors and colleagues spent several months having weekly meetings using avatars in virtual worlds. Our characters were dressed for action and met in our custom-designed conference room complete with a nifty white board, a slide show screen, period paintings, the requisite plants, and other artifacts from the in-world digital library. Periodically, we invited business partners to join us.

You might expect (we certainly did) that our in-world collaborations would quickly get to substantive issues, giving us good visibility into the collaboration of the future. Not true. We spent a good half of early sessions just trying to make things work. Can you see me yet in the room? How do you turn on the voice channel? Ann's on a slow connection at home and can't keep up with the conversation. Does this run on a Mac? What do I do if I'm behind the firewall?

We eventually solved each problem (the good news), and every month that passes means you'll be able to solve them more quickly as technology and interfaces improve, and especially as virtual worlds and games are hosted on websites rather than local machines. But the problem list is still troublesome. Like many technology disruptions, enthusiasm for these solutions is ahead of technology details, meaning that infrastructure bugs often trump substantive discovery during the first experiences. No wonder the consultants who are experts in serious uses of avatars and virtual worlds prefer that you call them *after* your first virtual-world experiment.

Expect the Unexpected

You're behind a virtual podium in a virtual world, lecturing to twenty other avatars about the benefits of new collaboration technology. The session is going well, in part because everything—the setting, costumes, appearances— is more engaging (for better and worse) than at the same meeting in real life. There's nothing seriously edgy, however, and so far, everyone's well behaved. Until a penguin hops up to the podium, stands right next to you, and lights himself on fire. We watched this happen to a respected colleague, and no, neither of us was driving the penguin.

Public virtual worlds and games are the new Wild West. And the penguin is just the tip of the iceberg. There will be a lot of surprises, and we think most will (and do already) meet with criticism from those trying to run a business. It's possible to curtail some of the shenanigans with a firewall, passwords, and corporate rules, but even with more structure, there is a degree of anonymity and anarchy in a virtual world that isn't customary in the physical office.

The trend in the next years will be to regulate our way around the problems with avatars with style sheets for appearance, rules for behavior, and protocol for meetings. This may partially work but will be as hard as any other corporate behavior change programs aimed at technology use (no cell phone use in the conference room, no Internet clothing purchases on company time, no sexy jokes via e-mail or promiscuous use of the Reply to All button). These programs gain compliance at launch but often wane over time because of the difficulty of enforcement; for games, the attraction of misbehaving is common.

Even if the rules could be sustained, however, they might not be advisable. It's the tension between playfulness and seriousness that makes avatars interesting. The reason you might want to work longer, communicate more, or take greater risks is precisely because you get to be a penguin at work (or whatever other persona suits the mood and job). We'll have to get used to a new blend of fun and seriousness to take full advantage of games and avatars, but this may be no different from other blends that brought entertainment to previously serious contexts.

Leveling Differences

A serious problem where avatars might help is in minimizing differences in personality or culture that can inhibit collaboration. Here's an example.

A large computer chip maker has development teams around the world. They're not skunk works designed to isolate people from the rest of the company, but rather groups that must work closely with other teams around the world. One new design depends on ten engineers from Korea working with a counterpart group in Silicon Valley. The engineers are peers with respect to intelligence, experience, and good ideas. But every time they meet, a daily requirement averaging about ninety minutes per session, nine of the Koreans politely defer to their shy boss to make comments at the meeting. The Valley engineers, over the objections of their boss, impolitely interrupt with all sorts of ideas, including those in need of more oven time. The result of the meeting is often confusion and frustration, attributable to differences in culture and style and not engineering prowess.

That part of the story is familiar. This part isn't, but might be an advantage for avatars. Imagine the same twenty engineers meeting as their avatars in a virtual world. The reports from first uses (there's no empirical test of this yet) suggest that when people appear as avatars two different changes happen. First, people may regress to a more balanced communication style, one potentially better at fostering innovation. Second, shy people disclose more and outgoing people talk less. Self-disclosure, confidence, and communication style all move in a direction that equalizes the group and facilitates collaboration.

This is not to say that avatars sterilize identities. In fact, the playfulness of avatars might actually encourage people to customize and personalize them in a way that emphasizes, like badges on a uniform, their unique identities. What is true for personality or cultural differences might be even truer for people who could use an avatar to neutralize *disadvantages* in communication. On the positive side, avatars have the potential to subtract from a conversation potential distractions such as personal handicaps, beauty, age, race, and gender.

It might be well known that a particular person has an avatar that looks nothing like they do in real life. The company directory may even show a picture of both. The effect of the avatar, however, depends more on the representation than on background information about the person controlling it. It's just too hard for people to see an avatar (its smiling face, body proportions, and coordinated behavior) and then somehow change the effect of its appearance and behavior because they know that the person controlling it looks and behaves differently. Even if mismatches might be obvious on occasion (likely for only the most noticeable of differences), it's way too difficult psychologically to keep up a constant dual processing. What you see is what you get, even if people are capable of determining otherwise if they think real hard.

Hiding Behind an Avatar Can Cause Problems

There is, however, a negative side to the separation of avatar and avatar owner. It certainly makes it more possible to hide, if that's your goal. We know from studies about other digital communication that even the *feeling* that people are hidden can make for fireworks that might not otherwise occur. There's good evidence, for example, that e-mail escalates angry flaming, most likely through depersonalization of those involved in the communication.[13] It's easier to get mad if you don't have to look someone in the eye.

With avatars, there's a potential double whammy of negative effects from depersonalization. Like e-mail, *you* don't have to look anyone in the eye (at least not until you meet them in the real world), but your avatar does. You escape the immediate discomfort of confrontation, but your message has the effect of a real face-to-face encounter because you have a stand-in who's more interesting than mere angry words, exclamation points, or all caps in text. And your avatar does the dirty work for you.

Flaming is frequent in the games because communication feels (and sometimes is) anonymous. But that doesn't mean it's any less offensive than in real life. Here's a comment from an MMO guild leader about a flaming incident during one of their raids (game lingo is translated in brackets):

> The raid began smoothly but the raid leader began to act
> erratically and pull far more monsters [he tried to attract more
> of the enemy into the fight] than was prudent for the situation.
> Needless to say, he caused the entire raid party to die. After he
> caused this "wipe" he began to make extremely rude comments
> about the healers, both of whom are my guild mates. . . At that,
> I ordered our guild to leave and let the raid group fend for
> themselves. So many people tend to forget that the Night Elf
> Priest that you are talking to is manned by a real human being
> on the other side of the screen. After I made my comment about
> not speaking to my healers in such a manner there was silence in
> the guild chat channel for a few moments before the priest
> replied, "Wow . . . that is the nicest thing anyone has ever said in
> this game." That has been one of the most rewarding experiences
> I have had while being a member of the leadership of this guild.

Another example of the communication errors that occur because people think they can hide is an experiment that was performed by a group of graduate students at Stanford who were among the first of a growing number of researchers to conduct interviews of players by talking to their avatars in virtual worlds. The study was about race.[14] In a virtual world, of course, you can have whatever skin color you'd like with the press of a button. In one world, players were given a choice of being "chocolate" or "vanilla." The students decided to interview other avatars in the world (players whom they had never met and whose actual skin color was quite unknown) and see how they responded to different skin colors. (Of the four students in the group, two were white and two were African American.) They created two different conversation starters to use when they approached other avatars, one nice and one mean. The nice script started with comments like "This place is cool." The mean script started with comments like "This place sucks." The students measured how much time the other avatars (who were all "vanilla") would spend talking with them and whether they got nice or mean comments in response.

The first surprise was that other players spent *more* time talking to avatars when they were rude than when they were nice, about two minutes more on average for conversations that took between eight and twelve minutes total.

It takes time to resolve conflict, a warning that there's a productivity cost to rudeness. But race made the differences more extreme, adding an additional two minutes for the "chocolate" conversations compared with the "vanilla" ones. It took even more time to resolve a rude conversation with avatars of the opposite color.

Avatar race also determined whether the responses were rude or not. The "vanilla" nice avatars received all nice responses. The "chocolate" nice avatars received one in five comments that were negative, evidence that there was some willingness to be mean to a nice avatar simply because of its color. The differences were even greater when the initial comments were mean. The "vanilla" rude avatars received more nice than mean responses (about 3:2 positive). The "chocolate" rude avatars received the opposite (about 3:2 negative).

This was good evidence that race matters, virtual or real. This isn't surprising, because the influence of race on interpersonal experience is well known.[15] But the ability to encourage responses based on race was easily and quickly done in-world. It's hard to imagine the negative comments uttered to the "chocolate" avatars being as explicit and easy to find in the real world, especially for conversations lasting five to ten minutes between strangers.

This is also a good reminder that virtual worlds provide opportunities to do research that would otherwise be difficult, and most likely impossible, to conduct. Sometimes, the fact that people can hide behind avatars might allow studies to be done that would be useful in business. What studies could you do with avatars that you couldn't do any other way? Maybe employees would be more forthcoming with management if they were talking to a CEO avatar.

Avatars Provide Ways to Get Lost (and Found)

If you're interested enough in avatars to find your way to a professional conference about virtual worlds (seems like there's at least one a month), you may be asked to provide two names and two pictures at registration. The second identity is your avatar. It should be easy to imagine the humor in the programs ("You're not at all who I thought you'd be!").

Now consider the matched identities (the directories with two pictures) with respect to a difficult collaboration problem. In business, teams need to be assembled quickly. The problem is epitomized in the IBM television commercial where a hip younger executive is bragging about his new social networking tool.[16] A more seasoned executive asks if the tool can help "put together a team of international finance experts who know merger arbitrage, have ten-plus years of experience, can speak Cantonese, and can hit the ground running Monday." He says no, of course, and the tool fails for now.

When you search for people in a large company, it's not the search that's hard; rather, it's the tagging of expertise that the search is based on that's the weak link. It's time-consuming and even socially awkward to tag yourself with information that will allow colleagues to find you easily and for the right reasons. Avatars could facilitate tagging. Badges, levels, and artifacts owned—all acquired in the game and attached to a player's avatar—could be all the tagging that's needed. In the games, the tags are applied automatically (e.g., Tom automatically got the merger arbitrage badge when he hit level 27), allowing the searches to work even better.

It's hard to disembody expertise, which is why we're able to remember information better when it's associated with a human body. That's how we attribute, categorize, and find expertise when we need it ("Check with Justin down the hall—he's the wiz on computer networking"). Avatars give expertise an important second identity, and if the avatars are cleverly constructed, perhaps an identity that could be more memorable than the person controlling it. Every successful virtual world has avatars who are huge celebrities in their own right, and it's because of what they have done more than how they look. Take Anshe Chung, for example, the tycoon who has amassed vast property holdings in *Second Life*. On the other hand, Nick's *Star Wars* character, mentioned in chapter 2, wears an extremely nice coat that must be earned with great talent and effort. So, with avatars, what you look like can be a direct representation of what you have accomplished. There are all kinds of useful stereotypes to play on that could allow people to be known in useful ways. You might not want to wear the computer networking uniform in real life, but on your avatar? Why not?

Guidelines for Avatar Use

The story so far is that avatars are inherently attractive, but with respect to the pros and cons of their use, the case is mixed. There will be opportunities *and* problems. How can companies take control of their inevitable presence in the workplace while accentuating the good over the bad?

Corporate Style Sheets

One strategy is to tell people how to use avatars. This won't be any easier than it's been to influence the use of other technology (as we've said, part of the attraction of avatars is a hint of anarchy), but it's certainly worth an effort. Some avatar evangelists, for example, think that the creation of an avatar style sheet may be what's needed to encourage hesitant participants to dive in and try something new. The presence of guidelines would sanction correct behavior and let people know what could get them in trouble.

IBM, a company well down the road in virtual-world thinking, has taken a first shot at such a style sheet.[17] It's appropriately general—maybe too much so for those looking to find out whether the flammable penguin will be prohibited—but the advice is consistent with the research about how people perceive avatars. The guiding principle in IBM's style sheet is based on the reality that a lot of mediated life is just like real life. So be a good citizen, build trust, be truthful, don't discriminate or harass, and generally do unto others. . . On business process, a bit more specific advice reminds users, for example, not to discuss intellectual property with unauthorized people. You could use pretty much the same sentences for either the real-world or virtual-world points.

Other IBM rules—and the most interesting and hardest to enforce, in our view—refer to appearance and personalization. For example, users are asked to be sensitive about their avatar's appearance when meeting with company clients. Another says that if you have multiple avatars, be aware that confusion about their interchangeability could diminish trust. There are no regulations on shirt color, but for some even these gentle rules are reminiscent of the Big Blue stereotype.

There's no stated IBM effort to become the sheriff (the policy is unclear on possible disciplinary action), but that may be what any guidelines will end up communicating. For many in the gamer generation, the seamlessness of the real and virtual worlds is assumed, and special rules may seem to pander to game stereotypes of too much virtual sex, too many dragons, and too much fighting. We wonder what Mike would have thought about these rules and the company that made them if they had accompanied his orientation invitation.

Personal Guidelines for Avatars

OK, now I know what my company would like me to do. What about my own *personal* style sheet? If avatars will determine whether I win friends and influence people, what are the best practices?[18] Here's some advice that Mike (and you) might keep in mind when using avatars at work. Some of these practices might seem like persona micromanagement, but all are based on recent research, much of it from the lab of Professor Jeremy Bailenson at Stanford. That research demonstrates powerful, even if sometime subtle, effects. It also suggests outcomes and social errors that could result in disaster. Danger ahead!

- *Avatars that look like the people with whom they're interacting are the most persuasive.* Here's a good reason to give up on penguins. When your avatar looks like the real person who is driving the avatar with which it is interacting, that person may like the avatar more, remember more about it, be more likely to do embarrassing things in front of the avatar, and think the avatar is better looking.[19]

  The practical implication is to build avatars at work that look like the people whom the avatars are meant to impress. Interestingly, the research suggests carrying this to an extreme. One dastardly digital trick might be to have your avatar actually morph (visually blend, either quickly or over time) its face with another person. (This is easy to accomplish with several different software applications, although it's not a feature of virtual worlds—yet.) In the laboratory, an avatar will have the advantages mentioned previously even if its face is imperceptibly blended with the face of the person you're trying to impress. That is, if you make your avatar's face look even a little bit like mine, even if I can't recognize the trick, I'll respond more favorably.

- *It's good for an avatar to look like the "in group."* Maximizing the entertainment value of avatars might suggest that you create avatars noticeably different from the group. Although that will indeed get you noticed, it may not be the best route to winning friends. People show preferential treatment for "in group" avatars; that is, avatars that have the same gender or race as the rest of the group.[20] Avatar similarity also enables people to work together better over an extended period. So beware gratuitous differentiation; you'll get noticed, but possibly to the disadvantage of group cohesion.

- *Virtual touching is like real touching.* You'll remember the first time your avatar bumps into another avatar. It feels almost physical—even more so if you're a male player and bump into a female avatar (or vice versa) or if you run as opposed to walk into another character. Your own brain will process the collision similarly to a real-life run-in (remember the mirror neurons), creating a real enough mental experience of the virtual event. Your memory for the event will also be better. Be careful how you move.

  And be careful what you touch—the results for bumping also apply to touching. Research shows that people "touch" avatars more

gently than they touch inanimate objects in virtual environments.[21]
They also touch avatars more gently on the face than on the torso.
And the effects of virtual sexual touching are even stronger.
The latter is common in some virtual worlds (not so much
in games), a reminder that real-life rules apply when avatars are
at work.

- *Realism isn't necessary to be influential.* There's an assumption that
  photorealism will make avatars better or more influential. It's true in
  general that better pictures will be taken more seriously, but it isn't
  necessary that avatars have your photo on their face to be influential.
  (There are new technologies to allow photos to be used in avatar
  creation, and more new tricks are on the horizon, including the
  creation of 3D avatars using photos.)

  One study showed that the more realistic an avatar looked (photorealistic versus cartoonlike), the less likely it was that people were
  willing to disclose personal information to that avatar when they first
  met. If your job involves interviewing, there's no need to impose on
  the interviewee with great pictures—a cartoon might do just fine.[22]
  One other caution from the same research: beware mismatches
  between the realism of an avatar's appearance and the realism of its
  behavior (for example, a photorealistic avatar that moves awkwardly).
  It's better to have less realism on both dimensions than a mismatch
  between them.[23] Game designers are obsessive about maintaining
  verisimilitude and would flag this as a major error.

- *It matters where you look.* When you control an avatar, you get to
  decide the direction it faces and even where it looks. Not all worlds
  offer this level of fine-grained avatar control, but they will. Choose
  your virtual visual targets carefully. Eye gaze is one of the most important determinants of the quality of interpersonal communication, and
  this is also true virtually.[24]

  Here's what we know so far about avatar gaze. Avatars that don't
  look at strangers when they advance are more likely to encourage
  other avatars to stand closer. Avatars that maintain mutual gaze are
  more persuasive than ones that don't. And when collaborators use
  avatars that allow for head movements and mutual gaze, they do
  better on tasks and like each other more than when avatars don't
  perform these realistic behaviors.[25] Look down at the wrong time or
  stare too long and you diminish your likability and influence in the

virtual world. Can you guess what happens to rapport when your avatar checks its BlackBerry?

- *It matters where you stand.* There are virtual rules about where you should stand that parallel those for real interactions. In real spaces, for example, men stand farther away from other men than women. Cultures also have different customs about the amount of personal space they favor when people meet (e.g., Spaniards stand closer than Americans).[26]

  The same rules apply in virtual worlds.[27] Give your new virtual colleagues some space. Be aware that it's quite possible to literally (not virtually) violate gender, cultural, or situational norms based on where you position your character in a 3D world.

- *Go ahead and be tall and good looking.* Sizes, shapes, and faces do matter. This is a well-tested result in psychology (e.g., tall and attractive political candidates do better than opponents with less striking features).[28] The same advantage accrues to virtual people, except that you can far more easily make the desirable changes.

  Remember that tall and attractive avatars are not only influential for the other players whom you'll meet in a virtual world. As long as you're playing in third-person mode (you get to see the other players and your character), the advantages are also true for *you*. People behave in ways consistent with how their avatar looks. For example, if you're playing a taller avatar, you are more likely to behave confidently. Attractive avatars are more likely to be social. Your avatar will not only influence others but you as well.

Avatars Are Just Like Real People—Take Them Seriously

The point of all of these rules is not to suggest that players should carry a cheat sheet of persuasive tricks as they conduct their work. In fact, remembering this one rule might be enough: what works in real life generally works in virtual life. In spite of the virtual opportunities to easily and dramatically change a virtual presentation, you should do so only on purpose.

Avatar creation will be a constant balancing act between retention of character features that make games fun (dragons, warriors, special powers, extreme physical features, interesting gear to wear and brag about) with a sensibility that preserves what is valuable and similar between games and real life (have good manners, don't misrepresent, avoid hypercriticism).

The next "virtual" is money. The same theme occurs about the differences (or the lack of them) between the real thing and a synthetic copy. In the case of money, what is being copied is not people, but rather incentives that work in the real world that can change real behavior.

Meet Claire. She's about to spend some virtual money to change some real behaviors.

Chapter Six

Virtual Money

8:30 a.m.: Claire rests her first cup of coffee next to the computer as she waits for the company security system to log her in to Windows. She doesn't actually mind the wait, because her first task will be wading through unwelcome e-mails to find the handful that really matter to her. Her thoughts turn to the research project she'd come here to pursue, if only she could find the time and get the key people in her organization to buy into the idea. But it's always such a struggle to get stuff on their radar screen; they're as swamped as she is.

8:32 a.m.: The computer is on and the e-mail downloaded, and her research dreams are crushed by an inbox consisting largely of useless information and uninvited requests. She joined the company to work on big ideas, but can't seem to dig out of the minutia. When she tries, her ideas get lost in other inboxes that look just like hers. There's not enough attention, not enough feedback, not enough action. So she completes assignments that do get others' attention and plays her part in official initiatives, but she yearns to expand her role and advance her career.

8:37 a.m.: Back to the inbox. "Hmmm . . . What's this?" as she notices a note titled "Invitation" from Joe. The subject sounds like spam from another social networking site, but the sender is a respected colleague.

Dear Claire,

Joe Anderson has invited you to open a free Serio account with an initial balance of one hundred Serios. Serios are currency that you and your colleagues can use to signal each other that some e-mail is more important than others, and to reward valuable correspon-dence. When you receive an e-mail with Serios attached, you get to keep them! But sometimes, it's useful to return Serios to the sender if you find their message valuable.

If this sounds like it's worth a try, click to Download.

8:39 a.m.: "Sounds a little complicated. Who else got this invitation?" Claire wonders. "OK, let's give it a go. For Joe." Claire downloads a new piece of software that works with her e-mail application.

8:44 a.m.: Claire sends her first note to Joe, still skeptical. But she uses the new tool and attaches five Serios to Joe's note, out of her initial allowance of one hundred, curious to see whether they will help get his attention. "Hey Joe," she writes, "I signed up for your Serio thingy. Hope it's fun or you owe me!"

3:44 p.m.: Claire continues attaching Serios to notes during the day, including twenty-five that she sent with a new idea for Harry, the senior manager in her group. "Couldn't hurt," Claire thinks. "He hasn't responded to anything else on this topic." To her surprise, there's a reply from Harry within the hour with fifty Serios attached. "A 100% gain," Claire thinks, "and it's on the record!" Harry agreed that her outsourcing idea would save two weeks on the next round of trials.

5:00 p.m.: At the end of the day, Claire looks at a couple of new features in her inbox and can see all of the Serios sent and received. A net increase—"that's kinda fun." She also takes one last look at the remain-ing messages to see if she's missed anything important. But first, she rank-orders the messages in her inbox according to the Serios attached to the notes. The ones with the most currency go to the top.

2:00 p.m. the next day: Claire receives an e-mail from Joe that says he'll send each team member twenty Serios if they come to a planning meeting. She might have gone anyway, but the Serios are a good signal that Joe thinks the meeting is important. Claire is surprised that the meeting actually advances her own project, so she sends thirty Serios back to Joe for including her project on the agenda. With this experi-ence fresh in her mind, Claire attaches twenty Serios to one of her own meeting announcements. Unlike previous invitations, she only invites the people most central to the agenda. "Don't want to waste Serios on unnecessary invites," she thinks to herself.

4:00 p.m.: Harry has given Claire a new deadline for a follow-up experiment on lab results she submitted yesterday, but the instrument lab is booked solid for the next two weeks. Claire scans the first-come, first-served queue for the lab and sees that Roger is scheduled tomorrow afternoon for what looks to be a block of routine work. A new use for Serios pops into her head. "Roger, I'll give you thirty Serios now if you'll let me have your lab slot tomorrow" Roger, a nice guy, says, "Sure Claire—my stuff can wait. Just send the Serios over in an e-mail."

6:00 p.m.: Claire spends some time playing with the network maps that show all recent currency trades by people within her group. It's readily apparent that Louise is an outlier. "We all know that she's a loner, but we can never finish our projects without her unique skill," Clare muses, wondering how Serios might be used to make Louise feel more identified with the group.

6:02 p.m.: Claire runs into Joe at the elevator and starts a conversation about Louise that gets around to his and her own priorities. "I was wondering why you didn't give me any Serios back for yesterday's e-mail about the scheduling problem. I thought it was pretty good stuff. Did you just forget or is there something wrong with my idea?"

It's the Economy, Stupid

Claire's pain points are not unique or especially remarkable. Working in complex social groups such as today's large companies involves lots of trade-offs between one's personal aspirations, those of colleagues, and the formal requirements of the organization. Her experimentation with a synthetic currency at work is still novel, of course, but making the trade-offs explicit exposes deep parallels between today's multiplayer games and what could be a more productive, efficient, and happier workplace.

The phrase "It's the economy, stupid," a relic of the 1992 presidential campaign, began as an internal reminder to the Clinton team by James Carville to keep the economy at the forefront of the campaign.

This chapter takes the advice to heart by looking into the origins and variety of the vibrant economies in today's games, followed by an exploration of what might be missing from the barter system that characterizes most company discussions about priorities, resources, attention, and goals. (For the 2008 season, we nominate "A crisis is a terrible thing to waste".)[1]

Choice Under Scarcity

If you read Edward Castronova's *Synthetic Worlds*, you will find a new and improved version of Economics 101 by a tenured professor of the dismal science who has spent more than nine years immersed in the massive multiplayer games we have been describing.[2] Instead of the classic treatment that others inflict on undergraduates, his students are treated to a lucid, bottom-up case that economics is less about money than it is about making choices in the face of scarcity. (More about the utility of money later; let's stick with the fundamentals of scarcity for a bit.)

Think about the first video game you ever played. Was it Pong? Pac Man? Mario Brothers? Tetris? Doom? Wii Golf? You'll date yourself with the answer, but we assume your first video game did not have anything like synthetic currency or a marketplace where you could send your avatar to spend gold pieces for the latest virtual doodad to enhance your ability to get to the next level in the game.

In most single-person electronic games, the striking scarcity is that of *time*. The concept is so important that we include it as the final one of our ten key ingredients in chapter 4. There are tasks that must be accomplished, and the clock keeps on ticking. In the early hand-eye "twitch" games, the trade-off was "Do I move the cursor left, right, up or down in order to gobble, shoot, collect, or escape before something bad happens?" Typically, the clock ticks come faster and faster and faster until you eventually fail. The *fun* games give you a sense of accomplishment before the inevitable catastrophe. Then they give you a chance to try again and make better trade-offs.

In addition to time pressure, the user experience in today's persistent online games includes a vastly more complex landscape of objects, space, characters, and challenges in which to make choices under scarcity. To advance from level to level, MMO players must obtain or create certain virtual objects to carry out their quests, and some of these objects are rare. These items may contain the vital clues to puzzles or confer special powers on the holder. Many are a necessary means to a valued end. Some are simply cool. Some objects (or the raw materials to make them) may "spawn," or appear from time to time, at a specific location. Others may need to be "crafted" using natural resources that are gathered by players using their special skills. Or they may be given to the player by nonplayer characters (NPCs), essentially robot avatars that are controlled by game software.

Desired objects can often be obtained from other players by trading something of value. Frequently, there are alternative ways to obtain the same object. The challenge to players is to find the most efficient way to accomplish tasks because the clock is ticking. Humans seem to enjoy (and may excel at) solving these mental equations provided there is sufficient information to tackle the problem and the task is not so difficult as to be destructively frustrating. It is also fun to be able to talk about the problem with others and to seek and get advice about solutions. Gamers love to gossip about their trades. The talking usually occurs in the game, but increasingly, it also occurs in the ecology of online websites and social media that grow up around successful games.

For All the Rest, There's Money

Money appeared very early in the development of electronic games involving multiple players. As the richness of choices evolved in a landscape of diverse scarcity and opportunity, game designers experimented with new forms of play money. Julian Dibbell, an early game aficionado and game industry writer, provides a wonderful introduction to MUD money, the synthetic currency that appeared in the early text-based adventure games played among university computer geeks and known as multiuser dungeons (MUDs).[3] His comments go far beyond MUDs, including the observation that money itself may be the oldest virtual reality technology around.

Castronova reminds us that money is not the economy but rather a convenience for recording choices and the effects of choices that take place in the economy.[4] Although economies are about *choices*, not money, it is clear that the design of *synthetic* money can have a huge impact on player experience. Players in the early text-based games experienced "mudflation," a pernicious form of currency inflation that occurred when game designers mismanaged the balance of sources and sinks for synthetic currency in the game. Victims saw the value of hard-earned virtual gold pieces plummet as new gold, minted at the (in)discretion of the publishers, flooded the game. The rapid inflation caused the gulf between established players and newbies to widen, making the game less fun.

A well-designed currency solves a lot of problems for players who are making choices under scarcity. The ancient Assyrians discovered that it was easier to carry around clay tokens rather than the warehoused sheaves of barley each token represented.[5] Following Dibbell, we would say that these tokens were essentially virtual barley. Portability may have been one key driver for the adoption of Assyrian money, but game designers have other ways to help players with the inconvenience of bulky goods, since these are only bits set in a computer's memory (designers could provide a magic sled to carry around heavy gold pieces, for example).

Money in games has useful properties other than portability. Gamers enjoy benefits related to all of the properties in the standard definition of the concept: money has the ability to serve as a unit of account, a means of exchange, a store of value, and a source of liquidity.[6] As a unit of account, money is more easily divisible than most objects, including game pieces such as special swords or magic rings. In the classic argument favoring money, the alternative barter systems of exchange are inefficient because they rely on a coincidence of need between two people lucky enough to find each other at the time and place where each happens to have a specific good desired by the other and which can be exchanged without destroying value by chopping something up to make the trade come out even.

Provided that someone keeps an eye on inflation, money is useful as a way to store value between moments in time when you want to sell something (say, when it's scarce) and when you want to buy something (when it's plentiful). These circumstances are common as play proceeds in an MMO, and time-shifting creates a way to keep options open—you might change your mind about what you want to buy. Money is like a time machine for value, at least in the forward direction.

The economy in games also serves as a bridge connecting feedback and rewards. If you win a prized object that you already have, you can sometimes sell it for gold pieces. Not every prized object in a game can be transferred from one player to another. Players say that some objects are "soul bound," in that some items can't be sold directly using game currency. Even so, money indirectly helps players acquire these objects because it can be used to buy special powers that in turn enable players to compete to earn the soul-bound items. (The next chapter has more discussion about how teams deal with such objects.)

The introduction of money almost always introduces liquidity into a market, and this goes for markets in games as well. Think of money as spraying WD-40 on the clankety machinery of a barter economy. The definition of a liquid good is one that can be sold rapidly at any time with minimal loss of value. Money is the ultimate liquid good, and its availability in a marketplace makes everything easier to buy and sell. More liquid markets are more efficient, and so on. Money makes it easier to know when the value of things goes up and down, and money makes it a lot more fun to talk about and keep track of prices ("You paid *what* for that?").

It didn't take long for players to discover another form of liquidity: they could trade virtual property and virtual money earned *inside* a game for real-world currency outside a game. We mentioned this earlier in the discussion of cheating on reputations in chapter 4. The practice became firmly established in the 1990s during the era of *Ultima Online*. Now the practice is called *real money trading* (RMT), and it has generated serious interest from economists, entrepreneurs, players, and game publishers.[7]

Economists point out that the value of virtual goods exchanged for real money can be used to calculate the gross domestic product per capita of a particular MMO population. Some come out ahead of countries such as Bulgaria and Russia.[8] Individual players have found they can scratch out a living in real dollars by selling virtual objects, game currency, and even entire characters on eBay.[9] Companies have been set up to hire cheap labor to grind out game pieces and high-level characters for sale in RMT, a practice known as farming. There are even currency exchanges to facilitate trading among game currencies and government currencies.[10]

Players have strong opinions about RMT and the practice of farming. For some, it degrades the game experience by puncturing the membrane separating the game world from the rest of the world. Whereas all players are supposed to start out with equal advantages, some who are wealthy in real life (but have little free time) can now purchase privileges that others had to earn by hard work in the game. Although a virtual object purchased on a trading website may be indistinguishable from one earned in-game, players are quick to smoke out elite-level characters and their gear that are played by people who purchased the assets but don't have the reflexes and knowledge to participate authentically in the group challenges available at rarified levels of play. Not surprisingly, the companies that own successful MMOs have also taken notice, and in some cases have taken legal steps to prevent trading in what they consider to be their intellectual property and a violation of their terms of use for the game software. One publisher, however, decided to get in on the action and sponsor its own currency marketplace.[11]

What's Fun About Economic Activity?

There weren't any experts on the "economics of fun" when Edward Castronova decided to study the field from the perspective of a classically trained economist. He brought an unusual combination of playfulness and incisive analysis to the problem, augmented by his own experience spanning a thousand-plus hours playing all kinds of electronic games, and particularly MMOs. After observing what worked well and not so well in game economies, he produced a list of design features that are important for creating entertaining economic experiences for players. We are happy to leave a discussion of the formal production equations to economists, but it is instructive to review the qualitative observations here.[12] These are the reasons that virtual economies will be useful at work.

People like to consume and acquire things. Pretty obvious. But what makes this interesting is the extent to which people care about consuming and acquiring things that *don't even exist*, at least in the real world. Virtual goods are merely ideas encoded in bits and represented by light on a screen. They have real value based on the labor required to create them and the value (similarly derived) of other virtual objects for which they can be traded. People like to *create* things that are valued by others. In the games, this is called crafting, and it's carried out by following a series of steps to collect and assemble components. The recipe for crafted virtual objects is defined in the game software by the designers. Specifications are complex and sometimes need to be discovered by solving puzzles or by trial and error. Sometimes players will personalize virtual objects, expressing individual creativity. And remember that most of these work products aren't just eye candy to adorn an avatar or virtual living space; many confer special powers on the user's character that can be used to fight, defend, solve, or explore—and to level up.

Trading currency between the virtual and real worlds provides compelling price information that can be used to set the value of virtual goods. But even without that data, the behavior of players exerting personal effort to create objects is evidence enough that they have economic value, even if the players are having fun in the process. You wouldn't argue that the output of a successful artist wasn't economically valuable just because she enjoyed the process of creation. Of course, consumption, acquisition, and production are meaningless in a context of abundant plenty; it's the fact of scarcity that makes these behaviors interesting to players.

Players also enjoy what economists call "fair returns to work and skill." This means that a player community can tolerate, and even celebrate, vast differences in wealth provided that starting conditions and opportunities were equal for all. In other words, consistent rules, no cheating, and no side deals between players and the powers that be (the so-called game authorities). Competition is good, so long as it isn't rigged.

Surprise plays an important role in making economies fun. Human sensors are tuned to detect variations. Appearance of the unpredictable is what captures attention. Market fluctuations and even chaos make game economies more interesting.

Finally, it's important to note that economic activity for its own sake is not what keeps players engaged, but rather purposeful activity driving toward a larger goal. This may be assembling assets needed to complete quests and leveling up to higher status or becoming a more effective member of a raiding team in a highly challenging group activity where peer respect is based on capabilities and effort.

Prescription for a Fun Economy

So how would you ensure that a vibrant and interesting economy is taking place in your game? Castronova offers a nonobvious prescription. If you want to generate lots of economic activity, you must create a *lack* of individual self-sufficiency and ensure inconvenient geography, obscure and complex objectives, and, of course, some chaos. Once again, it's scarcity that counts. The tougher the world, the more useful and interesting the economic activity.

If that doesn't sound right at first, think about what happens between two players who each have a crafting skill that the other lacks, and the product of both skills is needed to be successful in the game. Trading will take place. Now consider a more complex social game in which players entering the game can choose among different occupations, each of which is characterized by having only a few skills, but many different needs. You can be sure that this group will trade with each other. In a well-designed game, the resulting market is a mechanism for aggregating collective intelligence. Acting together, the group "derives an efficient production function" optimized for individual and group success. By the way, even if a game doesn't provide a currency, we've watched players invent moneylike instruments to enable trading and facilitate complex deals.

Geography can also drive economic activity. Recall that some important objects must be crafted by using acquired skills to process natural resources that spawn in the environment. Game designers should keep the raw materials needed to make finished objects as far apart as possible in the virtual landscape so that it is inconvenient to combine them. Then designers should take advantage of the trade routes that players ply to situate cities at the intersections. Once again, the virtual parallels real life.

As long as you're making things difficult for players (in order to make the economy more interesting), be sure to include planned obsolescence, so that goods decay over time. An economy rich with consumable products rather than durable goods is livelier. Players can't rest on their nonperishable laurels but must continue to be economic participants. One can even contrive to make game currency slightly perishable via modest inflation or taxes that serve to reward income more than wealth.

Work Needs a Better Economy!

The prescription for inconvenience to ensure a fun game has a lot in common with the current state of affairs in real-world work environments. Enterprise workers are pretty much by definition *not* self-sufficient. After all, the enterprise was invented to aggregate complementary skills. Today's multinational teams must collaborate and assemble solutions across distant time zones. They must solve complex production problems in which the objective is all too often poorly defined. Then there is the matter of chaos: plenty of that to go around in the modern enterprise, whether from competition, government, technology, or management churn. So why isn't working there more fun?

Of course some people are having fun, at least some of the time. We're convinced that one of the ways to improve the situation is to encourage more overt economic behavior in the workplace and to do it, initially, with a synthetic currency. The wonderfully inane behavior depicted in Scott Adam's *Dilbert* comic strip could never happen unless the characters were *disconnected* from economic incentives. It's as if someone cut all of the wires between Dilbert's world and the rest of economic society.

Fun isn't the only reason to consider letting a thousand marketplaces bloom. Economists and business theorists have been making the case for years that corporations would be much better off if they allocated scarce resources inside their walls using the same powerful mechanisms that serve to allocate resources between corporations—that is, better markets.[13]

To address the challenges of running a large-scale service organization, McKinsey & Company has invested heavily to create internal systems that create marketplaces for talent and, separately, for knowledge. Their talent market is intended to leverage "individual self-interest to drive enterprise-wide collaboration rather than by relying on top-down mandates to rotate jobs."[14] Key elements of this market include a reputation system for employees and protocols for job definition as well as human resource "talent brokers." McKinsey consultants also contribute to and draw from a massive knowledge management system with overt economic elements that reward workers for contributing their tacit knowledge so others can be more effective. McKinsey is using its internal experience with talent and knowledge markets to lead clients in the direction of market-based mechanisms for addressing the central problems in today's global enterprises. So far, these McKinsey markets rely on informal and indirect rewards where enhanced reputation is eventually reflected in promotion and compensation is reminiscent of a thriving barter-based marketplace.

In most companies, the give and take among managers and workers is accomplished in an informal market of favors, quid pro quos, office politics, and sometimes intimidation. Barter is especially subject to perverse mismatches in the timing and adjustment of feedback. Some decisions that should be revisited frequently are forgotten or off the table for social or structural reasons. Some decisions that should be given time to ripen are hurried or tweaked beyond recognition.

Better markets lower the cost of transactions. Better markets allow participants access to the same information about what is being traded, and they create transparent prices. A lot of learning goes on in these circumstances. Traders get smarter about how to get what they want, and if money isn't already provided, they'll invent something like money to make the market better.

Thomas Malone, in *The Future of Work*, makes the case that internal markets are one of the key ingredients of an engaged and decentralized information workforce.[15] In The Management Lab workshop on radical ideas for adapting management to the information age, Malone led a breakout discussion on just how far one could push this idea.[16] What the participants came up with is a pretty good checklist of ways one might use economics to make work more fun. Here are two highlights from the taxonomy that apply to game economies at work.

One of these is already gaining attention as a result of widespread interest in James Surowiecki's book *The Wisdom of Crowds*.[17] So-called *prediction markets* use economic behavior to aggregate opinions across individuals instead of using typical surveys and focus groups. In most variations on the idea, people express their opinion about specific events in the future by "investing" money (real or synthetic currency) in an idea or proposition, with the expectation that they will earn economic rewards if the proposition turns out to be true. Surowiecki cites evidence showing that if the individuals in a group represent a reasonable range of diversity of opinion and experience, their forecasts are frequently better than they are for other methods that collect opinion, such as surveys and focus groups in which the respondents don't have skin in the game when they communicate their expectations.

As in games, no one gets a survey to fill out; players pay up and take their chances. Others have been developing formalisms to explain these observations about prediction markets and support the notion that we can create value from diversity.[18] Prediction markets are an example of a larger idea some call *crowdsourcing*, or outsourcing a task or job in an open-source model.[19] By one compilation these prediction markets have been the subject of experiments at companies as diverse as Abbott Labs, Arcelor Mittal, Best Buy, Chrysler, Corning, Electronic Arts, Eli Lilly, Frito-Lay, General Electric, Google, Hewlett-Packard, Intel, InterContinental Hotels, Masterfoods, Microsoft, Motorola, Nokia, Pfizer, Qualcomm, Siemens, and TNT.[20] This idea has generated so much interest that the U.S. Commodities Futures Trading Commission (CFTC) has sought comment in preparation for issuing guidance on whether these markets (which CFTC calls "event markets") will be regulated like traditional futures markets.[21]

Another way to adopt the idea of internal corporate markets is to establish *resource allocation markets*, in which corporate assets are auctioned to the highest internal bidder. Not long ago we interviewed a key product manager at one of the world's largest enterprise software companies who gave us a good example of how this could (and should) work. His company has a vast investment in computer hardware running 24/7 as a test bed for evaluating the never-ending stream of new products and upgrades coming from the company's thousands of software engineers. How do you suppose the machine time in this array, worth perhaps tens of millions of dollars, is allocated? It is done on a first-come, first-served basis, with occasional exceptions dictated by a vice president *if* the project manager cared enough to use political capital to jump the queue. Maybe all of the projects in that company were of exactly equal importance and there were no last-minute surprises that moved up the true urgency of a particular software test, but that's not the world that we know in Silicon Valley.

There is a strong argument that a well-designed internal market would be a better way to manage valuable resources. For example, a continuous auction for each block of time on segments of the array could be set up in software so that a project manager could bid for the capacity. At any given time, the project manager who "owns" the capacity for a project could also see what others would bid and, if there was sufficient interest, post an asking price to yield time to another project. Sometimes, a clearing price would be met and the resource would be reallocated based on a market determination (with lots of mid- and lower-level manager input) of importance and urgency. This is a good example of how Malone's thesis about how a distributed, democratic workforce could make decisions.

If you're having trouble imagining that your company would let people actually make serious cash money by betting in a prediction market or auctioning off corporate assets to peers, you have good company. The prediction markets are generally organized so that the winnings are personal to the individuals participating; that is, individuals pocket a bit of cash. Funds paid and received in resource allocation markets could be paid into and out of employees' pockets or, in other models, be attributed to resource pools controlled by managers on behalf of the enterprise. Today, there are serious barriers to such market practices, ranging from legal restrictions on gambling to payroll taxes for earned compensation to withholding requirements. Significant earnings in such markets could also run afoul of other compensation and incentive programs long accepted in the enterprise.

Many of these objections can be dealt with by running internal markets using a synthetic currency rather than government-sponsored money. In the course of The Management Lab meeting described in chapter 3, we heard from Hal Varian, Google's chief economist, about how his company is using such an artificial currency, experimenting with auction processes to allocate server time for engineers testing or deploying new applications.[22] At Google, the currency for these markets is "Goobles," invented for the purpose of experimenting with internal markets that track predictions and allocate resources.[23]

Industrial-Strength Play Money

We've been encouraged enough about the value of a synthetic economy at work to participate in the creation of a computer application based on our broad thesis. In 2005, we and colleagues designed a synthetic currency system intended for all manner of trading inside companies.[24] Our aim was to create and test a currency that people could quickly understand and trust using a few simple rules.

We wanted to make it as convenient as possible to use and move the currency around at work so people could invent markets wherever they were needed. But first, we needed to help people get acquainted with the idea in a user-friendly application that dealt with a specific and important pain point. The goal was to place the tool *on the way* to work, but not *in the way* of work. We didn't want to start our experiment with a totally separate application that would have to be launched and navigated outside of the primary places on a computer where work was done. We chose to start with everyone's e-mail inbox.

In a meeting with researchers at a large pharmaceutical company, the pain point we sought presented itself under the general heading of information overload. E-mail is the most pervasive culprit, but the collateral din of instant messaging, intranet-based workflow, wikis, and the growing presence of tools in the genre of social networking contributes as well.

Tom Davenport and John Beck, in *The Attention Economy*, drive home the argument that an enterprise's most valuable asset is the attention of employees.[25] Managing attention, far more than managing time, is the greatest challenge of all. Before winning hearts, engaging minds, or harnessing creativity, you must first get people's attention. In the world of digital communication this is both easier and more difficult than it's ever been. It's easier because the marginal cost of electronic communication is nearly zero, but much harder because of the clutter that ensues when other people's inboxes (a prime place where attention is allocated) are turned into a free good for all to abuse. Even after taking into account recent success with filters for commercial spam, corporate friendly fire via e-mail remains a major drag on information worker productivity. One analyst pegs this problem at $650 billion for the entire U.S. economy, and scientists at Intel have estimated (painstakingly) that the problem costs that company over $1 billion a year.[26]

Therefore, the first arena we targeted for the synthetic currency is the market for the attention of you and your colleagues in today's large enterprise. Our vehicle for moving currency is e-mail. The software we designed runs the bank so we can manage the money supply and let people use the currency across companies as well as internally.

The software that enables people to exchange synthetic currency makes a small modification to e-mail applications so that senders can attach whatever amount of currency they would like to use to signal others about the importance they place on a particular message.[27] Of course, they can't send more than they have in their account, which is why the signal is so much more informative than using the red exclamation point or typing the subject line in all caps. This is choice under scarcity—real economics.

Recipients can see the incoming currency and even rank-order the messages in their inbox based on this field if they find it useful ("I'll read the messages that my colleagues value most first"). And they get to keep the incoming currency and use it to get the attention of others. This is in contrast to schemes for "virtual postage." Asking or requiring a sender to purchase a digital stamp has a similar benefit of signaling from a pool of scarcity, but like stamps in the real world, postage ends up in the trash after the virtual envelope has served its purpose. Money, on the other hand, has a past *and* a future. Someone using money usually has a sense of where it came from and how hard it was to obtain. Spenders often have a sense about what the recipient will do with the money. People already know what to do with a well-designed synthetic currency because they know what to do with money. It's just like real money (but it's not).

We first began experimenting with virtual currency among the dozen-odd people who were designing and building our software. The rules were set up to make the system easy to understand and to support a sense of fairness: everyone, regardless of rank in the organization, receives the same allowance of currency (arbitrarily 100 units per week), the amount of currency selected for any message is transferred when the message successfully arrives in the recipient's mailbox, and you can't send more currency than you have in your account. The only source of currency is a weekly allowance, and the only drain out of the system is a yet-to-be needed wealth tax to be imposed by our Open Market Committee after public discussion. That tax wouldn't be needed unless there was inflationary evidence of a supply–demand imbalance or evidence that individual balances were large enough that a small number of collaborators could disrupt the system.

It's been interesting to observe how much "player-created content" emerges from such a simple system (you can think of it as a game—small "g"). Because anyone can send any amount of currency (up to the limit of his or her balance) simply by sending an e-mail, there is almost unlimited potential for people to invent private treaty transactions using the currency for all manner of trades. The first thing we noticed was feedback nested in social reciprocity. When replying to messages, people enjoyed sending currency back to the original sender if they found the e-mail useful. Sometimes people weren't sure how much currency to send with a message to make it stand out or whether they would offend someone by not sending enough currency back with the reply. It didn't take long for people to realize that this was a multiperiod game and that the real social signals were aggregated across many transactions. When those who repeatedly sent a lot of currency to bid for attention found that it wasn't getting returned, they changed their behavior. People found it easy to express appreciation for useful messages by sending extra currency in return, so that the initiator's investment in the thread was rewarded.

Over time, people figured out how much currency it took to have an impact. In a published study of e-mail behavior using this system, we got a glimpse into how this simple game-inspired feature can change behavior.[28] Senders behaved as economists would expect them to with real currency: they sent large amounts less often than smaller numbers, conserving currency for future use. We were also interested in whether the amount of currency sent had any impact on how long it took for the recipient to open a message. There was an interesting (and statistically significant) biphasic curve. Compared with messages with the average number of currency units sent (about five in our study), messages that arrived with more currency than average were opened sooner.

Our empirical results were early evidence that people attended to the currency signal and changed behavior accordingly. We liken these results to paying real money for a virtual sword or, more important, changing behavior in a game to acquire it. The wall between real and virtual isn't high. What matters is what you can do with the virtual sword in the real game or what you can gain from real attention signaled with virtual coins at work.

Some of the private treaty transactions made with the synthetic currency provided delightful surprises. People used the currency for conditional offers, as in Claire's scenario at the beginning of this chapter where currency was used as an incentive for meeting attendance (and feedback). The currency may also serve as the basis for any of the variations on prediction markets and resource allocation markets already described, but without some of the important problems expected if government-sponsored money is used.

As people gain more experience with synthetic currencies in the enterprise, we'll surely be surprised by new use cases. People already know what to do with money, and it's entertaining to invent new uses for play money. We trust that we'll see creative applications that solve business problems, but it would be surprising if we did not also see people gaming the system for personal benefit or just for the devilish fun of causing grief. That goes with the territory (these folks are well known as "griefers" in the games) and will require monitoring and adjustment at work.

Here's a final and huge opportunity for using synthetic currencies. Because a computer tracks all trades, there is the potential for unprecedented visibility into trading activity. Data (and especially visualizations of the data) about who trades with whom can be a highly informative tool for evaluating collaboration and relationships. We found that a map of e-mail connections based on the sender's *valuation* of messages exchanged looks significantly different from network maps based on the *frequency* of correspondence. Up to now, social network pictures of communication patterns in large groups have depended on *how many* messages people exchange and often merely on whether or not any message is sent. Two people who e-mail each other frequently will appear close together in the map, with the link between them visually thicker than links between others. But that can be misleading. What if all the messages are about a company party? When maps of the same groups are drawn using currency exchanges as the measures of "closeness," new roles appear for people in the network. The person in marketing who *infrequently* sends one thousand units of currency to the engineers (and vice versa) will now appear close to the engineers, potentially revealing a hidden communication channel that adds significant value to the business.

Transparency on prices and trading is interesting, generates fun conversations, and can help people become better market participants. But it also has risks. Complete exposure of trading activity has the potential to embarrass people, and some experimentation will be needed to find the right cultural fit for different environments. We hope that judicious use of transparency features will help curb misbehavior and provide a basis for organizations to learn about the trade-offs they are making.

This brings us to our third "virtual"—teams. Games are about groups, and the best prospects for business impact require multiple players. Much of what we've said about virtual people and money applies. But there are some specific team and collaboration problems that appear particularly amenable to game sensibilities.

What could dragon kill points have to do with the problems of virtual teams? Meet David.

Chapter Seven

Virtual Teams

WHAT DO I GET WHEN WE WIN?

For David, the answer depends on dragon kill points. DKP for short, this is the mechanism by which success for David's entire guild can be apportioned among individual players according to the quality of their participation. DKP is awarded for everything from the amount of time David spends on a raid (in particular, punctuality and staying until the finish) to the quality of his play (more DKP if his firepower or healing potions are well administered and effective) and to the assets he prepares for the event (extra DKP, for example, if he gathers the raw materials needed to mix the healing potions needed in the raid).[1]

David's guild keeps a detailed account of DKP for each player posted on its website for all to see. The guild DKP manager updates the site regularly and is experimenting with third-party software that will automatically tabulate DKP during play. The automation and transparency of the guild's system gives David confidence that the system is fair and the data are current.

Here's how DKP helps David solve the "me"-versus-"we" problem. Gamers want to know how a plundered item, itself not divisible, will be awarded. David might spend an entire evening helping the guild bring down a dungeon bad guy. When defeated, the monster might drop the Axe of the Gronn Lords. This is a highly desirable game piece, worthy of serious bragging rights and useful for battle advantage in subsequent raids. But you can't split the axe into twenty-five equal pieces so all can share.

What to do? Hold an auction. David bids on desirable fallen items using his DKP stash. Sometimes, the allocation is merely prioritized based on DKP standings; that is, David will get first dibs if he's willing to cash DKP. This could even happen during a raid, maximizing David's interest in the quest and acting as reinforcement for participation and performance.

DKP is a huge advantage for those who have a lot of it. The more DKP, the better the stuff you get when "we" win. With DKP, the group has a quantitative system to motivate play. Even for those with low numbers, there is certain knowledge of where they stand, mitigating disappointment and conflict when the bidding begins.

You Would Die for Dragon Kill Points (Well, Maybe Your Avatar Would)

Why have a DKP system? Fights break out otherwise. We are going into a bit of detail here because there are compelling implications of DKP for all kinds of real-world collaboration. It's just one of the innovative ways that games and gamers have discovered to address collaboration problems that have vexed business for many years.

David uses DKP to acquire items of personal value that can't be shared. Remember, these items have a lot to do with David's interest in this game: if he can acquire a legendary dagger or a primo white mount he has guaranteed bragging rights and better protection or faster travel the next time he plays. David wants those game pieces. Another advantage of DKP has to do with the fact that some treasures are not only indivisible but also nontransferable. That is, some especially valuable items can't be exchanged in the normal commerce of the game, for example, by trading for game currency. We've already labeled this property as "soul bound," which means that the game software only allows them to be owned by the person who originally picked them up during a raid.

DKP systems bridge the gap between the game's global currency and local barter (or something worse—for example, fighting). DKP makes it possible for David and teammates to trade time and expertise for rewards that matter to them using what amounts to a private money system that gives the guild a sense of community. (Note that one guild's DKP isn't welcome in other guilds.) New points are created constantly, and DKP accounts increase, sometimes with inflationary speed, over time. To combat inflation, some guilds create zero-sum DKP systems. Here, there is a finite amount of DKP such that when one person spends DKP on loot won by the group, it is distributed evenly within the group (i.e., if I spend forty DKP on a cool sword, and my guild has forty other players, they would each get one DKP from my purchase). This twist has the advantage of taming inflation because no new points enter the system from the outside.

What's astonishing is that these systems are self-enforcing, operating outside of direct influence from game designers. It's not baked into the game, and there's no court or supervisor to arbitrate disputes. It's all up to the players. (Some third-party DKP management software is sold or given away to the guilds.) DKP is an emergent game element, not built into the game software but added by gamers via "mods" ("I'll change what you made to something I like even better"). Don't make the mistake of thinking that being a game add-on means such systems are of secondary importance. Our observation is that player-inspired content such as DKP is part of the value of the game.

The nuances seem endless. David's guild conducts auctions for items that individuals want but the group owns. Bidding, which can even occur during a raid (there's no sense in delaying reinforcement for participation, and the item might be needed right away), is moderated by the DKP manager and can have a time limit of a few minutes. Other guilds set fixed prices for items. This is typically accomplished by a small group of volunteers who must not only assess the fair value of items to players but also the value of the item to the group. There are some items, for example, that at least one guild member must own for the group to be successful in an upcoming battle—but after that, the item's value is just for show.

The trust that emerges in David's guild isn't totally a result of the DKP algorithms. Of the twenty-five or so raiders any given evening, David knows five of them in real life (that is, he has dated them or shared a dorm floor or office corridor with them in real life). Many guild members feel (and they're backed up by substantial research) that a group of total strangers might encourage a bit too much competitiveness. A light seeding of familiarity is the right antidote.[2] This allows established and trusted relationships to be influential as trust in the larger group grows and strangers become friends.

Furthermore, David and his guildmates are playing a multiperiod game composed of discreet segments of intense collaboration interspersed with time for reflection and planning in between. This bursty pattern of collaboration has interesting consequences. Getting the magical sword today is good because it will be useful next week. David knows personally (or at least expects to know soon) the people with whom he's playing with and on whom he'll depend—today and tomorrow. He has a reputation to maintain over time. Furthermore, people can try out roles. Frequent opportunities to try again against the same challenge set the stage for new ways to mentor and manage risk.

Collaboration in the Real World

Now back to the real world. One middle-management information worker in a *Fortune* 100 company told us this: "I work on seven different teams that average 9.2 members each from twelve different company offices on three different continents. I have four different bosses, two of whom I've never met personally and one that just set my salary for next year. I use a lot of technology to stay in touch."

The amount of technology deployed to support information workers is staggering. Collaboration software and platforms are a big part of the $73 billion in spending on collaboration systems, with 16 percent growth projected this year, for an average cost of $1,224 per employee.[3] Big numbers; important problems.

Much of the current spending on collaboration is about infrastructure—just making it possible to connect better, faster, and cheaper. We project that new spending will focus on enabling closer personal, social, and emotional connections that feed innovation. It's one thing to allow groups to transmit information; it's quite another to allow them to do so in a manner that engages, persuades, and changes. By now you know that this is the sweet spot for games.

Multiplayer games demand collaboration: *I* can't win unless *we* win. But in both virtual and real worlds, there's a tension between "me" and "we," a battle royal between the psychology of the individual and the sociology of the group. The manner in which "me" and "we" are reconciled may hold the key to success in both worlds.

What's Hard About Collaboration and Teamwork?

To make business collaboration more effective using ideas from games, let's first take a look at how business defines the collaboration problem.

There aren't many secrets about why business organizations and those who study them think that collaboration is hard. Many of the reasons are very similar to the issues David's guild confronts in the game. Teams, increasingly more than individuals, are charged with the most challenging and mission-critical projects. Leaders need to evaluate and motivate from a distance. And the makeup of teams is increasingly complex—they're bigger, more diverse, more geographically distributed, composed more of specialists than generalists, and much more dependent on technology than in the past. And difficult economic times only accent these challenges.

That's the familiar story. But there are underlying challenges to group success that exacerbate the logistical ones. Players at work care about the same thing as David: what do I get when we win? If they can't answer that question, and even more so if they don't like the answer, they're hesitant to share their knowledge and their talent.

Why Share?

A company's wealth increasingly depends on its knowledge equity. The value of knowledge is growing, in large part as a result of advances in the information technology that collects it, but also because of the increased value of intellectual property, the increasing complexity of business processes, and the greater decentralization of work groups.

The best way to get this sharing going, if the purveyors of knowledge management software are to be believed, is to deploy expert systems that will automatically collect, organize, and make available important information to anyone, especially a new employee, who needs to know what and how things have worked in the past. The responsibility of individuals is to pony up all their best stuff—regularly, completely, and preferably with useful tags—so that the organization can profit from the personal knowledge that the company pays people to collect.

But not so fast. What do *I* get when *we* win? People easily understand that contributing to collective knowledge helps the group, but it's less clear how it helps them personally. Actually, research shows that it often doesn't. This particular answer to the familiar game question is therefore the most difficult challenge in corporate collaboration.[4] Individuals are often valued in a company to the extent that the information they hold personally is *unique*. When personal knowledge becomes corporate knowledge, that's good for the organization, but not for the individual who was the source of the knowledge. The individual's relative intellectual capital might decline. There is the risk that you may give up power by giving up information.

In addition to hiding information, people sometimes hide their agendas. This kind of hoarding can be even more damaging to teamwork. So why share? Somehow, the enterprise needs to invent better private rewards for creating a public good. Economists are serious about this "free rider" problem on a societal scale, but there is also a literature on how it applies to teamwork.[5] People are even starting to invent systems that sound a lot like DKP for business teams.[6]

Tacit Versus Explicit Knowledge

One reason to share is that your boss may demand it, even though such a dictate is almost impossible to enforce. How can you make someone tell you something that you don't even know that they know? The fallback strategy is to make it easier to share. The technology scene is alive with opportunities to comply: wikis, blogs, social networks, and a hundred software services that help people share, co-create, edit, and critique information that was once held by individuals, and transmitted only by them one to another.[7] So called knowledge management systems offer an impressive collection of technology that is intended to expand community knowledge. The impact of such systems is sometimes disappointing, perhaps because the kind of sharing that's enabled may not be the most important part of the knowledge story.

Information specialists have long recognized two types of corporate information. One is personal knowledge about the company that resides with individuals (this is often called *tacit knowledge* and was introduced in chapter 3).[8] It's informally gathered, learned from experience, generally not codified, and defined more by *how* to get things done than by the details of *what* one should know. Tacit knowledge is really useful practical information about how to attain personal goals. It may be as simple as a comment at the water cooler such as "In my ten years here, any plan to change the organization has to have Frank's blessing first." This information isn't in the company files.

Other knowledge (often called *explicit knowledge*) is formal and usually more public. Much of it is conditional (when this happens, do this), and it's fairly easy to formalize, record, and make it available to large groups. This kind of information is the mainstay of knowledge management systems. Think of company SOPs and many of the documents stored on a project wiki.

Groups benefit when tacit knowledge morphs into explicit knowledge. When that happens, everyone can access the best procedures *and* they'll have the informal information about how to make the best use of them. Personal mentoring meets public expertise.

There are at least two barriers that deter translation of tacit into explicit knowledge. The first is that it may take effort that is not easy to see and reward in the typical enterprise environment. The second barrier is the potential loss of personal power mentioned already. The transition from tacit to explicit might work pretty well when everyone is on the same hallway, where trust and interest in mutual success is easier to create, but can break down when people try to collaborate remotely. The greater the reliance on electronic communication ("We've only met on a conference call; I've never negotiated with my boss face-to-face"), the more likely tacit knowledge is to remain tacit ("I'm not sending you my valuable personal experiences because your status may increase at my expense"). In geographically challenged groups, new hires often learn tried-and-true methods of talking up cooperation while at the same time competing ferociously with little sympathy for the failure of others.

Knowledge about how to *coordinate* groups, and especially the tacit knowledge that a group has about the right way to go about work, may be more important than the *facts* that the group produces that are the results of their actions. Let's look at how today's businesses and games address the problem.

Attacking Collaboration Problems

How do you promote collaboration that coordinates expertise? Prescriptions for better collaboration generally agree on some key principles. Here they are, initially without comment about how games might help (we'll apply game sensibilities to each next). If you did these things well, so say the experts, you'd be on your way to effective collaboration.[9]

- *Recruit and hire for cooperation.* To create a culture of collaboration, start with the right people. Find out whether job candidates can collaborate by having them meet large numbers of current employees. Give people collaborative scenarios and ask them how they'd respond. Instinctive free riders will try to fool management, but at least they will demonstrate the intellectual capacity for teamwork. Better yet, ask candidates to tell you their own stories about tough collaboration challenges and check references to back these up. Ask the best collaborators in the group to do the interviews (it takes one to know one).

- *Model collaborative behavior.* The collaborative styles and abilities of senior executives aren't always on display. But when they are, they're influential. Even the perception in the larger group that leaders collaborate often and well increases the chances that others will do the same. Make executive collaboration more visible.

- *Teach collaboration.* It's possible to teach collaboration, and those companies that make training part of their human resource (HR) offerings fare better. Instruction is particularly useful in the first days and weeks on the job. That's when the competitive versus cooperative tone is set. Longer term, mentors are important drivers of collaboration, especially when they volunteer services.

- *Support a strong sense of community.* The more an organization interacts, casually and informally, the better. When organizations sponsor events that create a sense of community (things such as special interest networks, group travel, or sports) and when they encourage informal places and times for casual interaction, people will feel more comfortable reaching out and will be more likely to share information. The cost of setting time aside to build trust is cheap compared with the cost of lack of trust when attempting collaborative work. The "ropes course" cliché has grounding in theory.

- *Build on established relationships.* Groups of total strangers are handicapped. Seeding groups with established relationships (a fifth to a third of participants is recommended) ensures there are some pairs that can jump-start collaboration before the network develops poor communication patterns. Even casual acquaintances count in the seeding because they decrease the amount of time necessary for introductions and help build trust early.

- *Reward collaboration in performance reviews.* You can't champion collaboration if it means a subordination of personal goals and then only reward individual achievement. Rewards need to accrue to groups, with distribution of the rewards (tangible and intangible) among members. Not only should individual rewards depend on group success, but also peer group rewards should depend on each other. This encourages accountability across groups as well as individuals.

- *Find leaders attentive to tasks and relationships.* Collaboration depends on trusted relationships in addition to good business strategies. A fair summary of the long debate about the relative desirability of task versus social orientations in good leaders suggests both are important. The half that often gets short shrift, however, emphasizes relationships. Social and emotional connections determine whether and with what amount of enthusiasm people will contribute.

- *Invest in collaboration infrastructure.* Organizations can demonstrate a commitment to collaboration by building an infrastructure to support it, including office assignments, physical architecture, mealtime amenities, and social uses of technology that encourage sharing and relationship development.

Current Technology: Friend or Foe to Teams?

Does current information technology help or hurt with this list? It's certainly true that it's easier to share information using new technology, *if you want to*. There are important caveats about ease of use, expense, and absent features, but it's true that many collaboration tools today do help deliver the right information, if it's available, to the right people as conveniently as possible—the right people on the video conference, the right slides on the right screens, the right files posted on the wiki, and the right forms in front of the right people. But many of these technologies miss on sharing and coordination in a manner similar to the advantages that David's DKP system brought to his group. The most difficult challenges for teams involve emotional engagement, social relationships, personal reputations, and, most important, information about individual reward for group success.

How Can Games Help?

The question that we asked in our research is whether gamers have different or better tools and tactics for implementing the best practices list. Or do they have a different list? The answer is a bit of both. We start with the infrastructure challenge described earlier and then describe how players use the game environment to recruit, model, teach, support, and reward collaboration. We realize we may be overstating our case. Experienced gamers will point out lots of counterexamples to our sunny exposition. On the other hand, hundreds of thousands of people are paying good money to spend hundreds or thousands of hours each in these voluntary collaborations. We still have to pay people to do stuff like this at work.

It's About the Environment, Not Just the People

A prevailing view in business is that good collaborators—and good leaders—are born, not made. Do gamers agree? We assembled a team of seven expert guild leaders to observe collaboration and leadership in the games and extract generalizations about why and how groups in the games succeed.[10] Their conclusion? It's about the *environment* more than the players. The places where collaboration happens and the processes by which it's managed are more important than the innate capabilities of the people participating. When asked about the most important implication of that conclusion for serious work, a guild leader comment was: "Change the game, not the people."

This conclusion emphasizes the last point in our list above all the others: collaboration infrastructure. In the real world, this usually means architecture: open seating, conversation pits, and, recently, the use of technology to create similar functions online. Games do a pretty good job of blending all of these components. Games create collaboration environments that redefine all the other points as environmental factors rather than attributes of people.

The multiplayer game environment that creates a setting for great collaboration is a blend of the designer's vision and emergent properties resulting from the way players organize themselves into guilds. Game designers do a good job of making clear the *objectives* of large-scale collaborative effort; what's hidden is how to achieve those goals. Designers make sure that it will take close coordination of many players with different skill sets to conquer a particular "boss," the powerful computer-controlled monster that is the object of a raid. The game provides persistent and transparent reputational markers so players can easily recognize relevant talent. Timely metrics on the performance of individuals in the raid can be pulled out of the game and analyzed. Using this extraordinary infrastructure, guilds create collaborative styles and systems that reflect the group's personality. DKP systems are one of these emergent properties.

Nonmonetary Incentives

We believe a DKP manager could be a great addition to enterprise teams. This might be awkward to many people, so first remember that the degree of awkwardness will be correlated with age and game experience. For gamers, this is a familiar feature of collaboration. Interestingly, variants of DKP systems have popped up in class projects at Stanford—projects where the single reward for individual work is a group grade. Some students complain: "Can I please do a project by myself?" "No—and welcome to the real world." But you also can't hide behind the good work of your peers. Students now keep track of who does what, distribute points accordingly, and make the data available to all. Jeremy Williams describes a similar peer reward system tried in a Singapore setting.[11]

A DKP system (or some corporate variant) has community, transparency, and fairness. And there's nothing subtle in the communication. The mere fact of such systems means that a group recognizes an "I"-versus-"we" tension, has a transparent system for moment-to-moment information about what's going on with all the "I's", and has records of transactions (who got what and when) that are publically posted.

When it's possible to capture and observe the flow of these points, or DKP, this is collaboration with high visibility and a staggering amount of useful performance information, all in one place. There's no need for lengthy one-off conversations in hopes of divining how the group works or who are the most recognized. Compared with real life, substantially fewer awkward conversations are necessary to learn how to succeed. The participation and modeling by group leaders is perfectly apparent. I can learn the group collaboration algorithm by watching it work (no HR training session required).

Cheap, Plentiful, Fun Transactions That Matter

You don't start playing the complex games without consulting the guild website. (Is this true for your organization's intranet?) The guild site is Information Central, with not only plenty of features that are required viewing (that's where you see the raid calendar and DKP spreadsheets) but also features that chronicle fun, meaning they support a robust form of community socialization, such as social chat channels and raid team forums.

A guild website has pages that constantly update the action in blazing color, complete with game piece icons, rosters of avatars, and video grabs from the game. There's a list of recent raids (check it to see if you missed a successful raid or a team wiping, or send a link to a nonmember friend to brag about a recent success), a list of recent booty from legendary raids (with pictures of the players who ended up with each item), and lively interviews with players about tactics, mistakes, relationships, and ideas for future action. And there are always lots of picture postcards from the game—and yes, all the avatars turn to face the camera before the scene is snapped and posted. All of this contributes immensely to a sense of community. There is a poignant combination of hard success metrics intimately mixed with light play. It's the contrast that creates engagement, and it's the engagement that enables success.

Guild websites feel a lot like other familiar social media. Page layouts look like social network home pages, with personal pictures and annotations of shared experiences. But the sites also feel different because they're about the game, a single common activity with its own strong narrative and clear challenges ahead. Social networking in or outside work may indeed be like a game, but the winning condition is ambiguous, the rules are often unknown, and the levels, skills, and expertise aren't transparent. On the game sites, the game narrative guides the conversation, everyone remains in costume, and the relevant expertise, ranks, and accomplishments needed for what's ahead are available for all to see.

Tacit Knowledge Moves Front and Center

If good collaboration requires better methods to share informal knowledge, especially when it's virtual, then the gamers have a good formula. The guild websites, as well as other formats for communication, move tacit knowledge front and center.

Within one minute on a guild website (after secure login, of course) you can know who's doing well, who's contributed recently, who's being credited with new points, and who's talking with whom. The contrast between formal information (schedules, rankings, bank account information, auction purchases) and informal information (postcards, tags on pictures and prizes, gratuitous humor) is striking. If it's a good idea to closely link these two forms of information, and we think it is, these sites are wonderful examples of blending serious and casual: after-event photo sharing meets the office wiki.

The feeling you get from the websites, and from the informal conversations available in multiple chat channels during play, is one of inclusion and transparency, especially related to tacit information. If a player knows how to get something done, it's reflected on the website or volunteered easily in conversation. The same is true for disagreements about group management, information about who's joining and leaving the group, and especially information about who's doing well (or not). There's the formal DKP and level information, but also a lot of informal acknowledgements of group contributions. Players feel a need to give due credit: it's encouragement that promotes future participation. Everyone knows that everyone else is a volunteer.

Performance Reviews

Good collaboration occurs when performance is tracked and when it is consequential. This is where computing helps. It's hard to imagine a work environment that automatically produces as much relevant, valid, and transparent data about how individuals and groups are progressing as seen in an MMO. Replication of that environment is a wonderful challenge for the workplace of the future.

Let's listen in on a guild performance review (transcribed from a conversation recorded during play). Our commentary is in brackets. The guild leader is a thirty-year-old MBA student at a top-ten university; the officer is a fourteen-year-old high school freshman from Iowa.

Leader: Ok, Let's talk about Minwur.

Officer: Umm . . . can only play two days a week [officer examines DKP for attendance and punctuality]. And when he does show up, he doesn't perform very well [examines DPS—damage per second—charts based on raid logs].

Leader: Have you talked with him about his performance problems? [Leader doesn't see evaluation in guild review folder on website from last review opportunity.]

Officer: Ummm . . . well, he's barely online enough to raid [DKP chart again]. He has a lack of feign death on bosses [a major error for a player]. He tends to pull them. For example, Brood Lord. That was not a good performance [again looking at damage and threat data]. I will speak to him the next time he is on.

Leader: Pulling bosses is something a hunter should never do. You know—it's something that once you tell somebody, they should be able to prevent it from happening again.

Officer: Because with a boss like Brood Lord, where he has the agro dump, you can pull agro very easily, if you're stupid.

Leader: The issue is that I'm loath to remove this guy when we really haven't given him feedback on what his problem is.

Officer: Oh, I see . . . I see what you're saying.

Leader: Obviously, you seem to be interested in encouraging him to find another guild but before we do that let's have a real serious conversation.

Because he had easy access to performance data, the guild leader was able to evaluate several different behaviors, quantitatively, to produce an aggregate evaluation of the play. Criticism was objective, and the numbers were public and trusted because they were computed within the game and not by someone who might have it in for a competitor. It's certainly possible that a player could be trashed just because others didn't like him (for example, he talked too much during the raid or wasn't encouraging of newbies), but that doesn't happen often without evidence. The game is multiperiod. You and your guild will get a reputation for trash talking without data. Recruiting, and more, will suffer.

Intragroup Encouragement

One obvious form of encouragement in information-rich game environments is certain evidence of a personal reward for group success. There are numbers to prove it. There are some game players (we called them the achievers in chapter 2) for whom the numbers are enough. But for many, encouragement needs to be social as well as empirical.

There are both simple and complex behaviors that get social rewards. On the simple side, some guilds give DKP for mentoring. This is actually more profound than it first appears. You get a share of group rewards, not just for battle performance (the business counterparts of which might be making the sale or finishing the computer code) but for making the group better, even if you had to compromise your own battle success.

We've seen guilds that offer tangible rewards for behavior such as answering questions in the guild forum, preparing for a guild quest by helping to gather scarce resources, or allowing a newbie to shadow you in a raid ("Just to learn; don't do anything stupid!"). One guild even devoted one night per week to helping new players level up. There were no victories to brag about on those occasions, but a wise investment in future ones. Quantification helps again in the teaching session: the lesson is over when seven new priests and five mages reach level 30, allowing them to at least enter the dungeon the guild has in mind for the raid next week.

Multiperiod game interactions facilitate teaching collaboration—and by doing rather than talking or reading. It's one thing to read about the rules associated with an activity (like the material that HR might assign to you when you start a new job), but when you're trying to learn the tacit rules of a *process* that defies formalization, it's far better to give it a try—and not once, but several times. It's even better if the initial consequences of possible failure are few. A former manager of semiconductor manufacturing plants told us that when starting up a billion dollar factory, it was routine for newly assembled teams to be given complicated assignments that took days to complete but that were only for team practice. When Honda Motor Company decided to test the mettle of American factory workers with its first U.S. plant, it started teams out building motorcycles and then taking them apart at the end of the day to assess quality and technique.[12]

Games are also wonderful collaboration simulators, so much so that we're beginning to invite managers with no game experience to participate in guided (the Stanford students again) and accelerated (they'll help you level up quickly) guild experiences as part of formal collaboration training. It's cheaper than having people fly or drive to the executive training center (people can join using their computer from a drilling platform, union hall, hotel room, or the study at home), and the experiences—sometimes intense and usually fun—add informal training about collaboration to formal courses that are part of the official curriculum.

Forming Collaborative Groups

Just as some businesses recruit for collaboration, gamers want to have the best people they can get on their team. In business, the only practical strategy is to draw out the interview process. In extreme cases this might mean that there will be tens of interviews over many weeks, as is true, for example, at Google or Goldman Sachs.[13] There aren't many other options for smoking out clinkers. It's hard to formalize probationary periods, and although hiring and then firing is always an option, it's inefficient, not to mention unfriendly.

In the games, interviewing typically means trial by fire: join us for the raid tonight. Gamers don't discuss hypotheticals or simulate play when the real thing is readily available. This takes advantage of game collaboration that is a series of short, intense "projects" that are highly monitored. After the raid, forum comments are securely posted for guild review (with the most likely negative comment being "I didn't enjoy his/her company"), the votes are tabulated, and offers made (or not). When work becomes more like the games, it will be easier to ensure that new members are the ones you really want. The transfer from interviewee to new group member becomes blurred, with good value to group effectiveness and culture.

We envision an even more fluid transfer between stages of involvement, one that includes seamless shifts from recruitment to first job to movement up the corporate ladder. So you'd like to work here? Sit down at the computer and start playing. When you can convince a guild to let you join, you're hired. When you get to level 7, we'll let you talk to real customers. When you get to level 70, you're in charge.

Mass Collaboration

The collaboration we've discussed so far, in the games and in business, is about better, deeper, and more connections between relatively few individuals. Even though game guilds often number in the hundreds, the teams that venture out on most of the quests are fairly intimate groups of twenty-five people or fewer. Corporate work groups we meet, on average, are even smaller.

Some game collaboration, however, turns intimate small-group cooperation on its head. What if larger groups need to collaborate? What can games offer collaboration that requires orders of magnitude more people to be successful?

What's the Right-Sized Team?

At Procter & Gamble (P&G), a team of 1,500,000 seemed like the right number. That's the size of the innovation network they tapped to supplement the 7,500 internal researchers who were trying to keep up with the frenetic pace of innovation needed to feed $8 billion worth of new products annually into company growth. P&G changed the name of its research and development operation to "Connect and Develop" and sought contributions from independent labs around the world: research universities, industry consortia, technology entrepreneurs, retired scientists, and even housewives during shopping trips.[14] A team that large will never achieve the intimacy possible in small groups, but there's plenty they can do together that will result in solid contributions.

By many measures, the model worked. Now, more than a third of P&G's new products and almost half of the ideas in its pipeline are attributable to collaborations within its innovation network, not just its internal labs. In this case, the question of how to grow revenue through research had a new answer: bigger is better.

Larger networks have a better chance of delivering the right minds to the right problems, a daunting task for companies as expertise becomes specialized and distributed.[15] Someone might know the answer to a problem that will drive innovation, but unless the mind and problem are linked, nothing will happen. For some problems, the value of collaboration is consequently related to large numbers: the more people in the network, the greater the chance that a mind and a problem will match.

What's interesting is that all large networks are not equal. Creating the most value depends on driving participation, but the amount of value created depends as well on the nature of the connections within. Consider three different types of networks—broadcast, transaction, and affiliation networks—that we believe are good, better, and best. We add an example of how games apply in each case.

Broadcast Networks

When someone broadcasts invitations to participate, one to many, the value of the network created increases simply as a function of the number of people who hear the call and participate. For P&G, 1.5 million created a distinct advantage over 7,500.

In this kind of network the best way to maximize value (V) is to attract a large number (N) of people: the value formula is merely $V = N$. Attraction will depend substantially on the extent to which people find engagement and interest in the content of the problems. Consequently, the best broadcast networks, similar to familiar entertainment networks in traditional media such as television, will be those that deliver the best content.

Bring in the games. There's a lot of mind share available in the games, offering the opportunity for a crowd to achieve success at a level of performance beyond what an individual could accomplish, even if the individuals in the crowd have relatively little expertise.[16] The owner of the network will benefit in proportion to the number of players.

The Wisdom of Crowds and Information Diagnosis

As they work their way to elite levels, gamers are called on to make many types of classification decisions in a variety of puzzles, quests, and challenges. Sometimes they work hard to develop the skills to make these calls accurately. There is the potential to harness these skills in a form of crowd-sourcing to assist in a variety of real-world diagnostic problems in which input can be aggregated to produce something of real value. (Let's defer for now the important discussion regarding when it's appropriate, if ever, to secretly tap the efforts of players paying for entertainment to obtain real work for someone else—what we call "stealing work.")

Potential classification problems range from diagnosing computer malfunctions to evaluating cyberattacks and other threats, from production delays and engine failures to aesthetic judgments, and even to the potential for medical diagnosis. Most of these problems involve pattern identification and matching images or information to an imperfect set of criteria leading to a final black-or-white classification.

Nick's character in *Star Wars Galaxies* (you met Nick at the beginning of chapter 2) had to use medical instruments to examine wounds on the warriors he was being paid to heal so he'd know the best course of treatment. There's a scanner in the game hospital that displays the medical images, and it gives Nick's character buttons to push to see different views and register a final diagnosis.

The information that appears on the scanner is, of course, as fictional as the virtual hospital room in which the scanner is located. But what if the images weren't fictional? Imagine a video feed into the game that replaced images of avatar body parts with medically relevant scans from real people (anonymously, of course). A radiological scan could be substituted in the game, for example, with the player's task being to diagnose whether disease was present. The motivation to register a correct evaluation would be high if the better judgments produced gains for players in the game. What would it take for a bunch of gamers to generate useful data?

The advantages of more than one brain could be substantial. Consider four possible classifications. Two represent correct diagnoses: for example, cancer when cancer actually exists, and good health when cancer is absent. There are also two possible errors: disease when there isn't any, and good health when there is disease. Each of these errors has important implications for health as well as business. Given that false positives may be more tolerable in this case than false negatives (i.e., it's better to be safe than sorry), substantial resources are required to track down many diagnoses that will eventually be proven wrong. If a reduction in false positives can be achieved without increasing false negatives, resources could be freed for other worthy health care objectives. Many real-world classification decisions have these same characteristics (see the story about Vinnie in chapter 11 for another example).

There is a literature on what happens to accuracy when expert ratings are aggregated in radiology or tissue diagnosis.[17] We think there will be conditions where lower levels of expertise can be combined to yield useful accuracy. Games could be designed to train and aggregate many classification skills relevant in the real world.

No one would delegate a surgical decision to results obtained from a crowd of gamers, but their work could serve as a valuable signal to raise or lower the level of additional investigation needed by real experts. The point is that games are an important place to look for the requisite diversity and engagement to achieve the benefits of crowdsourcing.

Limits to Crowd Wisdom in Broadcast Networks

The true wisdom of any crowd that gathers in a broadcast network is far from guaranteed. There are situations where crowds can be dead wrong. Four attributes of large groups increase the value of large collaborations: diversity, independence, decentralization, and aggregation. All play to the strengths of MMOs.

Diverse groups with many points of view will do better than those whose members all know the same things. Diversity could mean multidisciplinary skills (computer scientists and English majors; marketers and engineers), experiential diversity (young and old members), or hierarchical diversity (line workers and vice presidents). In spite of the stereotype of gamers as male teenage nerds with too much free time, the data shows substantial diversity in age, education, and expertise, with gender catching up. It may be relatively easy for games to bring more diversity to the workplace than would normally be possible, especially if a business were willing to open the network to outsiders.

Large groups do poorly when they merely circulate the same wrong answers. Creating independence among group members is an antidote. When the multiple connections are used to exchange information, to critique options, or to brainstorm, that's good. When the connections merely facilitate the spread of wrong solutions, that's bad. The design of game infrastructure and feedback could readily ensure that groups have the requisite independence.

Finally, group intelligence depends on an ability to aggregate work across individuals. It's entirely possible to miss the wisdom of a group if input is uncoordinated or undocumented. Game infrastructure facilitates aggregation because every keystroke is captured. Metadata is generated and displayed on dashboards showing progress that constantly aggregate and update individual actions. These features are already mainstays in the games. No new inventions are needed, just inventive implementations.

Transaction Networks: What Happens When People Can Talk to Each Other?

Successful broadcast networks will attract participation because of great content, and value can be extracted by aggregating judgments. That's good. But what if the people participating could interact *with each other* about the content? That's better.

When people in the network are also connected and can communicate with each other, informally or as a requirement of their work, the value of attracting new participants, so says Metcalf's law, increases exponentially ($V = N^2$).[18] For example, to the extent that the independent entrepreneurs working on P&G ideas are communicating with *each other* about their ideas in addition to a central hub, the value of the collaboration increases dramatically as new members are added.

Again, games fit this model nicely. Diagnosis from the doctors in Nick's game, for example, need not depend on interactions between players, but it's easy to imagine making that happen. There are plenty of opportunities for players to communicate during play. This includes player-to-player chat channels, messaging, and, increasingly, voice communication. One-to-one communication between the nodes in a network will increase the value of any given collective judgment, and the payoff for adding people is substantial—that is, exponential.

Affiliation Networks

The nodes that interact in a transaction network (*Star Wars* game doctors or P&G scientists) need not be individuals. Many networks support the connection between groups as well as individuals—a network of networks. Called *affiliation* or *group forming networks* by David Reed, they offer an important increment to shared knowledge.[19] When groups overlay individuals, as is the case with online communities such as those in the games, Reed argues that the value of the network becomes the *exponent* of the number of participants ($V = 2^N$), dramatically accelerating value creation as a function of participation, especially when the number of groups added becomes large. Groups could be all sorts of collectives: for example, chat rooms, buddy lists, trading rooms, discussion groups—any group that shares something in common.

It is difficult to imagine any community that connects as many *groups* together as MMOs. In addition to guilds, there are raiding groups and groups that share the same role in the game narrative (e.g., all the priests in a guild). Higher up there are servers that collect different guilds, and it's now the case that entire servers, encompassing several guilds, will brag about their progress above and beyond the achievement of individual guilds: "Our server raised the Gates of Ahn'Qiraj." (This actually happened while we were watching guilds at play. Over five hundred avatars from all the guilds that played on one particular server were invited to the event, the highest number of characters we've ever seen in one 3D environment.)

The value of these larger collaborative networks is getting notice beyond P&G, and promises to move beyond the significant value that P&G has already achieved with broadcast networks. Innocentive, a new company that makes available scientific problems to independent scientists internationally, offers financial rewards for being the first to send in a solution. The company runs a virtual lab that has tens of thousands of potential solvers who have been, until now, disconnected. A next step would be to create communities among the solvers so that scientists can *collaborate* to find solutions. And the next version? Why not a game?

Similarly, LiveOps, a new company that offers stay-at-home workers the opportunity to work as telephone customer service representatives, has thousands of agents who can be flexibly deployed on multiple projects. The creation of additional value through interacting online communities is similarly a goal for their virtual workforce. These type of organizations can add significant value to their network with agents who can compete collectively as teams in competition with other teams.

These new companies, and new ideas at older ones, have a common theme: people want to interact. An executive at Innocentive said to us that a frequent request among his relatively disconnected solver community early on was for new ways to share information—chat rooms, forums, legal help with team formation. The plaintive request of one scientist summed up the community urge: "Can I at least post my picture if I win?"

The final "virtual" we discuss involves the role of leaders. They're viewed differently in the games and in ways relevant to decentralized, fast-paced business. We start by listening in on a raid leader barking instructions during action.

Chapter Eight

Virtual Leaders

Take your flask . . . take your zanza. Do it now!

Let's finish it up. I need spiritual healers active. Good. They're all down.

Shit, what group are you in? No, no . . . you need to be near the wall.

Class call coming in 3 seconds. I need everyone to de-curse at all times. Ok. BOP on net. This is good.

Can we get a threat meter reading!

I need you to take your shadow protection potions on the count of three . . . one, two, now!

Healers, stay out of the fear! Go to max range.

Let's start DPS [damage per second] on Nefarian.

All right, guys. We're in the home stretch here. Don't screw this up. We can do this.

Leadership matters in games. The dialogue above is twenty seconds of voice instructions we recorded from a raid leader guiding twenty-five players against Lord Nefarian. Imagine avatars running, loud battle noises, gasps from a dying monster, metrics updating, and queries from guild members interspersed with this dialogue. We recorded three hours of nonstop calls like this in a single evening's raid. This leader really needed to know a lot about the game to coordinate a successful raid (and Lord Nefarian *did* eventually drop). Game play for leaders can be complex.

Although other instances of leadership in games are not as fast-paced as this kind of military staccato, the work of leaders doesn't end after the moment-to-moment action during battle. Leaders recruit, set policy, choose associates, give promotions, arbitrate disputes, analyze multiple streams of constantly changing and often incomplete data—just about everything real leaders confront. But leaders in the games have an even more complex task: they do their leading with a workforce of volunteers who not only don't get paid but who pay real money themselves for an opportunity to have some fun.

Virtual Worlds, Real Leaders

Gamers are aware they're doing something difficult and relevant to the real world. The following are comments from real people about virtual experiences that they believe are relevant to real life.[1]

> Being a guild leader has affected my RL [real-life] ability to lead people and stand up and do what is good and needs to be done. I have received numerous promotions at work into leadership positions and I make almost 8 times more now than when I started [playing] last year. [Male, 24]

> I learned several things; I could manage events for a few hundred people, I could mediate arguments, I began to notice traits in individuals that were helpful in predicting what they were most likely to do next or likely to be interested in. I learned to delegate authority without releasing responsibility. I am very proud to say that my experience strengthened my diplomatic skills that had never been a strong point prior to my experience. I also learned more about the Internet, building sites, and moderating forums that I didn't know before. [Female, 56]

> At first, I was a bit concerned about my ability to organize 100 some people from all over the world but, as it turned out, I learned that I was much more organized that I had thought I would be, and that I had an uncanny knack for diplomacy and leadership. It's hard to describe very eloquently why EQ [EverQuest] helped me feel like I could do it . . . but it has. It's given me confidence in myself, and made me realize I make good decisions, and am pretty smart, and that gave me the push I needed to make a "scary" real life decision. [Female, 34]

*I was approached by several of these friends to assume
leadership of the guild and agreed, even though I was uncertain
of my suitability. I've grown more accustomed now to directing
various aspects of running the guild and providing a vision and
leadership to the members. Follow-up and assertiveness now feel
more natural to me even in real life. [Female, 46]*

From players like these, we learned that being a leader in a game *already* makes people think about their real-world jobs, good evidence that gamers will be predisposed favorably to the idea that business processes explicitly include game mechanics.

Leadership activities in games turn out to be both substantial and mandatory. Groups in games can't succeed without coordination, even though many contributions to groups and game play are from the bottom up. In response, each guild creates its own website complete with officer roles including guild heads, executive committees, specialized raid leaders, DKP managers, and forum organizers.

In our research, a key question has been to determine the extent to which leadership in the games resembles leadership in real life. If it's similar, are gamers better prepared for work because they get more practice? And if it's different, what unique expectations will gamers bring to work? How will work need to change to take full advantage of gamers' skills?

What Are the Characteristics of a Good Leader in Real Life?

Working with Thomas Malone of the MIT Sloan School of Management, we started our research by examining leadership best practices in real life.[2] Models of leadership have gone through phases. Definitions in the early twentieth century emphasized traits of born leaders (they're self-confident, emotionally stable, and have personal integrity), switching in the 1960s and 1970s to an emphasis on situational attributes (be autocratic if a decision isn't critical to success and engage the group if it is). In the last thirty years, integrative models have prevailed, and we chose one of those definitions to guide our own analysis.

The Sloan model has been used since 2001 as a basis for MIT workshops on distributed leadership.[3] The model describes four core capabilities needed for effective leadership: *sensemaking, relating, visioning,* and *inventing.* Good leaders have at least a minimal competence in all four capabilities, but no leaders are perfect in all of them. The following are descriptions of the four dimensions. Next, we'll look at how they play out in the games.

Sensemaking

Sensemaking is the ability to notice, evaluate, and communicate about ambiguous situations.[4] It often involves creating mental maps, stories, or useful points of view. The key to effective sensemaking is to create a map or other method of representing a situation that is useful for the people who need to respond to that situation.

Examples of sensemaking behavior include using many different types and sources of data; going beyond existing frameworks to see the world in new ways; checking interpretations with others; and trying small-scale experiments.

Relating

Relating involves developing key relationships within and across an organization. Effective relating balances inquiry and advocacy.[5] *Inquiry* involves the ability to listen to and understand what others are thinking and feeling without imposing your own point of view. Leaders who are good at inquiry are good at suspending judgment and understanding how others move from data to opinions. *Advocacy* involves effectively articulating your own points of view, explaining how you arrived at them, and convincing others about the merits of a perspective. Too often in business, the focus is on advocacy, but successful relating requires a balance of both.

Examples of relating behavior include trying to understand the perspective of others (What data and reasoning did they use?); articulating your point of view and reasoning clearly (What data and reasoning did you use?); and building strong relationships with many different kinds of people.

Visioning

Visioning is about creating compelling images of the future, not of what is, but of what could be. Leaders who are good at visioning provide *meaning* for what people do and motivate them to bring their best to the task of fulfilling a vision.

Examples of visioning behavior include describing a desired future state; connecting organizational goals to personal or societal values; and painting a picture of the future.

Inventing

Inventing means turning visions into reality by creating methods for people to work together to achieve their goals. Terms such as *implementation* and *execution* are relevant. Inventing implies a creative, and not merely routine, orientation to getting things done. Effective leaders need to create new ways for people to work together and to overcome obstacles.

Examples of inventing behavior include thinking about who will do what, by when, and how; tracking progress and overcoming obstacles; not assuming that the way things have always been done is best; and coming up with new ways of organizing.

Traditional Leadership Skills Also Work in the Games

Our first big question was whether these four capabilities are useful for game leaders, and if they are, what the relative value of each is in defining leadership among gamers. Here are our conclusions, based on interviews with prominent guild leaders and hundreds of hours of observing and recording guild action.[6]

- *Game leadership requires a breadth of skills.* Our first conclusion is that leaders in complex games have experiences consistent with all four leadership capabilities. This is evidence that good leadership behavior has constants, regardless of context, and it means that games are at least an important source of practice for the real world (and vice versa), even if the games do not add or subtract skills. If the two worlds were different, the implications of games for serious work would be less clear.

- *Relating and inventing are emphasized in the games.* We found all of the capabilities in the games, but there were differences in relative emphasis. Complex games reward leaders who are primarily good at relating and inventing. Leaders need to recruit and retain the good will of top players who have critical roles in guild missions and creating communities, and they must invent procedures for accomplishing both. Invention emphasizes organizing players with effective moment-by-moment tactics linked to the challenges in the game, as well as inventing community experience that motivates participation. We expect experienced gamers to have a leg up on these two skills at work.

- *Mainstream game narratives require less sensemaking and visioning.* The emphasis on relating and inventing applies primarily to mainstream games that have highly structured challenges with known tasks and tactics and at least some common knowledge among players about the best methods for successful completion. In the structured challenges of the most popular games, sensemaking and visioning are less relevant because these dimensions are often defined by game narratives. One might say that the game designers are the "leaders" who supplied these components. It's tempting to simplify this further and say that the game dictates strategy while players in leadership roles manage tactics by recruiting players, providing a good community experience (website forums, mechanisms for celebrating and sharing group success), and then planning and executing the tactics that allow groups to advance in the game. However, assuming a complete exclusion of strategy from guild leaders' roles would not do justice to the strategic work they do in selecting the challenges to tackle in the most complex games.

- *Games and virtual environments without strong narratives require different skills.* In some types of games, visioning and sensemaking are more important to success than relating and inventing. This is particularly true for virtual environments that explicitly avoid narratives. In those worlds, the fun is up to you: they only provide the infrastructure. Doing well is usually defined as designing activities and building structures and digital objects that others will want to use or purchase. This requires having a larger vision in addition to a plan to execute.

The Characteristics of a Good Leader in the Games

We now review the four capabilities in their order of importance based on comments from players and experts who participated in our research. These echo many comments from our gamers who supplied examples for the O*NET work taxonomy reviewed in chapter 3.

Relating

When asked to comment on leadership activities in games, guild leaders mention relationships more than any other topic. Here's a typical comment:

> *The toughest thing about being a guild leader is maintaining relationships with all of your members on a personal level, and realizing that no matter what, you're not going to please everybody.*

Many say it's a rude awakening, especially in an entertainment context. Opinions are divided on whether it's the best part of play or a burden too similar to problems in the real world for casual entertainment. But in either case, the conflicts are real and the lessons sometimes profound.

Relating Is Rewarding and Hard

Many comments from players describe a tension between recognizing the importance of relationships and bemoaning the effort that it takes to maintain them. This player is a perfect example:

> Being a guild leader has its ups and downs. On the positive side, it's nice to feel the accomplishment of bringing a group of people together to work towards a common goal. However, there is an awful lot of handholding and personal conflict resolution that you have to do. I know in my first guild, I would find myself dealing with interpersonal player problems for 1 to 2 hours a night. I knew it was time to change when I found myself creating an alt just to play without guild headaches.

(Creating an "alt" refers to an alternative character or avatar; in this case, presumably one without leadership obligations.)

Games provide poignant lessons about the tension between the rewards and the costs associated with different roles. The lessons are certainly available elsewhere in life, but for younger gamers, this may be their first chance to ponder details of this trade-off.

Recruitment Is a Critical Context for Relationships

Relationship concerns are common when recruiting. Attracting good members can make or break a guild, and although some players stay in the same group for months without issues, others are constantly evaluating their membership and keeping an eye out for greener pastures. For younger players, this may be their first lesson that recruitment doesn't stop when membership is conferred. Keep in mind that nearly all of these relationships exist without face-to-face contact, but via game play behavior and chat and voice channels supplied by the game and add-ons.

We've had a chance to eavesdrop on guild leaders discussing players who'd either like to join the group or who were being considered for removal. Reminiscent of business, the recruiting talk was about what to ask for in guild applications, appropriate trial periods, who should do the interviewing, frustrations during interviews, the difficulty of finding good players, the necessity of overrecruiting to counter desertions, and forced dependence on third-party recommendations because there's not enough time for adequate trials during actual guild play. That's a lot of HR training, and all in the context of home entertainment.

Game Leaders Try to Understand the Perspectives of Other Players

A good leader needs to make an effort to understand the perspectives of other people. This is certainly true in the games, and constitutes one of the better applications of real-world lessons from work.

In one performance review we recorded, a guild leader solicited comments from each of his officers before making any summary conclusions or taking action. The most important decisions are usually whether or not to retain a member whose contributions are suspect. In the exchange cited in chapter 7, the guild leader heard about poor game play from an officer who wanted to kick a player out of the guild. The leader said a better method would be to first make sure that the player was aware of his mistakes and had a chance to fix his poor play. That's not only fair but also a shrewd calculation, because the guild leader went on to explain that arbitrary action against players could harm guild reputation. "We'll see that guy again," the leader continued. "Let's make sure he feels like we treated him fairly."

Game Leaders Get to Know Other Players as People

Businesses are getting better at melding the differences found in diverse workplaces to produce stronger groups. Games offer opportunities to observe the extremes of this variance. It's quite likely that players' ages will range from adolescence to retirement, their occupations from engineers to teachers to carpenters, and their cultural background from the developing world to Wall Street. Here's one leader's lament:

> The toughest thing about being a guild leader for me was making the hard decisions while dealing with people of multiple ages, ethnicities and time zones. I was continually balancing our 'guild rules' as they applied to loot, to ensure the largest numbers of people remained happy. I adopted a 'firm but fair' leadership style that seemed to appeal to nearly everyone—younger guildmates saw me as a father-figure type, while older guild-mates saw me as their 'boss.' I found it very difficult, however, to schedule guild events for people in nearly every time zone; ensure that everyone had adequate help to gear up/prepare their characters for more difficult content; prepare myself to lead us to victory in that difficult content; and balance the contingent of 14,

*15, 16 year olds versus the late 20s–early 40s people—that was
the most difficult task, as those two age groups tend to have some
friction when placed into a setting that is equal. Different views
on life, different manners of speech, less respect from younger
folks . . . it was crazy.*

A subtler version of diversity exists because players have different motivations for participation on a continuum from casual to serious interest.[7] Leaders need to understand where participants fall on this continuum, and they need to encourage people with different game motivations and personalities to cooperate. That's not always easy, as this female guild leader, age thirty-seven, mentioned:

*The toughest part of being a guild leader is that my guild is
comprised of people who have great personalities and get along
really well, but are a real mixed bag of playing styles. You've got
the guy who has ten level-30 characters, you've got the guy who
levels at a glacier pace, you've got the guy who hits 60 in a month
but only wants to solo, you've got your hardcore raiders, the guy
who has eight level 60 toons, your casual players, your night
crew and your stone cold PVPers [people who like "player-
versus-player" game style]. Trying to come up with goals and
content for people like that, people who are all my friends, but
have a million different goals, has been a really stressful balancing
act. On top of which, I am a casual player who has a busy job
and a RL of her own, and can't be on every night of the week to
make sure everyone is happy. Being a guild leader has taught me
about personality types and how to manage people more than
any job I've ever worked on. While it's not always a fun lesson,
it's definitely the most valuable thing I've gotten from the game.*

The leader in this example clearly understood the value of reconciling different interests. But she also understood the costs. This echoes the cost–benefit trade-offs in relationship management mentioned previously, and highlights one of the most frequent reasons people give for retiring from leadership positions—too much stress!

Relationships Often Involve Sensitive Self-Disclosure

Relationships in guilds can extend well beyond game play. In spite of game norms that often discourage disclosure of personal information, it's inevitable that conversations, when they are as long and intense as is necessary to succeed in the game, will turn personal. And when they do, it's often the leaders who hear the most powerful personal stories. There are plenty of stories in the popular press about sex and romance that started in the games (e.g., there's been more than one marriage proposal offered in a game, several weddings, and even a funeral), but more commonly, the stories are about detailed personal experiences. Every once in a while the stories are intense:

> The hardest part about being a guild leader is listening to
> people's real life problems. I am sort of a 'mom' to people in the
> guild and a lot of them confide in me. I listen to some really sad
> stories and it's very difficult to hear them, they affect me greatly.
> Probably the most difficult was when a 27-year-old woman in
> the guild told me she had terminal breast cancer and that she
> just needed to talk to me because she was 'so scared.' I think the
> toughest part about hearing things like that is the realization that
> these folks had to confide in someone that they don't even
> know—I feel so bad that they don't have a real life friend or
> family member that they can reach out to.

It's difficult to pursue guild goals in the midst of intense personal stories. Leaders report difficulty in balancing the two, particularly when the personal information is shared with only one other player while the entire group is involved in a collaborative activity. Welcome to the real world.

There Are Limits in Relationships

Even though relationships are critical to guild success, there are limits. Several of the guild leaders recognize, sometimes painfully, that they can't please everyone. One of the most difficult lessons is balancing group happiness against an obsession with perfect relationships. There are times when you just have to make a decision, stick with it, and accept the consequences.

> The hardest thing is trying to decide what is good for all.
> Currently we have a problem with materials for special fire
> resistance gear. Several of the materials have been distributed
> between the members, but we are seeing that many are being
> sold. At the same time people are complaining that we don't have
> enough fire resistance gear to survive and win certain battles. No
> matter what we will choose to do, some people will not agree

with our decision. One of the lessons I learned as a guild leader
is that you can't make everyone happy and sometimes you have
to make a decision and stick with it, even if you don't completely
agree with it.

Inventing

Inventing (which in the Sloan model is more about implementation than gadget innovation) was the second most common capability found in the games. Mainstream games provide a structure and narrative that define the broad actions necessary for advancement, but it's up to the leaders to decide exactly what to do and when. Consequently, there's a premium on leaders who not only hold relationships together but also figure out the best way to accomplish tasks.

Good Game Leaders Are Focused on Execution

Details matter. Timing and sequenced actions are critical, and it often takes constant instruction to guide the guild. Guild leaders have written and oral contact with tens and sometimes hundreds of players, responding to adversity by assigning and reassigning roles and responsibilities in a highly fluid action. Without attention to detail, raids fail and people quit.

The brief narrative at the beginning of the chapter demonstrates the detail that's required to succeed. Those instructions were the *invention* of the raid leader. Although there is a general goal that the game imposes, and there even might be a well-known trick that could be usefully applied, there are many different routes to success. Inventions are welcome.

Game Leaders Do Deals

Designing and inventing incentives to keep players happy and participating is one of the most creative parts of guild leadership. As we reviewed in chapter 6, synthetic currencies offer a flexible system that enables new inventions about how to compensate players—a useful feature for guilds as well as individual advancement in the game. The guild leaders are the most frequent authors of the schemes to share loot based on player contributions to the action.

Sensemaking

Sensemaking involves organizing information to create a useful picture of the environment. The following two features of the games help explain why.

Built-in Game Narratives Drive Sensemaking More Than Players

In most mainstream games, there are elaborate narratives that define the big picture. You already know that the Horde has been battling the Humans for two thousand years, and the characters, costumes, and places constantly remind you about the details. Sensemaking can involve more than just understanding the larger backstory, however. It can include any aspect of the internal or external environment. Guild leaders are sensemaking when they realize that guild members are unhappy or dissatisfied, or when they assess what members can do well.

Sensemaking Is Often Distributed Across Multiple Roles

Another reason that sensemaking may be featured less in game leadership is that it is often distributed across several players. A raid leader may not be the same person as the guild leader; one coordinates detailed action, usually within a single session, whereas the other specializes in recruiting, creating incentive systems, evaluating players, and resolving disputes. There is no single position in a guild for which sensemaking is a natural primary task. It might be a mistake to think of guild leaders as CEOs for whom sensemaking is their primary value to the organization.

Visioning

The conclusion about visioning is similar to that for sensemaking: mainstream games don't often require players to supply a compelling story about what the guild or game might be like in the future. Of course, each guild owes its existence to the vision of the leaders who founded the new tribe, and there are players who, when asked, have stories that would qualify as visionary. Compelling epic stories supplied by successful MMO designers fulfill much of the need for leadership vision. The attraction of these stories is certainly one of the reasons people come to work in the games.

Visioning Is Critical In Games Without Strong Narrative

A good counterexample is *EVE Online*, a game built around economic competition, allowing players to specialize in skills related to mining, manufacturing, research, trade, and corporate management. The space-faring narrative of *EVE* is more open ended than some MMOs, and the economic rewards are player driven. The game designers do not identify opportunities for guilds and leaders. Leaders have to first and foremost create a compelling vision around which a corporation can galvanize and action can be structured. That sure sounds familiar.

Visioning Is Important in Virtual Environments That Are Not Games

Another exception is play seen in *Second Life*. As explained previously, *Second Life* is a virtual environment and not a game per se. Consequently, players must initiate group behavior (the environment doesn't tell you what to do), and some activities involve substantial visioning. Players build discos, promote political, social, and religious causes, organize hobbyists, and open up businesses (e.g., developing virtual real estate and selling digital clothing). Some of the best organizations in virtual environments completely bridge the two worlds. For example, several companies have opened for business in *Second Life* using visions similar to those that guide their brick-and-mortar counterparts (early arrivals include Starwood Hotels, Sun Microsystems, Reuters, Accenture, BP, Wells Fargo, and IBM).

Leadership Differences in the Games

In traditional businesses, leaders are appointed to managerial positions for months or years, they are not often encouraged to take risks (despite the lip service), they have lots of time to make decisions, and most have only limited opportunities to practice before showtime. In online games, the opposite of each of these characteristics is likely to be true.

Leadership Happens Fast

Whatever constitutes good leadership in the games, it happens fast. To someone unfamiliar with the games, the pace of play and the speed at which people make decisions, meet people, coordinate tasks, and plan action make a huge first impression.

The negotiation of who will lead can be quick. We watched player-versus-player games (essentially five-on-five capture the flag games) that took, on average, twenty-two seconds for five players to decide the roles they would assume in a group action. Some of the roles were determined at the outset because the capabilities of a game character are defined by a character's role (for example, priests are better at healing than warriors are). The chat exchanges during the quick planning session include self-nominations about the best roles for a character ("My character is a mage—good long-range damage but very fragile") followed by a short negotiation when there are two or more characters that could take on a similar role ("I've done this before; I'll take the lead").

Being quick can be more important than making everyone happy. It's true that maintaining good relations with a team is critical for guild success, and particularly for recruiting. But it's also true that quickness sometimes trumps relationships. Gamers make numerous comments related to the pace of play that demonstrate the trade-off between time and consensus. This is an important lesson, and an early one for younger players. It's hard to make everyone happy and there is often no time to waste on consensus.

Leadership Roles Are Often Temporary

Leaders in real life are identified and trained for roles that endure across situations and even years. A rising star is offered mentorship, training, and eventually a promotion, and unless problems occur, that position may last anywhere from several years to the duration of a career.

Games have no such expectations about the permanence of roles. You might be a leader for ten minutes or ten days, more like a turn in the barrel, trading leader and follower roles back and forth between sessions. Leadership is a task and not an identity, enabled in part by the quick and organized pace of play. Leaders are chosen (or they volunteer) in minutes, with no expectations that the role will last beyond a single game episode.

Good leaders are often also good followers. Whoever leads will have people following who have a better sense of what the leader is trying to accomplish because they have been there themselves.

Stars do emerge, and they're most often the leaders who build the larger guilds. Some of these leaders last longer than a year, an eternity in this new medium. Many stars, however, are surprises. They are people you'd never expect to identify—and who would never expect to *be* identified—as appropriate for real-world management. The surprises are easy to find, we've noticed, because it's much easier to give leadership a try. There's no long-term commitment and consequently very little risk in an audition.

Some of the fluidity of leadership is because people get tired. Leaders retire and others take charge out of frustration more than a desire for a prominent role. These two comments from players are good examples; the first is from a thirty-six-year-old woman and the second from a twenty-seven-year-old man.

> *I became guild leader of my guild after several guild leaders took the position and stepped down. I got tired of the ping ponging and took it over.*

> *I became a guild leader when the guild I was an officer in was struggling to merge with another. When things didn't work out to*

*plan, the previous guild leader called it quits. The guild was left
without a leader, and when no one volunteered to take over,
I stepped up to the plate. It wasn't my desire to lead, but I knew
if I didn't, everything we had worked so hard to build would
crumble.*

The fact that you can get out of leadership responsibility as fast as you can get into it encourages experimentation. Experiments sometimes fail, and when people leave out of frustration rather than when their turn is over, guild chaos and player exodus may result.

Game leaders are often volunteers stepping in to help, which has an interesting implication for business. No one is appointed from above to lead. There's an expectation in the games that someone will step up to offer temporary leadership if groups go awry. What if work groups were more dynamic, allowing for continual changes as a group developed, including the opportunity for self-nomination?

Risk Taking Is Encouraged

An accelerated pace causes a more relaxed view of risk. It's easier to get past mistakes in the games, in part because you don't have to wait long to try again or try something different. Trial and error becomes a preferred strategy, and failure, at least on occasion, an expected feature of play. This contrasts sharply with the more deliberate strategizing in companies, where leaders form ideas and theories, carefully debate options, and only then execute. In the games, failure isn't a career killer, just a piece of data for strategizing about the next attempt.

Here's an example: We watched seven guild members attempt to get their whole team across a lake protected by a gruesome monster. A brief chat yielded an initial strategy, but the conversation was short. Everyone was comfortable with the high likelihood of failure. Why? Death (or "wipe") to their characters did occur. But that was quickly followed by "Let's try that again," and "This time no one step on the protruding stones."

Neither shareholder stock value nor the livelihoods of real employees were at stake when the group first tried and failed, but it would be wrong to assume there was nothing ventured. Resurrecting a dead character takes time (less time if you pay in gold), and continued failure does erode reputations and hard-earned privileges. It's fine to trade some short-term pain for long-term reward, but in the words of one gamer, "No one wants to be a member of a guild that *always* wipes."

Gamers are practiced in weighing odds under uncertainty, and often under conditions more chaotic than might exist in the real world. This practice is valuable leadership experience for real-world business environments that have increasing uncertainty and equal dependence on execution *and* innovation. There are plenty of places in business where we could encourage more fast-paced experimentation with the opportunity to fail and learn. One example is the effort enterprises give to handling exceptions to standard business processes. The unending flow of these challenges represents a good place for teams to experiment with better and more efficient exception handling without risking mission-critical results.

Practice Is Plentiful

In business, leadership training may be five weeks at an elite business school program, a weekend at a company retreat, or on-the-job mentoring— all good. In the games, however, there are endless opportunities to practice leadership strategies and tactics and get feedback on how they worked. Games can be virtual leadership simulators, offering players informal, realistic, and any-time training many years before they would see similar action at work.

There is already a developing field of business simulation that will help serve the need for practice at leadership skills. Just do an Internet search for words such as "business simulation leadership training." We know that some of those developers are studying the games to ensure they have the right ingredients for engagement. We also believe that companies could explicitly include multiplayer entertainment games as part of their leadership development programs. These would be like "management flight simulators" for softer aspects of leadership, as opposed to the more analytical aspects for which simulators and spreadsheets are already available.

Most practice in the games, of course, is with really diverse people, and not the homogeneous groups that might typically participate in a formal corporate training exercise. As already discussed, the games have substantial breadth of players, and they don't eliminate players who might pose the greatest leadership challenges because of casual or unpracticed play. Ironically, management training in a large MMO might offer more real-world experience in dealing with people than any business simulator.

The leadership learning accomplished during game play is the epitome of *informal* learning. Substantial evidence in the learning science literature points to the benefits of learning in informal contexts, and new programs in corporate training are attempting to take advantage of this tendency.[8] Like learning math at the racetrack, learning leadership while *playing* may be just the distraction that creates enough engagement to make progress.

Finally, leadership practice benefits more than just individuals. There are plenty of opportunities for *groups* to rehearse leadership. Games allow experimentation about different ways to create entire leadership hierarchies. In one game we watched, there were groups competing based on shared convictions about leadership roles as defined by capitalist and socialist systems (no victor was declared by press time). It's difficult to imagine where you could gain similar practice and learning absent a complicated production involving the cooperation of several people over a long period of time.

Leadership Environments

Remember the gamer comments about collaboration in chapter 7—that it's more about the environment than about the people? Gamers think that's equally applicable to leadership.

Most writing about how to make corporate leadership better is about how to select or develop *individuals* who are the best suited to lead, usually based on background and natural talent. Leadership is something that you are either born with or learn, but in either case, the expertise resides with the individual. Common practices to identify leadership include performance reviews and recommendations from peers, and common practices to develop skills include classroom instruction, career planning, and mentoring.

The gamers ask, "Why not change the game instead of changing the leaders?" We believe there are three game-changing properties of environments that facilitate effective leadership: quantitative *incentives*, particularly in the form of synthetic currencies; the *hypertransparency* of important and conveniently organized information; and *connections* through a variety of specialized communication channels.

These features allow people to manage themselves to a larger degree than is familiar at work. If you give them the tools, players know what they should be doing, and it's easier for leaders to be effective. The strongest (and still speculative) conclusion may be that the traditional expectations of an individual leader may be less important as environments and their metrics support individual action.

Many of the important environmental features have already been discussed. Here's a review of their unique application to leadership.

Nonmonetary Incentives

Incentives are usually discussed from the perspective of the people receiving them. For example, DKP (see chapter 7) turns out to be a great answer to the question of what I get when we win. These systems are also powerful tools for leadership. Because the game keeps exquisite track of individual performance, guilds can tie their group reward system to data. Leaders, even if their tenure is short and the pace of play frenetic, can motivate and keep track of participation in ways impossible to imagine otherwise.

When assessing the performance of team members in real life, "scoring" can include financial measures and subjective measures such as performance reviews, reputation, and peer ratings. Leaders in games use synthetic currencies to achieve many of the psychological benefits of real-world financial rewards, but they can be used more broadly to provide explicit incentives for things that might otherwise only be done out of loyalty or bartered quid pro quo.

The opportunity to closely align personal and group goals is a central promise of applying game ideas in the workplace, and this is accomplished without real money. Effective incentives are both compelling and task relevant.

Business leaders must worry about multiple time domains, championing strategic goals over the course of years as well as tactics during the day. It may be obvious that game incentives are well tuned to short time domains because players receive feedback moment by moment and leaders can redirect attention, behavior, and tactics quickly. Motivation can be evaluated and ramped up, if necessary, in the course of minutes. Because the commercial entertainment games are also subscription businesses, publishers are also interested in longer-term motivation. Key contributors are the "equity" that players build up over time developing their character, including virtual goods, and especially the character's reputation in a compelling social context.

Game incentives also create motivation systems that can be uncoupled from long-standing social relationships (*who* you know), unlike real life. This may happen because data relevant to the quality of play is transparent. The environment facilitates a fluid meritocracy. The perception of advancement based on merit may be as important as the reality. When it feels like the only thing a player needs do to get ahead is to play well, motivation to excel and the perception of fairness both increase.

Hypertransparency of Information

Game environments make lots of information available to leaders—and to entire teams—on dashboards that are continuously updated and are leadership relevant. One obvious value is that leaders have information displayed on a single screen that gives a complete picture of the state of the world at any given moment. The screen is crowded, but it's customized, so at least stuff is where the player wants it. A leader knows which avatars are available to serve, their capabilities and performance history, detailed information about their locations, and their health (as in near death or plenty in reserve).

All of this information makes *leading* easier. But the information also makes *following* easier as well, which may be even more important. Players can easily see for themselves where they fit in and how well they are contributing and adjust their behavior accordingly. This is a huge advantage and, we think, an important explanation for why lessons from these environments are the next frontier for enhancing leadership functions.

The idea of an über-dashboard for the CEO has received a lot of attention. Many products that offer "business intelligence" technology deliver the dashboard in only a few offices on the higher floors. We believe that leaders will benefit when they make that information available for all to see, as part of managing in a looser hierarchy where people are expected to make their own decisions or organize organically in groups that could process the information together.

The information found on game dashboards is empowering. One icon gives players information about themselves (e.g., health status and currency reserves). Others help them locate and evaluate players, contact them individually or by using lists, take notes during play, access market information during trades, and even open a browser within the game. The dashboards in games are like a streaming video of players' résumés. A huge bonus is that much of the information doesn't have to be provided by the person it's about (the biggest problem with any system that depends on human creation of metadata). Much of the information is *automatically* made transparent as the computer tracks play.

It's hard to lead when people aren't capable of doing the tasks that need to be done. In business, if groups don't have the right expertise (engineering, marketing, sales), they may not be successful. Games present detailed information about each player that is available for all to see. Persistent reputations are revealed through the use of ranks, levels, and numerous other indicators that show what people can do. Levels define capabilities, and people can make choices to seek help (or stay away) from players based on that information.

Players (and leaders) learn to trust game metrics, in part because it's difficult to cheat. It's important for gamers to know that the data are objective and less susceptible to social influence than might be the case in settings with fewer environmental confirmations of performance.

Taken in isolation, a lot of game data would look familiar to business-people—numbers and progress bars—although the display is generally a lot more colorful and easier to process than typical enterprise software user interfaces. More striking is the integration of the data into the game screens. Everything is open at once on the same screen—there is no need to open several applications and move between windows as information needs arise. A similar feature in enterprise software would be a dashboard *on the way to* and not separate from the places where people already work: metrics baked into ubiquitous e-mail and browser applications, for example. Outside of work, social applications such as Facebook, with its myriad of customizable plug-in applications, illustrate the point.

Transparency goes beyond data. Leaders (and everyone else) can also see the actual players (or at least their avatars) in addition to the data attached to them. You know (at least virtually) where people are located and who's ready for action. You can place the "camera" at any location in the scene to view the action (e.g., top down, from the eyes of your avatar, or next to the immediate group), and leaders can scan with great flexibility, tracking everyone in the group. People tracking the emerging enterprise technology related to "presence" in the field of unified communication will appreciate the parallel between awareness of others in the game and knowing where they are at work.[9]

The Future Is Here

At the beginning of this chapter, we quoted gamers who had, without instigation, made strong connections between their play and their work. Are there also people in large companies who believe that's true?

We helped IBM find out.[10] Through an intranet newsletter, experienced gamers who worked at IBM were invited to comment on the connections between real and virtual leadership. (The invitation included a promise that no negative evaluation would be held against anyone for admitting significant game experience). It was quite easy to find 135 IBM leaders who also led online guilds. Here's what they had to say.

First, more than a third of the respondents (39 percent) believed that leadership techniques in the games could be used to improve leadership effectiveness at work. The mechanism for formalizing the transfer, most felt, should be straightforward—document what works in the games and map the skills and techniques to virtual business environments. They saw no need to even mention the games when work is being redesigned—just steal the best methods and apply them where they are useful.

Others felt the games could be used explicitly as training grounds for sophisticated leadership lessons. Nearly half (49 percent) said that game play was not only linked to real-world needs but also that it had explicitly improved their own leadership capabilities. Commenting specifically on the environmental influences we discussed (currencies, transparency, and communication systems), 75 percent of the IBMers said they believed that game experiences could enhance leadership among a larger group of managers than would be possible with traditional methods of training.

The one caution from the survey was the widespread belief that the adoption of game sensibilities about leadership would require a change in company culture. For example, one person noted that failure to achieve a goal on the first try is generally viewed as a learning experience in the games, after which you "reattempt with new knowledge." That's in contrast to the corporate world, where, he acknowledged, "reattempting is hard."

There seems little question that a new crop of leaders will bring game-informed ideas about leadership to their work. Ultimately, the entire workplace may be transformed by 3D environments and game mechanics, and that will enhance not just leadership but all forms of collaboration and innovation as well. The metrics by which the new systems will be evaluated will be efficiency and productivity. But the mechanism responsible for the success will be straight out of entertainment: I'm having more fun.

Beyond the Obvious About Virtual Versus Real

This part of the book dealt with four important virtual experiences—people, money, groups, and leaders—and how they could change business practice. For each, there are differences between how they work in the games and real life (e.g., your avatar can look like anything you'd like in the games, but you can't in real life), but it's the *similarities* that are even more useful to the thesis that games are powerful.

There are three critical points to make about the similarities, and that's our goal in the next section. One is about the nature and importance of *play*, whether it's accomplished virtually or in real life; one is about the power of *media* to alter how people think and feel; and another is about *ethics* and business issues that will emerge when work and play merge.

These three discussions—of play, media, and ethics—offer a critical intellectual framework for evaluating our thesis, one that we think will be necessary to sustain a serious new field. In our experience, evaluations of serious games often hinge on judgments, and sometimes quick ones, about the *in*appropriateness of play, the *in*ability of media, and especially entertainment media, to be taken seriously, and the *un*ethical potential to engage people in an activity that may seduce them to participate with more enthusiasm than seems warranted.

We start with the topic of play. Work is not the opposite of play, as we'll show. Meet Marc, a twenty-year-old student who thinks advanced calculus can help his guild perform better.

Chapter Nine

Play Is Not the Opposite of Work

Marc was thumbing through two-year-old class notes from sophomore calculus. He was looking for the section about polynomial algorithms that used quantifier eliminations to find symmetric Nash equilibria. He'd been lucky to get a C+ when he had originally taken the course, but now the stakes seemed higher.

Marc was sure there was a better way to systematize game tactics in upcoming raids, and he was dead set on making sure that his group had the benefit of the most sophisticated analysis. The game publisher had just made available new APIs for up-to-the-second reporting about each player's progress. He'd already figured out how to build the necessary spreadsheets. All that remained was hooking up the differential equations to the raw data.

Even if some in the guild might not appreciate or understand the math, Marc was more than willing to do the work. He was oblivious to the noise his friends were making in the dorm. The hours passed without notice. He lost self-awareness and had no thoughts about failure. He'd found a perfect balance between challenge and skills. Marc was having a blast.

Marc was playing a game, but a different definition of *play* is required to describe the experience. His story is solid evidence that some game play may be fun, in the street sense of the word, but it's also a clue that play is more complicated than simple definitions of laughing, parties, or mindless wasting of time. Play is not the opposite of work. Rather, it's an important component of attention, involvement, and productivity, and it's capable of energizing behavior of all sorts.

Play and Productivity

There is good and new evidence that enjoying work—being engaged and emotionally involved—can positively influence productivity and a host of other desirable outcomes.[1] Positive emotions at work are associated with less absenteeism and lower intention to change jobs. Positive affect can facilitate creativity and the likelihood that people will help each other and cooperate. Positive emotions decrease aggressive responses, and they lead to greater self-efficacy, including a greater likelihood that people will think they control their own fate within work groups. Emotionally involved workers are also more likely to be evaluated positively by bosses as well as coworkers.

Taking "Play" Seriously

How seriously do we take the term "play" when evaluating work? There's a fundamental tension between classic and newer ideas about work and play. The old-school view is that play is a diversion to be extracted as completely as possible from business. Play is trivial, unguided, and irrelevant to the achievement of serious goals. For many, the word *play* trivializes loftier goals.

For others, simple words like *play* (and we'd add *fun*) are important terms that define delight in serious work. Play allows work to transcend a sense of time and place and produce focused concentration, if not a continuous smile. Time flies when you're having fun, an adage that is often said sheepishly as if to hedge against a reaction that fun is out of place at work. When engagement goes away, however, the word creeps back into serious conversation—for example, when people quit because "I just wasn't having fun anymore." Among those who study this field, play looks pretty serious. It is organized, purposive, and influential. Who's right?

To answer the question, it's important to know the details of how play works. What exactly does it mean to play a game or enjoy an experience? This chapter looks at several important definitions of play and relates them to business objectives and the design of work.

The Modern Convergence of Work and Play

Studies about play constitute a relatively new direction for thinking about organizational behavior. Work and play have traditionally been considered separately, especially with respect to the software that helps people do their work. If you're having too much fun, somehow the business process must be getting short shrift. Enterprises, and the software that runs them, are about efficiency—time on task, keystrokes per transaction, total cost of ownership—

and, to the extent necessary, about ease of use. Up to now, whether technology promoted a fulfilling sense of *play* hadn't been an issue. Play is for consumers (and mostly young ones), and its place is in the home. The software products that enable play, far from garnering the distinction of *productivity tools*, are labeled *media entertainment*.

But things are changing. There's a growing business trend, and a parallel scholarly and scientific effort, that is reevaluating the segregation of work and play. Human experiences are increasingly chaotic and complex, and cut across boundaries. Those who are adept at new digital skills bridge these boundaries and are redefining what it means to be computer literate in a digital world.

Knowledge about systems at work and digital life at home covers the same expertise. It's more often the case that the systems at home are *more* complicated and capable than those in the office. If you have the right tools, social networking, for example, works pretty much the same way whether you're planning a weekend party or forming a collaborative work team. For those who study and build technology, digital expertise is being similarly reshuffled, expanding the boundaries of knowledge relevant to the design of work and its tools. Sociologists, anthropologists, psychologists, and other flavors of entertainment experts will increasingly be involved in the design of work.

The convergence of work and play means that workers are engaged by the same media sensibilities—great pictures, meaningful interactivity, compelling narratives, constant feedback—that drive consumer experiences. And if you're selling software, productivity isn't the lone advantage. Among substantially similar software offerings, what could be a better differentiation in the market than a technical review that concludes "and on top of that, workers actually enjoyed the experience!"

What the Experts Say About "Play"

What does it mean to *play*? One classic summary of the serious literature about play concludes—surprise!—that the meaning of play is ambiguous. Brian Sutton-Smith starts an extensive review with the observation that "we all play occasionally, and we all know what playing feels like. But when it comes to making statements about what play is, we fall into silliness."[2] The central ambiguity (Sutton-Smith even titles his book *The Ambiguity of Play*) is that play is at once what it seems to be and also *not* what it seems to be. When young animals bite each other while playing, the playful nip *means* a real bite, but it isn't *really* a serious bite.

To define *play* here, we have borrowed extensively from the literature about a broad range of play experiences, much of it unrelated to games per se. You could reasonably say that you're playing and have the comment apply to activities far more diverse than games: gambling, playing the piano, golfing, sailing, playing with the dog, traveling, pulling pranks, watching TV, dressing in costumes, cooking, or sky jumping. The serious treatments of play throw in art, politics, teaching, and writing. It would be a mistake to separate today's computer and video games from this list. There's much to learn about play and work by embracing a larger category of experience.

The following sections describe nine forms of play that help define where play fits between fact and fiction and help organize ideas about what it means to play a game.[3]

Play as Frivolity ("That was fun but useless")

In 2006, Mayor Bloomberg abruptly fired Edward Greenwood from his job as an assistant in the city's lobbying office in Albany after spying him playing Solitaire on a computer during business hours, saying that "the workplace isn't an appropriate place for games."[4] The mayor had the notion of play as frivolity nailed: play is the anathema of productivity and success in serious endeavors.

Many a boss or a parent would say the same, at least on first thought. They might be coerced to admit that there's a place for play, but only if crisply separated from work. Defining play as frivolity is an important part of the Protestant ethic and its influence on industrial-age views of time and work.[5] Work is good, honorable, hard, and obligatory, and play is the opposite. Play is frivolous, valueless, nonsensical, and a waste of time.

With all due respect to the mayor, defining play as useless frivolity is not taken seriously by anyone who studies play, including many thoughtful treatments of the concept in psychology and education that are especially relevant to challenges at work. There's even a Dutch study that showed a little Solitaire at work actually *improved* productivity and job satisfaction.[6]

Thinking that play is frivolous is behind most gut-level critiques about games at work. Our most important counterargument, and one supported widely in the literature, is that play is *valuable*, and that games, by organizing play and engaging workers, can positively influence serious behavior. This might be accomplished using different methods (there are several quite different ways in which play could influence work), but regardless of the mechanism by which it works, *play is important*.

Play as Power ("When we compete, we're at our best")

The opposite of frivolity is play that defines power. The essence of most modern computer games is conflict: worlds at war, galaxies in revolt or guilds aiming for the high spot on a leader board. Game play allows conflict to be practiced in ways that promote a connoisseurship of competitive skills. Doing well—for example, receiving badges, reaching the highest levels, accumulating synthetic currency—is prized by individuals and groups, and it's something worth bragging about to friends. And, we think, eventually to colleagues.

Although playful contests are as old as humans, recognition of their value is historically new. Through the first half of the twentieth century, the Protestant work ethic clashed with the idea that play had merit. The inversion of that ethic began with a radical treatment of play by Johan Huizinga published in 1949 (*Homo Ludens: A Study of the Play Element in Culture*).[7] Huizinga boldly suggested that play, especially playful *contests*, was the same as those activities that shaped the essence of culture, including politics, law, scholarship, and the arts. Anybody who challenges himself or herself in comparison with others in a way that requires skill is engaged in essentially similar behavior, and the behavior could be defined interchangeably as work *or* play—take your pick.

Homo Ludens went on to define for the first time the inner structure of play, emphasizing elements of tension and uncertainty. Play has its own rhythm and tempo, in which tension is created and then resolved. It has its own rules, and it has a beginning and end. Most important, play can't be commanded; it is voluntary, and those who participate honor themselves by explicitly acknowledging that they're in it to win. Successful game designers have deep intuition regarding these principles.

This hardly sounds like frivolity. Although the games in 1949 weren't driven by computers or presented on fancy displays, Huizinga's ideas seem even more relevant today. Defining play as power may be the highest compliment to a modern computer game. By turning a contest into play, there is a commitment to win or succeed, and it's the public and enthusiastic vow on entering the game that elevates contributions, making everyone better. We might argue about the importance of outcomes in computer games (are we really better off if the Hoard defeats the Alliance?), but if the goals of play were aligned with those of good business—create jobs, build families and communities—the value of a contest might rise to the level Huizinga envisioned for all forms of competitive play.

Many argue that there's more to play than power, as the next definitions show. And it's also worth noting that power definitions aren't universally favored, especially among those who view them as unnecessarily macho. Maybe the related concept of "potency" or "competency" is a better label than Huizinga's use of "power." On the other hand, there are plenty of links between combat and modern work. War games, for example, are used extensively in the enterprise, although mostly for training and planning rather than as a context for actual work.[8] Recently, the 2,500-year-old Chinese classic *The Art of War* became a business bestseller.[9] Others have written about the explicit connections between business processes and less serious contests. More than one noteworthy book, for example, touts the close and useful relationship between poker and financial investing.[10]

There's much to value, we think, by characterizing work as a contest. Most people already believe this to be the case, with victory coming in the form of a better salary, longer tenure, or the corner office. Yet many at work also feel that the game they play is unfair, mostly because the contest fails on the very qualities that make computer games work: specific and transparent rules, continuous feedback linked to goals, and awareness of how play fits within a larger narrative. Maybe there is a thoughtful way to imbue business processes with features that acknowledge and celebrate work as a contest. If so, we think it will by by embedding it within play that uses the best game ingredients.

Play as Developmental Progress ("Now I know what to do")

A second strong definition of play highlights development. Play, as much as any other experience, enables personal progress, but with far less bother, more opportunity for practice, and less risk than waiting to experience the real thing. Playful imitation is how the young learn motor skills, how to think, how to engage in social relationships, and how to make moral decisions. Developmental play offers chances for experimentation, repetition, and repair of behavior. Play encourages children to practice taking the perspective of other people (like using an avatar to interact with others) and to develop fundamental skills necessary for social interaction.

Workers also need to make developmental progress and can benefit from use of business simulations. With the flexibility of virtual worlds, avatars, and 3D environments, the possibilities for simulation increase. There are employees who are now being trained in the areas of safety, persuasive skills, and even sexual harassment using make-believe conversations in a virtual world.[11] Practice matters, even if it's simulated. There are pilots, surgeons, welders, and retail clerks who perform better on the job because they've "played" with simulations ahead of and in between the real experiences.[12] Simulations are more easily accepted as first uses of games and virtual worlds in companies, possibly because they *seem* more serious because they better disguise a primitive playful attraction. But remember where in the computer store you go to buy simulator software—the game aisle.

Most business simulation tools don't take full advantage of game psychology to drive engagement and productivity. When you add game components such as points, levels, time pressure, and feedback to simulations, performance gets even better, as has been shown, for example, with surgical simulations.[13] One study showed that playing *any* video game requiring close hand-eye coordination improved real-life surgical practice, and using a simulator that mimicked the actual procedure helped even more. But the best preparation for the real thing was playing a *game* using the simulator—for example, more points awarded for *Top Gun*–level speed and accuracy, with the leader visible to all.[14]

Play as Community Identity ("I'm with *them*")

Remember when Helen left work early in chapter 4 to ensure that she wouldn't let her guild down by showing up late for a raid? Her play was centered on identity with a community, although not necessarily a community that scholars typically consider when studying play (they're more prone to study countries, cities, or schools) or even the type of play that most often causes strong identification (events such as festivals or parades or big sporting events such as the Olympics).

Although new, we think that guild and group identification in multiplayer games fits this definition perfectly. Whether the groups are virtual or more traditional, games allow people to confirm membership in a group and communicate that membership to others, often in ways that celebrate the connection. When anthropologists analyze group identity, they say that play offers group members an occasion to persuade each other that they *belong together*.[15] Guild meetings offer the same, with an emphasis on communication practices that maintain the group in the face of numerous and attractive alternatives.

Community identification doesn't depend on competitive play, even if it might be accentuated by it. In the case of identification with guilds, there's value in the mere definition of who's in and who's out of a group (it's nicer to be in, of course). This is a powerful motivation for social interaction as well as a prominent feature of game design, as discussed in chapter 7. Games can promote teams in the workplace as well as players' identification with them.

Effective teams are critical for business collaboration and innovation, and those with the best sense of community are often the winners. There are plenty of play opportunities for work groups that aim to heighten team cohesion and identity. (We have previously mentioned, for example, a ropes course where the expectation is that those who jump together will work better together.) These opportunities, however, don't yet merge the venues for work and play as we are suggesting. Games at work can create community identity by helping to determine who's in and out, celebrating those within the group, and offering opportunities for confirmation and repair within the community—all while usefully confusing the place where the work is accomplished with the place where the team is encouraged. Smart use of game principles can tap the power of team identification, even when the work is essentially a solo endeavor, by coaxing individuals into groups with identity and rewards.

Play as Imagination ("Here's an idea from a totally different time and place . . .")

Multiplayer games are like jazz. There's a basic structure to the play (like chord progressions), but much of the actual experience is improvisational. Individual players decide the details of how to play their characters, the best way for a story to unfold, or how a group will identify itself to others. You have to follow the general narrative, but there's substantial room for creativity and imagination.

The imagination that play encourages and requires is invaluable for innovation. Players need to transform themselves, making what is present absent and what is absent present.[16] This represents an inversion of the more linear and rational expectations about ordered thought, yet it might be the essence of thinking outside the box.

Imagination is also less about the contest than it is an entirely different way to think. The philosopher Immanuel Kant said that a playful imagination is the link between mere sensory experiences and formal thinking.[17] To our ears, he's making the case that play could be a link to innovations at work.

Games provide a structured environment where you can play with ideas, more like a novel than nonfiction, but without the immediate burden of trying to figure out the details. What if we *temporarily* freed workers from questions such as "Will the boss like it?" "Is it fiscally plausible?" "Does it break a rule?" When play allows workers to lighten up, get beyond the details of the present, and imagine the otherwise unimaginable, the opportunities for profound innovation increase. This happens in the normal course of playing games.

Play as Fate ("I won! [Even though I know I was just lucky]")

Playing games of chance can be a great escape from complex work. (Is anyone playing Solitaire during work hours at *your* company?) One reason that it's fun to gamble, whether for dollars or virtual gold, is because players feel like they are transferring destiny to powers beyond themselves—to the gods, magic, planets in alignment, or a found piece of clover. Those powers *seem* to control events that are independent of a player's own expertise. It may seem harder to make a case that fateful play has serious value at work, in contrast to the potential case for play as power, identity, or imagination. But it's also true that games of chance dwarf all other play in terms of market share. Is there anything to learn from games of chance that could be applied to serious work?

Work supplies plenty of random surprises. As much as possible, however, workers should take charge of their own fate and that of their projects, and not resign themselves to external forces. Games that introduce randomness, however, might create a backdrop for problem solving by using surprise to motivate a workaround. In this sense, it may be worth saving a space for mini-games of chance that are embedded in larger games. Many of the most popular MMOs, for example, have small games of chance that players use for a break or just to pass time during a guild call or practice skills that are randomly reinforced. This works because even though games of chance provide reinforcement that we don't deserve, in the sense that luck and not expertise is what determines success, they nonetheless cause very real responses capable of sustaining engagement. For example, searching under countless rocks to find a special weapon (an embedded game of chance in one popular MMO) causes great excitement, and a quite real dopamine rush in the brain when success is achieved.[18] However random a reinforcer is in reality, people often take it personally when the result is in their favor. This is just one more psychological tool in the kit of successful game designers.

Play as Enjoyment ("This was just plain pleasurable—I'll be back")

The next definitions are about pleasure. Play keeps things exciting and makes time fly. Definitions that emphasize enjoyment fit the street sense that games are important because people just plain like them, without much regard at all for whether they represent development, power, or identity. These definitions are about "me" and "fun."

It's great when you get paid to play, as has been true for several of the student gamers who have been our guides to multiplayer worlds. But it's equally clear that for each of these students, the quality of their play experiences, quite apart from extrinsic rewards, was a central motivation. There's something about the experiences themselves that turns a casual interest into an avocation, and that's the essence that is often missing in work.

Recent game and media research tries to explain why play is attractive to individuals, with the common assumption that play is about pleasure. We concentrate on two concepts: peak experiences (called *flow*) and emotional arousal. Each contributes to an understanding of why games will be important at work.

Play as Psychological Flow

When a gamers say, "That game was fun," they often mean, invoking the stereotype of excitement-seeking adolescents, that the game was a *thrill*. We imagine that he (gender is part of the stereotype) was on the edge of his seat, with facial expressions changing quickly with every small victory or defeat. That may not, however, be the right stereotype for multiplayer games, especially those that are able to command sustained attention over long periods of time. What do players really mean when they say they *enjoyed* the play?

The psychologist Mihaly Csikszentmihalyi has an unlikely answer. He has shown that our best moments—those we say we enjoy the most—occur when we're voluntarily trying to accomplish something difficult for which we have the right skills.[19] Labeled as "flow," this high level of engagement describes a state in which nothing else matters, and experience is so pleasurable that people participate at great cost and for the mere sake of enjoyment. Flow has nothing to do with alcohol, drugs, or wealth, and it's more likely when experiences are risky—that is, when they stretch abilities and when they involve novelty and discovery. Sounds a lot like multiplayer games to us.

Often applied to more highbrow experiences such as music, sailing, and sports, the concept of flow has direct application to games at work. Flow helps explain how games create motivation, and how enjoyment should be understood as a precursor to involvement at work. Applicable across cultures, gender, age, and economic status, there are nine features of flow that contribute to a sense of enjoyment—each with strong links to games.[20]

- *Clear goals at every step.* In flow, it's obvious what needs to be done. This is a mainstay of the games but often the opposite of the ambiguous or contradictory demands at work.

- *Immediate feedback.* It's hard to fully engage in a process unless you know how each small behavior connects with a goal. Not only is the feedback instructive, as discussed in chapter 4, but it also defines how engagement is achieved. Each small step, whether successful or not, keeps attention centered on corrective action. This doesn't have to be a pat on the back from another person; often the feedback is embedded in the task.

- *Balance between challenge and skill.* If a challenge is beneath or beyond you, the outcomes are likely to be either boredom or anxiety. Games skillfully match challenges and skills, creating just enough uncertainty about an accomplishment that attention is required but not so much that flow is precluded or interrupted.

- *Merger of action and awareness.* There is a tight coupling of thinking and behavior in flow experiences. This describes a lot of game play. Specific thoughts cause specific behaviors, and conversely, actions determine thoughts. Great user interfaces promote this tight coupling.

- *Exclusion of distractions.* Flow involves intense concentration on the moment. This is achieved with effort, of course, but for gamers, the virtual environments help. These include advanced displays, sizzling graphics, and compelling avatars that minimize temptations to attend to other stimuli. It's all geared to make you keep looking and stay on task when it matters the most. (So what do we do to help keep people on task during a business conference call?)

- *No worries about failure.* This is different from thinking about failure and dismissing it as unimportant. In flow, involvement precludes thoughts about the end results of actions. Everyone knows failure is possible, but that doesn't determine thoughts and action. Keep your eye on the ball—nothing else matters, at least for right now.

- *Absence of self-consciousness.* Having to keep track of how you appear to others, although sometimes socially useful, is a burden. Actions aimed at ego protection tend to diminish flow. Games, especially ones where play unfolds with avatars, often relieve players of constant self-consciousness, allowing them to concentrate on goals.

- *Time becomes distorted.* In flow, perceptual time doesn't match clock time, often causing people to overestimate or underestimate the actual passage of time. In games, there are experiences that unfold at a slow and deliberate pace while the clock seems to speed ahead, making players feel as if they're moving in slow motion. Sometimes, the hours simply disappear.

- *The experience is an end in itself.* As people seek enjoyment, what they really seek is to be in a state of flow—that's the ultimate goal and even more valuable than a prize at the end. When the desire for enjoyment, achieved by just playing the game, can be aligned with the goals of an organization, games will have their maximum impact.

Several people who study the entertainment uses of games have proposed that psychological flow is important.[21] Game designers themselves think that flow is an important outcome of games, especially in games that involve long-term engagement over several sessions.[22] As far as we know, no one has proposed, as we do here, that games provide a way to bring more flow into the *workplace*, but the original author of the flow theories has offered intriguing previews of the role of flow in business, even if he doesn't identity games as a means to the ends.

Mihaly Csikszentmihalyi (in *Good Business: Leadership, Flow, and the Making of Meaning*), laments the dreariness of modern work. His antidote: "The best way management can help motivate workers . . . is by *providing opportunities for flow in the workplace* [italics in original]." His prescription has more to do with eliminating bad than adding good. He says we should "make certain that organizational behavior does not deprive workers of the enjoyment that comes naturally from being able to do one's best."[23] Going further, he argues that the primary reason that flow is important at work is that flow experiences are enjoyable, and that it's the *responsibility* of business to provide a relief from unhappiness and alienation.

That's a pretty challenging notion for business, and it's elicited some testy responses from executives who'd rather not employ a Chief Happiness Officer. We offer a slight twist that may make a better connection—in this case, between flow states and games. If flow is a common aspect of games, and if it's the state of flow that's more important than what you're doing when it's achieved, then peak experiences via games at work may not only increase self-worth for individuals but also increase the bottom line. How about a Chief Engagement Officer?

Play as Emotional Experience ("That was a thrill—keep it coming")

Play as emotional experience is the treatment of play most consistent with the stereotype about exciting games. It may take practice to achieve a state of flow that will last for hours, but emotional responses, and particularly arousal or excitation responses, can occur within seconds with no practice necessary.

Psychologists often separate experience into thinking versus feeling—or cognitive versus emotional processes. Thinking, so goes the distinction, is rational, ordered, and difficult to fool. Feelings, however, are subjective, irrational, and often occur problematically even when we try our best to control them. There are all kinds of dichotomies that capture the essence of the thinking/feeling distinction—mindful/mindless, rational/irrational, discretionary/involuntary, conscious/unconscious—but they all highlight a similar difference. It's easy to guess which ones the boss would choose. With respect to business, we should think at work and save feelings for the rest of life. We should do our best to quell emotional experience whenever it rears its irrelevant head.

Actually, nothing could be further from the way emotions and thinking work, and the way they should work together to encourage the best performances. All experience, even within time spans of seconds and even at work, is a complex interplay of thinking and feeling. Games choreograph the influence of emotions on how people think during play. Games are environments in which people experience quick switches between stimuli that promote thinking *and* feeling, promoting engagement.

What exactly constitutes emotional experience while playing a game? And what might be its use at work?

Defining Emotions: The Role of Arousal

The most common definitions of emotion name categories of experience, such as feeling happy or sad, which persist for at least hours (and maybe days), and may also describe a type of person.[24] Applied to games, we might say that Joan, a naturally cheery person, felt happy this afternoon after a successful raid with her guild. At other times, and in relation to other experiences, Joan may just as easily have felt fear, anger, frustration, sadness, disgust, or surprise. In any case, Joan played a game and experienced a particular emotion for an extended period—a pretty common understanding of emotions in games and life generally.

A different definition, however, is useful to explain how games will change work. In our conception, emotion is defined as *arousal*, not always the heart-pounding excitement associated with exercise or sex, but rather a constantly changing state of readiness for action that is an engine for thinking and behavior. Arousal is the excitement, caused by specific events in the environment, that engages our brains to process the significance of events and, if necessary, get our bodies moving so that we approach or avoid people and places as needed.

The following list offers seven attributes that describe what it means to be aroused when playing games, with comments about how each should affect serious work. Together, these features demonstrate the complexity of excitement and its value in maintaining attention and thoughtfulness. Each attribute helps define the role of emotions in play.

1. *Arousal changes quickly.* Unlike Joan's afternoon of *happiness,* arousal lasts for mere seconds and may spike repeatedly, even during short interactions. This means that the emotion engine is revving and idling alternately during any play experience. *Dispositions* and *moods* describe emotional experiences that last for hours. Arousal happens in seconds, with typically less than ten seconds between onset and return to a baseline. If this sounds antithetical to flow, consider how music, a great contributor to flow, is almost always composed of alternating phrases that create and release tension. The signal for flow is in the cycle.

   Brief experiences mean that good timing is more important than sustained arousal. For example, an arousing call to attention (maybe caused by a visual scene change or loud bang) one second prior to delivering an important piece of information *increases* memory; the same spike in arousal during presentation of the important information *decreases* memory for the information presented.[25] As with good film editing, the best games are engineered to sustain attention by including quickly changing features well synchronized to the natural cadence of human attention.

2. *Arousal is triggered by events in the environment.* Arousal isn't a response primarily initiated by the person who experiences it. It is a good skill if you can achieve some level of action readiness by intentionally saying "Now is the time to pay attention," but arousal is more typically triggered by events in the environment. Game environments cause changes in arousal without voluntary or even conscious compliance.

   Many different events in games can cause arousal—for example, features such as sudden movement, audio surprises, camera angles that focus attention, or the touch of another avatar. These features are so perceptually salient, even though they're virtual, that people can't help but be called to attention. They are unconsciously and involuntarily engaging. The cadence and tempo do matter. When put together poorly, the arousal pattern may lead to frustration. What type of pattern do you get from your enterprise productivity tools?

3. *Arousal is different from good and bad experiences.* Arousal can be triggered by either positive or negative experience (I just entered a cool new 3D environment, or my character just got whacked by a hidden villain). In either case, the arousal activates critical psychological systems that ratchet up people's ability to evaluate the significance of experiences and decide whether action (approach or avoidance) is warranted.

   This makes arousal orthogonal to a good–bad axis of evaluation. Arousal is the engine for action *regardless* of the valence of the experience. This is the essence of its significance. Arousal is motivation—dangerous to be sure, in that it's the engine for *all* behavior, not just the behaviors we want to encourage. No wonder researchers find that games produce antisocial *and* prosocial behavior.

4. *Arousal produces an impulse to modify.* When people are highly aroused (or extremely bored), there is an urge to seek experiences that modify the current state. This is counter to the popular notion that game play should or does sustain arousal at the highest level possible. Even the sustained arousal in console shooting games habituates (fades) eventually, well within an hour.[26] Sustained arousal doesn't explain the attraction of collaborative games, in which players are given numerous opportunities to calm down if things are too exciting or to ratchet up excitement if they are too boring.

   The *modulation* of arousal is important to game play and to how people manage media experiences of any sort. Any media can be arousing or not—depending on the state of arousal immediately preceding it.[27] People use games to manage arousal, not necessarily to increase it. That's what keeps them coming back over the long haul. I'm bored to tears (or stressed to the max), and in either case, I need to play for a while. The best information tools at work will be those that offer refuge for both boredom and anxiety.

5. *If there are alternatives to modify an emotional state, minimize negativity.* The fancy name for this in psychology is *hedonic asymmetry*.[28] It simply means that positive and negative experiences are not equal when it comes to urges to modify the arousal associated with each. Negativity gets top billing. There's an evolutionary background to this response—bad stuff can hurt us more than good stuff can help us—and it plays out in the games and generally in how people respond to all forms of media.[29]

   In many games, there's a potential for more negativity than in real life. You can get ignored, poked, stabbed, critiqued, and killed—all in a couple of minutes. Even though virtual, these experiences increase arousal; because they are also threatening, they demand attention and repair. And it feels really good when you fix it. Thus, game play benefits from the saliency of negative experience. By the way, people don't distinguish much between negativity experienced via media versus in real life, as we'll review in the next chapter, even though the result in the former is less consequential. There is plenty of negative stuff to deal with at work, ranging from annoying exceptions to business processes to interpersonal conflict to competitive threats. Using the negative side of these stories properly can be a good way to maintain attention at work, and games give us examples of how to make the resulting arousal a positive force for action.

6. *Arousal is an engine for learning and memory.* If arousal were the enemy of careful thinking, there would be little use in helping people sustain excitement. A better plan would be to minimize arousal to maximize productivity. But don't be mistaken that excitement is only linked to entertainment and therefore useless at work. Some would like to assume a clean division between the unconscious excitement experienced by the reptilian brain and the thoughtful work of the frontal cortex, but this would be wrong. As we have said, feeling and thinking are intimately related, at play and at work. Attention is high when the brain's emotional and memory systems communicate. Studies show that when neurons in the amygdala, the area responsible for emotional activation, are firing in connection with those in the medial temporal lobe, the location for descriptive memory, the result is that whatever is on the computer screen gets more attention and is remembered

better.[30] Game play thus has features that activate emotional response in the form of arousal that increases attention, producing better memory, learning, and performance. This could be useful at work.

These conclusions about emotions are part of the promising new literature about informal learning.[31] If excitement enhances learning, then you would expect that formal environments, such as most high school classrooms and corporate training settings, would be less than ideal places to learn. New studies tilt an advantage toward more informal environments such as playgrounds, living rooms, bar rooms, sporting events—and games.[32]

7. *Excitement transfers.* While playing a game, arousal fluctuates, and the excitement associated with any given segment of the experience in part depends on the level of excitement when the experience started. Pieces of experience are interdependent. A calm period in a game accentuates an exciting moment that comes afterward.

The interdependence of experience does not *only* apply within a single activity, however. Excitement from one activity can transfer to a separate activity, even though they seem unrelated. That is, excitement from a game can transfer, although not necessarily consciously for the player, to a real-life conversation that comes afterward. Generally, when coactivation of emotional and thoughtful systems is high, information will not only be remembered better, but also will be available when thinking about other similar experiences (learning scientists call this *transfer*).[33]

The transfer of excitement is interesting when one considers how most games are played. A stereotype of game play is that periods are extended, they are rarely interrupted, and they have a distinct beginning and end. There are game sessions that meet these criteria (in particular those that produce flow experiences), but often, game play works like any other information experience: there are plenty of interruptions. People go back and forth between games (or TV programs, Web surfing, and social networking) and other activities. Gamers are especially accomplished multitaskers. The consequence is that there is substantial opportunity for excitation transfer during play. This could be particularly important at work because all activities, even those *outside* the game, are candidates for an excitement boost from the arousal generated *in* a game.

This also means that the benefits of motivation will be most pronounced when the features that generate motivation are *embedded directly* in work activities. When motivation is separated in time from the work it might influence (I'm excited today but won't have a chance to take action until tomorrow), the influence of games is diminished. Excitement won't have a chance to usefully focus attention. When the excitement generated in play occurs in short bursts, however, the resulting arousal can be transferred quickly from one activity to another.

Summary

Our most important conclusion from this literature tour is this: play is a substantial force in how people think, feel, and learn and in how groups collaborate, share identity, and produce culture. Game play at work doesn't need to be about parties, laughter, and slaps on the back. The potential of games in the workplace cannot be dismissed, because games are neither frivolous nor powerless. Play deserves as serious a treatment in business as any other management or productivity tool—and given the current state of excitement offered by many information jobs, maybe more.

It is clear that the distinction between play and work is far from crisp. It's always been true that a lot of work is accomplished as if it were play and vice versa. We think that the boundaries between work and play will continue to melt because the need to engage workers is more acute than ever and because media technology will make it more and more possible to create convergence. Our advice is to take control. It's inevitable that serious play will invade the workplace, and the phenomenon will be disruptive. The only choice is to purposefully construct the play so that individuals and the companies who employ them both win.

If you find yourself agreeable to the idea that we need to design more play into the workplace, then there is one more important question: whether today's media are up to the task. Meet Judy. She's playing the simplest media game imaginable.

Chapter Ten

Caught Between Fact and Fiction

Judy is lying in a medical magnetic resonance image (MRI) scanner. You know—the body-sized tube that's actually a cylindrical magnet coupled to a very high power computer. She lies quietly on her back— as she was asked—and feels no particular discomfort in the cramped cavity. The scanner is often used to image subtle changes in blood flow to detect injured tissues in a knee, shoulder, or elsewhere. But today, it's recording blood flow in Judy's brain—while she's playing a video game.

It is the simplest of games. There are two different colored dots on a screen that she views in a mirror above her eyes (because the screen won't work inside the 30,000-gauss magnet). Her right hand is on a joystick, and when she moves it, one of the dots moves up, down, left, or right on the screen as expected. All she has to do is see how closely she can follow the other dot.

This isn't a game you buy at the computer store but rather one that allows researchers to watch activity in different regions of Judy's brain while she plays. The MRI scanner is taking detailed pictures of which parts of her brain are engaged at different moments during an hour of play.

The game has only one rule: follow the dot on the screen as best she can. When it moves, Judy moves a joystick to keep up.[1] But the game has two playing conditions. Sometimes, Judy is told that the dot she is following is controlled by a computer, and sometimes she is told the dot is controlled by a real person in another room. (In fact, the computer controls the dot in both cases, but Judy readily believes what the experimenter tells her.)

Here's her result, something exciting scientifically and critical to why multiplayer games are engaging. Depending on which condition Judy played (i.e., whether she thought the other dot was controlled by a computer or by another person), her brain activated differently. When she played the game thinking the dot she followed was controlled by another person, the brain regions that she usually uses during interpersonal connections were activated, just as if she were interacting with a real human being. When she thought a computer controlled the dot, her primary activation was in areas of her brain associated with visual tracking of moving targets.

Judy (not her real name) was part of a real study, and here's why her result, similar across several other participants, is important.[2] To get people's brains to process an interaction as if it were real, all it takes in the way of media tricks and gimmicks is a small colored dot on a gray background and a very simple story: there is a person connected to the dot. No complicated graphics, no high-definition display, and no humanlike characters, although all of those features might make the effect even greater. The secret sauce is the belief, quite easily established in this case with the simple instruction that the player is interacting with another human being. People then take the point of view that the computer is merely mediating (occupying the middle position in) a conversation with another person who is not physically present. Multiplayer games are simply a very rich version of the same phenomenon.

The last chapter established that play is serious stuff. But what about playing with *media*? Media games are different from chess, the piano, or the Olympics, venues for much of the classic literature about play. In computer games, there are little characters—dots, asteroids, orcs, wizards, bugs, and penguins—often crudely animated and shown with simple pictures that appear on a television screen or small computer. Can media symbols, mere fluorescent light on two-dimensional displays, be taken seriously?

The answer is yes. Media catch us somewhere between fact and fiction. And as Judy's time in the MRI scanner showed, there is good evidence that the needle points more to fact than fiction. Media generate psychological and social responses that can be every bit as consequential as responses to people and places in the real world.

The major point in this chapter is that media games have the horsepower to be a serious venue for work. How can mere pictures and words on a screen be so powerful? The answer, based on extensive research about how people respond to media, is simple but unexpected. People are not evolved to cope with media or computer technology. Rather, the human brain evolved over hundreds of thousands of years in a social world where *all* people and places were *real* physical entities. There's no switch in the brain that toggles between mediated and real, causing the brain to process the world differently depending on which way the switch is thrown. The consequences of this innate confusion between media and reality are profound.

If we can trick Judy's brain with something as simple as a dot, now think about what happens when a full range of visual and auditory details are added.

The Dots Get Faces

There's a greater impact when pictures are substituted for the dots. Interesting things start to happen when you think you're playing with other real people *and* the characters, pictures, and sounds are rendered with all the great special effects common in 3D games.

We tested this recently in an experiment at Stanford. Instead of following a dot, players manipulated avatars in a popular multiplayer game that offered typical opportunities for combat and cooperation.[3] Players interacted with other avatars in practice sword fights or a cooperative exchange of information. Each person had several opportunities to interact, some in which they were told (and believed) that the other character was controlled by a computer, and some in which they were told that the other character was a real person. Games commonly have both types of players. Gamers are used to figuring out who's who, and in this case we helped by telling them explicitly.

What's the difference between playing with a computer-controlled character versus another person? The answer is about ten beats per minute in average heart rate during play. When people interacted with characters they believed were controlled by another human, and this time in the context of compelling visuals and game narrative, their hearts beat faster, a good measure of arousal during play.[4]

So we find similar results for dots on the screen or characters in an MMO. This is another key piece of the argument that media are quite up to the task of representing social relationships in a virtual world in ways that primitively engage players as if the people and places in the game were real.

Popular Ideas About the *Un*realism of Media

However intriguing, these two experiments are counter to mainstream hunches about the realism of media. Most people assume that real life is quite different from artificial life that is controlled by a computer and that if there are confusions between the two, they are most likely caused by some deficiency on the part of the viewer. Who would actually believe that an animated character on a computer screen (or anything synthetic, including money, places, teams, and stories) had real consequences for them personally?

The excuses given for confusion are numerous. Children are too young to know the difference, novices don't know enough about how media work, or distracted viewers might let their guard down, but only momentarily. And if the two worlds *are* ever confused, most people assume it's rare, inconsequential, or correctable with education in the case of children or just some harder thinking in the case of adults.

Entertainment, so goes the lore, is a world apart from real life. Don't we all bring a willing suspension of disbelief to media in exchange for the pleasures of an entertainment experience? I'll just pretend these game characters and places are real because that's what's required to have the most fun in the game.

The Media Equation

The scientific evidence shows just the opposite. Extensive research shows that media, and particularly the people and places portrayed in games, are capable of eliciting a range of social and physical responses that are the equivalents of those in real life. We don't need to voluntarily accept media as real (that is, there is no *willing* suspension of disbelief required), but rather the believing is automatic and entirely human. In prior writing, we've called this *the media equation* to press a point about the equation of mediated life and real life.[5]

The media equation works for a range of responses, all of them relevant to games and their migration to the workplace. Here are some examples.[6] When characters on the screen move toward viewers, people have the same physical responses as they would in real life (they back up if the advance appears threatening and move forward if it's interesting). The motion of objects on the screen grabs attention just like real objects. Anything hurled toward the viewer, even though people know at some level that it's not going to burst through the glass, demands immediate attention. The match or mismatch between the personality of a game character and the viewer determines "liking" (characters that match the viewer's personality are liked better than those that don't, just like in real life).

Keep in mind that the general conclusions about the media equation were based on research using media that were far simpler than today's multiplayer games—that is, stimuli more like the dots without the faces. The similarity exists even with passive old media such as television, where viewers aren't allowed to be part of the scene. Games accentuate the media equation by adding features that strengthen the illusion: more interactivity, better pictorial representations of people and places, and the presence of multiple players in the same space.

There's obviously a limit to the media equation (e.g., you probably wouldn't let an avatar marry your sister) but the qualifications are few. The equation works for everyone, even those with special knowledge about how media work. Earlier results have been replicated with computer scientists and media scholars—people who should know the difference—because we're all built with the same primitive responses.

Thinking can limit the effects, but that's hard and it's a distraction. When a scary scene unfolds in a game, to calm down you might keep repeating "It's only a game; it's only a game." That fact alone is good evidence that the default response is to take the experience seriously. Rather than a willing suspension of disbelief (the game is unreal until I say otherwise), there's a default acceptance (the game is real until I can figure out why not).

The general power of media, and the specific enhancements that games add, helps make the case for games at work. The wall separating real work environments and virtual ones is not as high or impenetrable as one might assume, although some walls are bigger than others. We next turn to the features of media that make the illusion more or less powerful.

A Sense of Presence

The best games use powerful features of media to create a sense of "being there," or presence.[7] In the media psychology literature, presence is defined as the perception of nonmediation—the absence of thoughts about the technology that creates the experience.[8] The concept of presence is receiving a lot of serious attention. Journals are now devoted to the topic, as well as substantial research associations and projects.[9] One needs to watch out for confusion of this sense with the same word, *presence* (or *presence information*), being used elsewhere in connection with computer networks. There, the concept has to do with whether an entity is able or willing to communicate, especially across different communication channels. People who speak of this kind of presence have their own societies and standards.[10] In our view of games at work, these two meanings will converge. Games will work best in business when presence is high—that is, when people forget about the delivery mechanism and focus on the work.

Most of the studies and a lot of game design efforts concentrate on sensory experiences, and rightly so. The more pixels, colors, fidelity, and polygons, the more people will forget that they are looking at a screen. But the presence recipe, like the one for good games, also includes features that go beyond good pictures and sounds. There are two important dimensions of presence: vividness and interactivity.[11]

Game Vividness

Vivid games have rich environments with many sensory channels activated simultaneously and in high resolution. A large-screen, high-definition 3D world with surround sound audio makes vividness high; throw in a force-feedback controller that vibrates when your virtual car rumbles over cobblestone or a wand that allows you to manipulate on-screen objects by swinging your hand and you've got an even more vivid experience.

Some advanced features that make game experiences vivid will take time to migrate to the workplace. At the bleeding edge of today's entertainment technology, it's geeky hobbyists who have added CPU processing power that requires extra cooling fans to keep the best game technology running. (What happened to the days when you had to go to the office to access the best computing?)

Of the factors that influence vividness, most are actually within the purview of enterprise computing right now. The following subsections provide a summary.

Pictorial Realism

Picture quality has increased substantially in all aspects of media (HDTV, computer monitors, and the graphics software and hardware that drive them), but this is pulled together most stunningly in multiplayer games. The new visual experiences include recent inventions that improve rendering speed, picture resolution, and subtleties of lighting and color. It's no wonder that some players say they're in the games just to watch.

Image technology is about more than wowing friends with the latest and greatest. Games get more psychologically potent as the pictures within them become more vivid. Brain imaging studies show that realistic people (those rendered on the screen using the most polygons) better engage regions in the brain reserved for real-world social information, for example, brain centers associated with empathy toward other humans.[12] These are Judy's dots on steroids, and they're a good reason to believe that having avatars as coworkers and virtual spaces as workplaces will engage people without the need for a discount just because they are presented on a screen.

Picture Size

Picture size also increases interest. Big is better, but that's not the only interesting aspect of size. An important feature of most digital experiences is that they can be displayed on any number of devices. It's possible to watch the same digital file projected on the wall of a conference room, on your desktop, on a phone, or on some other personal hand-held device. The effects of the displays, even though the content is identical, are not the same.

Larger pictures are perceived as more real and are more arousing.[13] This will likely eventually increase demand for larger displays when work becomes part of the games. It'll be more fun to participate (and see yourself in the game) when people are nearly life size or larger. What's interesting, however, is the size that comes in second place. Small pictures, those only a couple of inches on the diagonal and usually displayed on a device in one's hand, are *more* arousing than the desktop screen sizes, which are usually around fifteen to twenty inches on the diagonal. There's something intriguing about tiny pictures. They're more novel relative to those that display people and objects at familiar life sizes. Games at work could make good use of tiny screens as the more complex multiplayer experiences allow the game to continue beyond the office on whatever screen you're carrying.

The Role of Audio

Realism is not limited to visuals. There are significant advancements in audio that make game play more realistic, including increased fidelity and spatial localization. It's pretty easy to include high-definition audio in most computer applications, the only limitation on quality being the speakers (or earphones in the office) that deliver the signals. Several of the games and virtual worlds can now deliver audio that is synchronized with the pictures such that sounds are reproduced in your headphones to simulate the exact location where they originate in the picture, including behind you.

Games at work should not ignore the influence of great audio. There is even evidence that audio features may be more important than visual fidelity in creating a sense of "being there," because compromises in audio fidelity are more likely to lessen arousal and liking of content than problems with visuals.[14] Realistic audio can even change the perception of pictures. High audio fidelity makes people remember accompanying pictures as being larger and better than when the same pictures are presented with poor audio.

Audio enhancements in the workplace, long criticized simply because they might bother coworkers, will increase with the availability and accept-ability of personal sound gear. The uniform for Gen-Y employees includes a pair of iPod earphones and Bluetooth devices. Gamers already expect great audio and instant voice access to other players, via always-on headsets. Look for convergence between teleconference headsets and game audio technol-ogy to confer a sense of presence in the workplace.

Putting on the Virtual Reality Helmet

To really go wild with vividness, you could add a virtual reality (VR) hel-met that puts the games on special displays right in front of your eyes and blocks out the rest of the world. There are screens in the helmet for each eye. When you move your head, the pictures on the screens move the same way they would if you were moving your head and body in a real environment, creating an effect called proprioception.[15] There aren't many games yet that work with this technology, but there is interest in serious uses of virtual real-ity from the military and others for simulation and training.[16]

Difficulties with VR helmets include cost, the bother of special equip-ment, and, in some cases, the problem of not being aware of what's going on around you in the real environment. Some people also experience motion sickness. These issues will prevent widespread adoption for some time, especially uses that build games into a natural workflow. There are great sto-ries being told, however, about the day when we'll go to work by donning virtual reality gear at home that will put us in a high-definition rendering of an office we've never physically touched. You may be reminded of the 1994 film *Disclosure* (based on a book by Michael Crichton), in which the Michael Douglas character uses a VR system to navigate his company's filing system to uncover the misdeeds of Demi Moore's character (all under intense time pressure, of course).

From the perspective of today's CIO buying technology in challenging times, these virtual reality stories will remain fantasy. Not to worry, however, because there are equally important aspects of presence that can be used now.

Interactivity

Interactivity is the biggest promise of new media and a mainstay of games. The rationale is this: when we get to interact—press buttons, move joysticks, or wave a wand—rather than passively absorb information, a sense of presence increases because the games become more like real life. So next, we need to explore what makes a media experience more or less interactive. And why would that be important in business?

Interface Features That Increase Interactivity

Interactivity is more than just having a lot of different buttons to press, although that helps. One influential definition names three components: *speed* (the time it takes for game action to respond to input), *range* (the number of different things that can happen in the game as a result of player input), and *mapping* (the match between the virtual actions in the game and natural actions in the real world).[17] The history of games can be easily linked to these features, and an analysis of almost any recent title will show that the action is faster, more varied, and feels more like real life than earlier games (just push a few buttons and see what happens).

Contingency: I Can Influence What Happens Next

Interactivity goes beyond interfaces and fast computer code. Interactivity creates *contingency*. Highly interactive experiences allow people to determine what happens at each step, regardless of what might have been scripted or planned when the interaction started. The players are the authors in games, operating within constraints set by the game creators, but also imposing themselves on the action that unfolds. The result is that the user feels important (I changed the course of the conversation) and feels listened to (I told the character what to do and he did it).

Many people experience a greater sense of participation in interactive media, but research shows that much of this response is primitive and unconscious. With passive, older media such as television, a basic response that people have to information is a determination of interest: "Is what I'm seeing worthy of further attention?" The physical signature of that interest is an orienting response or tuning of the body to evaluate new information for possible action. When we showed people pictures without allowing them to control *when* the pictures appeared on a screen, heart rate decreased momentarily at each new image to allow better evaluation of the new information, a classic sign of orienting.[18]

The response was quite different, however, when we allowed people to initiate their exposure to the same information by choosing which material to watch and when to watch it, a common feature of interactive game play. When people were allowed to control media with a mouse or joystick, there was an acceleration of heart rate (the opposite of an orienting response), preparing the body for imminent action. When people control characters in interactive games, their experience is one of *taking action*, not just evaluating whether they might be interested. Knowing that you can change what happens in the virtual world gives a sense of power that keeps people engaged.

A greater sense of contingency could do wonders at work by increasing the sense that people are using technology to *act* on their environment rather than merely respond to it. Things you build, places you choose to be, conversations that hinge on your input—all of these actions increase the sense of being in the world created by the games.

Interactive Intelligence

Interactivity may be so important that it deserves its own designation of intelligence—for games and at work. At the least, interactive intelligence will include basic familiarity with interactive interfaces. Those who excel will have the best access to new entertainment technology, and when at work will be in the best position to exploit the most innovative business tools. But interactive *social* intelligence means even more. Some claim, much to the chagrin of professorial colleagues, that the ability to interact creatively and fluidly in real time is as important or even more important than traditional language abilities such as reading and writing. Interactive intelligence may be the new liberal art of the twenty-first century.[19]

When you're in the games recruiting, organizing, evaluating, coordinating, or arguing, you're also learning how to interact, and it's not always as easy as face-to-face encounters. These are skills that benefit from practice, and games fit the bill as primary places where that practice occurs.

Vividness and Interactivity Considered Together

The two dimensions of presence, vividness and interactivity, can be combined to make a useful map of media. The dot experiment at the beginning of the chapter described a game that was low on vividness (no interesting pictures) but high on interactivity (good response to player input). The opposite of that experience might be a high-definition, large-screen movie experience—great pictures but you don't determine how the experience unfolds. The interesting combinations, of course, are examples that are high on each dimension, and that's where games shine.

Where should you spend your money if you can't afford to do well on both dimensions? There's a debate about which of the dimensions is most important for maximizing the entertainment value of games, and there are good arguments on both sides. Some say bring on the great pictures and sounds, whereas others prefer interactive strength, particularly good narrative and many opportunities to change how stories unfold. The easiest conclusion is that you do best with both and that this will apply to games at work just as it does to entertainment. Now, let's look a bit closer at the story about pictures.

Pictures Versus Words

There are great games that are totally dependent on words—no pictures, no gold pieces, no 3D environments—epitomized by the multiplayer games called MUDs (multiuser dungeons), which were played on early computer networks when the flashing green cursor on a monochrome CRT was the user interface.[20] Without using any pictures, MUDs managed to invoke many of the psychological elements of currently popular games, delivered via exchanges of text among players and the computer code. All successful recent games, however, enjoy the benefit of great pictures. It's certainly true that one can be moved to tears by a great book and be totally bored in a 3D virtual world, but it's also true that words and pictures have different capabilities with respect to creating a sense of presence.

The difference between pictures and words is as simple as a sentence versus a facial expression. Consider this sentence versus a picture of the same face: "He had a broad smile, ear to ear, but his eyes were pointed down, signaling a bit of shyness." Beyond mere preference, there are important psychological differences. Processing the words requires effort to translate arbitrary symbols to a mental image (i.e., to go from the letters on the page to the picture of the face in your mind). When you read, your brain is working harder and it depends on a fair bit of training. You're also more in control of the processing; you control the pace at which you take in the information and you decide if it needs a second look.

Processing the picture is different. First, no instruction is necessary. Even aboriginal tribes who have never seen modern media have little trouble deciding what to make of pictures.[21] Less mental effort is required to figure out what's going on. Social information is broadly available, and emotional extremes are much easier to communicate (just crank the smile up a notch).

It's easy to say there's a place for both words *and* pictures, but it's also hard to ignore the imbalance between them that exists in modern media. Pictures rule! With significant improvements in television, film, computing, and personal digital devices, pictures now dominate everything from advertising to politics to news to entertainment. The word industries—publishing and newspapers in particular—are in decline.[22]

An explanation for the dominance of pictures is the sense, however accurate, of psychological presence they convey. People trust television news more than newspapers because they feel they can see the people and events themselves.[23] People forgo the book for a movie because they feel more engaged by the faces and places compared with what it would take to process the same narrative in words. This feeds right into why multiplayer games are successful and why those experiences are shaping the gamer generation to be a pictorial one.

Like all aspects of our thesis about games and work, this conclusion points to a disruption that games will cause more than to something that is inherently good. The details of harnessing that reality to better organize and increase productivity still need work.

A Century-Long Trend: Personalization of Media Experiences Increases Presence

Games fit a trend in the development of media that's been unfolding for the last hundred years—that of *personalizing* experiences even though audiences are massive. Twelve million people can play an MMO, but each person has a personal experience. How does that work?

Among those who study communication, there used to be a crisp distinction between interpersonal communication and mass communication. Interpersonal experiences were real, face-to-face, communal, tightly controlled by the participants, and involved subjective feelings. Mass communication was unreal, impersonal, loosely regulated, and mostly rational, because mass media were assumed to be less personally consequential. These differences have actually been blurring for some time.[24] The history of media personalization is captured by milestones such as individualized mass mailings ("How did they know my name?"), advertising appeals that have changed from rational ("Here's the evidence") to emotional ("You'll smile too"), and news broadcasts that are more concerned with convincing an audience member they're part of a conversation than with delivering facts.

One goal of modern media presentations is to conceal audience size. No one will feel special if they're reminded that they're just one in a million. To maximize personalization, media must make people feel unique, and one way to do that is to engage them in one-to-one interactions that at least *appear* personal, even if the reality is that there are millions of identical interactions occurring simultaneously.

There's a book of tricks to help with this disguise. Most important, be sincere. Anything sophisticated and rehearsed will remind people that the experience was authored without their input. Presentations should be extemporaneous, casual, and cool. Good examples are reality programs and call-in shows, and any personality who is able to engage each viewer as if they were the only one in the audience. John Madden, Mister Rogers, and Bill Clinton come to mind.

Games may be the epitome of mass communication that is experienced interpersonally. When you first enter a typical MMO, a character walks up to you and invites you *personally* to enter the place where your first quest will be explained. It's classic one-on-one engagement. Every ingredient in the recipe for success is directed at a single player (my character, my level, my virtual goods, my bank account), even though the computer code by which the personalization is achieved is identical for everyone.

Games turn up the volume on familiar and contemporary methods for engaging audiences. Games are reality and call-in shows taken to an extreme. There should be a serious treatment of the ethical boundaries for these interactions. When is it all right to trick people into engagement that they might not otherwise give? The methods are now on the table for all to observe and use. Because it will not be possible to ban them from the workplace, the only choice is to use them fairly and productively. We deal with questions such as this in chapter 11.

Other Evidence That Games Produce Real Responses

Any extended discussion about the effects of games on business productivity will inevitably bump into an extensive literature about the effects of games on social behavior. That literature helps make the case that games are powerful rather than inherently good or bad. Much of the difference is simply attributable to game content. If there's a lot of shooting and killing, negative consequences are more likely. But powerful effects are also attributable to features of the games that are more difficult to peg as positive or negative—for example, an addiction to play that might occur in some *prosocial* games.

This section presents the major categories of effects that should be expected when people spend time with games. We recommend it as a watch list as business experiments are conducted and products are developed for games at work. This evidence could help to keep an implementation on target and critics constructively engaged. We start with the bad stuff and build toward the positive.

Aggression

Much of the concern about games is about violence. The research is pretty clear that playing violent games can increase aggression. Across thirty-two studies, there was a significant relationship between spending time with violent game content and levels of aggression generally.[25] The biggest effects were on aggressive thoughts (listing more aggressive thoughts after playing, and quicker and better memory for those thoughts after play). Violent game play also increases aggressive feelings (self-reports of general hostility and anger) as well as aggressive behavior (willingness to behave in an aggressive fashion and acceptance of such behavior as appropriate).

All games are not created equally, however, with respect to effects on aggression. The most recent titles are the ones that show the biggest effects, confirming the stereotype that games are getting more violent and that violent presentations are more compelling. It's hard to imagine delivering the second, third, or even tenth edition of a game that *reduces* a previously successful bad-boy allure. A bright spot in this literature is that effects do habituate over time, such that after considerable regular play aggression diminishes.[26]

As is true for all research on media effects, however, it's a challenge to study aggression and games. The causal influence of games may be overestimated because aggressively inclined players may seek out the games as much as the other way around. But it's just as likely that the effects may be underestimated because it's difficult to follow people over extended time periods to see how prolonged exposure influences longer-term behavior. Our summary is that effects on aggression do exist, although the effect sizes are small.

None of these results, of course, mean that business uses of games are destined to produce an aggressive workforce. There would likely be few, if any, effects on aggression if the games did not include explicit aggressive portrayals. The effects of games can be summarized as "You are what eat." Trying to beat your colleagues to the finish line of a business game that requires persuasive influence recorded by the accumulation of gold pieces probably doesn't count as aggressive behavior. You'd have to be slicing and dicing them along the way pretty explicitly.

Arousal

We've already said that emotional experience, including physical arousal, is an important component of play. Arousal does increase during game play, with benefits to engagement, attention, and even learning. But there are specific studies about games and arousal that are worth noting because they add to the previous discussion about aggression. Research here is consistent: game play, and especially violent play, increases arousal as measured by methods such as accelerated heart rate and specific patterns of brain activation.

Arousal effects from violent shooting games, for example, are strong but short lived, and they are attached to specific events in the game. Annie Lang at Indiana University found that shooting other characters in a first-person game increased arousal substantially, and the arousal actually increased over the course of a play session.[27] Virtual killing isn't the only source of arousal, however. The same study showed even higher levels of arousal for stalking (peeking around corners looking for bad guys), but that response declined during the play sessions. So the excitement of the hunt fades, but the shooting keeps you juiced. Another study found increases in heart rate during play (with a return to normal fifteen minutes afterward).[28] Another found a greater increase in arousal for women than men, possibly because for women the violent play was more novel.[29]

There are also neurobiological effects of game play that show cortical arousal. One study found evidence of dopamine release during game play.[30] Dopamine has some effects similar to adrenaline, and its presence can be a precursor to aggressive behavior. But dopamine is also important in attention, learning, and motor activity, so a better conclusion from the research is that game play has the ability to change the chemical processes in the brain in favor of increased sensitivity to a range of pleasures and pain.

A more recent study using brain scans during game play did a better job of linking brain responses to specific game content. Violent instances in the games immediately increased activation in the emotion centers of the brain, revealing that violent game play creates brain responses linked to aggressive behavior.[31] Those same brain responses, however, could just as easily be caused by prosocial or benign portrayals, another reminder that arousal is the basis of motivation regardless of whether it produces good or bad thoughts and behavior.

Addiction

Worries about addiction are common, especially for adolescent boys, and we believe this effect will be equally prominent when game critics voice objections to companies taking unfair advantage of people's natural attraction to something too compelling to ignore. What if workers have *too* much fun, so much so that their play could be fairly labeled a clinical addiction?

There are many uses of the term *addiction*, starting with casual self-description, and it's true that many gamers do say they're hooked. A running survey of gamers compiled by Nick Yee has asked over ten thousand players to agree or disagree with the following sentence: "I would consider myself addicted to the game."[32] On average, about half of respondents under the age of twenty-two agreed with the statement; surprisingly, females agreed quite a bit more (67 percent) than males (47 percent). The addiction self-description wasn't limited to youth, either. A little less than half of respondents over thirty-five agreed they were addicted, with females slightly higher (48 percent) than males (41 percent).

What does it mean to volunteer that you're addicted to media? The term *addiction* is probably overused in popular culture, often standing in for "I really like this" and often applied to benign objects and experiences from hit songs to Chapstick. What would a true physical addiction look like?

Here's what the *Diagnostic Manual* of the American Psychiatric Association (APA) says to look for when making a formal diagnosis: spending a great deal of time using a substance; using it more often than one intends; thoughts about reducing use; repeated unsuccessful efforts to reduce use; giving up social, family, and occupational activities to use; and withdrawal symptoms when you stop.[33] Most often, these questions are put to those at risk because of alcohol, drugs, or gambling. But they're intriguing with respect to games. The APA says that more research is necessary before it will list a specific diagnosis of "video game addiction," but it's easy to imagine that several people would say "yes" to the questions that are the basis for similar diagnoses.[34]

New research is pursuing a physical model of addiction applied to games. Habit-forming drugs cause more dependence when they leave the body quickly than when they wear off slowly because the user is more aware of the change. It's in part that awareness that perpetuates continued use. There's some evidence that media might work the same way.[35] If researchers interrupt a person watching a good television show, that person reports feelings of involvement and relaxation. The same question asked immediately *after* viewing gets responses of increased stress (a return to real life). Our take is that we will have to adjust thinking about addiction to encompass electronic media, but the similarity to substance abuse is at least suggestive. The caution for games at work is worth noting.

Gender Stereotyping

Games today are predominantly made by men about men and made for men to play. Men play more different games, they play them longer, and they're the main characters in the most popular titles.[36] Consequently, so the theory goes, this entire media niche is primed to generate inaccurate stereotypes about gender.

Gender content in games is indeed skewed. In one recent survey of interactive games, 64 percent of the characters were male.[37] And that doesn't mean the rest were female—19 percent of the characters had no explicit gender. On average, the ratio of male versus female appearances was 4:1 across all of the titles, a ratio even more biased toward males if you look only at player-controlled characters. And most of the stereotypes about the portrayals hold up well: females are thin, sexy, and young, as opposed to hypermasculinized warriors and rescuers of females in distress.

The data on use of games is equally tilted toward males. The most popular MMO games (medieval and outer space themes) have 80 percent or more male subscribers who spend several hours more per week in the worlds than females.[38] There's evidence that gender disparity is changing (one top title has gone from 10 percent to 20 percent females over the last three years), but the ratios are less extreme when you move from the game worlds to virtual worlds. Virtual worlds provide the infrastructure for whatever interactions people prefer (socializing, listening to music, touring virtual spaces, trading virtual goods), and the gender balance may be almost equal.[39]

The concern, voiced by parents, teachers, and even the Federal Communications Commission, is that the bias in portrayals and differences in exposure time will lead to undesirable ideas about gender in real life.[40] Gender effects are as difficult to study as those for aggression (i.e., do men hold gender stereotypes and as a result seek stereotyped content, or does the content cause their attitudes to change?), but there is a growing literature, particularly with respect to children, that finds support for the conclusion that games can alter how people view gender.[41]

One reason it's tough to do studies of gender bias in games is that it's hard to prove a link between the values learned in the game and the application of those values outside of the game. An ingenious study by Edward Castronova solved this by looking at how players valued male versus female characters in one particular virtual game world.[42] No questionnaires were used. Rather, the *price* of male and female avatars was compared. When players train avatars, they increase in value, and that value is priced when players sell their avatars for real dollars on various auction websites that allow trading in virtual people and goods. In this case, female avatars were selling for $40 to $55 less than their male counterparts—even though the avatars had the same capabilities in the fantasy world of Norrath.

Our summary is that whatever biases exist in the real world can be found in games, and possibly even more so given the gender imbalance that exists now in portrayals and exposure. One solution, critically important as the games migrate to the world of work, is to make sure that the same protections, laws, and sensibilities designed to mitigate this bias are applied in-game as carefully and fairly as they are in real life.

Health

Health effects of games also straddle the negative and positive. The negative focus has mostly been on adolescent couch potatoes and obesity, and there's good evidence that media do contribute to obesity, although clear responsibility has not been pegged specifically to games.[43] It's hard to imagine, however, that there haven't been a few outdoor activities missed because of a guild raid that lasted longer than planned.

An extremely rare but high-consequence connection of games to physical health is the potential for a seizure disorder to be triggered by specific visual features of game play. The seizures are visually induced (i.e., they are responses to the depiction of sudden movement and color, and are possibly connected to the electronic refresh rates of digital screens). These can occur even when people merely watch the games being played, although the effects increase when people actually take the controls for themselves.[44] These are not the effects of games per se, because most media have the same visual features that induce the seizures.

Less rare is a particular type of visual disorientation called simulator sickness. This occurs when the information streams to your brain from your eyes and inner ear disagree (the picture says you're falling over, but your balance center reports no physical movement to your brain). The U.S. Army Research Institute estimated that this effect occurs for almost half of the military pilots who use flight simulators.[45] For gamers, the frequency may be less (although most reports are anecdotal), but the influence seems to increase the closer you sit to the screen and for bigger (and especially wider) screens that fill your field of vision.

On a happier note, there is substantial new interest in using games to promote healthy choices and to solve important health problems. The general logic is the same as for games at work: higher engagement leads to more influential participation in behavior change. For children, games have produced better communication and self-awareness about diabetes and asthma, leading to a 77 percent drop in emergency room visits.[46] Major new health games are under way as the government and foundations begin funding new projects.[47]

One of the authors began his study of games by producing commercial software to support lifestyle changes related to diet and exercise back when desktop personal computing was just getting started in the 1980s. That software employed many current game sensibilities, such as characters with personalities and feedback in multiple time scales, including durations of weeks and months needed to practice new behaviors. Although it wasn't formally evaluated, users of this program reported meaningful benefits.[48] Games and virtual environments have also had positive therapeutic outcomes in contexts from chemotherapy to psychotherapy, as biofeedback training for attention deficit therapy, as treatment for phobias ranging from fear of snakes to public speaking, and as memory training for seniors.[49]

Spatial and Cognitive Abilities—and Grades

The most obvious games at work will involve strategies, role playing, and team collaboration. That is, there will not be as many "twitch" games that rely on perfectly timed hand-eye coordination, even if that type of play is used occasionally. There's little doubt, however, that experience with fast-paced games, especially those that require vigilance in stalking and exploring, do affect real-world attention.

One excellent experiment had people play the popular army action game *Medal of Honor* for one hour for ten days. Compared with those who played *Tetris* (a purely geometric hand-eye game) for the same time period, those playing the action game showed significant improvement in their ability to identify objects and to sustain visual attention.[50] This type of result has been evidence enough for the military to depend on games such as *America's Army* for recruiting and soldier training. The even fancier military simulators, of course, are the ultimate reality experiences, as evidenced by the excited and sweating service members who exit battle tanks, ships, and aircraft where participation was entirely virtual.[51]

Participation in any type of 3D world can also increase spatial reasoning abilities. For example, as game time increases, elementary and middle school children are better able to perform mental rotation tasks (i.e., to imagine what a shape would look like if one viewed it from behind), and the improvement occurs equally for boys and girls.[52] Games also provide an advantage in interpreting scientific information from graphs, measured either by correlating that ability with what people experience naturally or imposing games on them during a laboratory experiment.[53]

The results regarding grades are even more of a stereotype buster. Although complaints to Congress and admonitions from pastors and politicians are still common, there's good evidence that games don't deserve the bad rap.[54] Several studies found that playing games is related to better, not worse, grades, as long as playing time wasn't off-the-charts high.

Regardless of the specific grades that teenagers receive, playing games is also a good route to a technology major and eventual career. High school students were asked what informal learning experiences were most responsible for launching interests that persisted in college and beyond. For computer science majors, the number one influence was games, but unfortunately it was mentioned far less often for boys than girls.[55] A survey of MIT undergraduates showed that 75 percent were still playing video games all through college and were much more invested in games than in television, film, or books.[56]

With appropriate caution about those *over*invested in games, this is more good ammunition against arguments that games will dumb down a business.

Sociability

The stereotype of black-clad loners sitting in windowless rooms substituting trivial game chat for real relationships may need as much adjusting as that for games' effects on academic achievement. As mentioned in chapter 2, social relationships are a prime reason to be engaged in MMOs, and although the relationships are indeed mediated by avatars on a computer screen and are rarely face-to-face, they are still substantial. There's not much evidence that young people who play games do so just to stay home alone or to avoid social interaction with their peers, although instances of each are of concern.

Social interaction in MMOs is integral to game play, and not merely a byproduct of it. Although the content of conversations can sound strange to the uninitiated ("Watch out for the orc on your left!"), they are also fundamentally similar to interpersonal relationships in real life. Many who participate in the games view the social interactions as merely another way to connect with friends. A Pew Internet and American Life study of undergraduate students in American universities found that multiplayer games were integrated into established relationships (for example, a dorm floor might create a guild) at least as much as they were used to connect with new people.[57]

Several studies, most with high school and college students, show little cause for general concern about social isolation. Frequency of game play isn't related to popularity in school, but it is related to better self-evaluations of mechanical and computer skills, more family closeness, and greater attachment to school.[58] Players also help each other often with game strategies, which improves social and communication skills.[59]

Much of the conversation in games, like a lot of talk in real life, is casual. That's especially true for social content, such as sharing personal backgrounds and interests that occur in and around talk about game strategy. But it's also true that the game environments support deeper relationships. Nick Yee's online survey of thousands of gamers asked people to agree or disagree with the statement that "some of my friends in the game are comparable to or better than my real-life friends." Roughly half of the players of all ages agreed, with interesting gender differences for older players. For women over age thirty-five, 62 percent agreed, compared with 35 percent of men.[60] There are also countless anecdotes about in-game marriages, parents playing with their children, and real-life rendezvous and parties that begin in the games. The games are serious social places.

As with the other effects described here, sociability results can be encouraging or discouraging. Our conclusion is that it's tilted more positively in the research than in popular anecdotes. As popularity and familiarity increase, games are looking like convenient and engaging venues for social interaction—more like the mall and the street corner than a weird hangout for the severely introverted.

Summary

Taken together, the research evidence about how games engage via media is encouraging when applied to the world of work. Games succeed for many of the same reasons interactions do in real life: they attract attention, create social connections, and give people opportunities to gauge themselves relative to others. Importantly, games allow people to develop and hone communication abilities that other technologies replace and that travel expenses may preclude. What makes this possible is that media engage people in ways that are also true in real life.

We've now argued that play is substantial rather than frivolous, and that media are quite capable of representing serious interactions in spite of their entertainment specialties. We've also identified effects of games that are sometimes more positive than the stereotype suggests. However, there is still no guarantee that the *idea* of work as a game will succeed merely because the general thesis is provocative.

Meet Vinnie. He's struggling with the trade-offs between good and bad uses of games at work.

Chapter Eleven

Danger

MEET VINNIE (IF YOU CARE TO)

Gliding into his sling-backed game chaise, Vinnie can't believe that only three months ago he used to sit at a desk trying to keep track of a dozen video screens with nothing more than a walkie-talkie and a phone to summon response. Long before his first coffee break, his eyes had glazed over with the peculiar kind of boredom that comes from a task that is impossibly difficult because it is so easy. Watching for evildoers in an endless stream of ordinary people doing ordinary things would be unbearable if it weren't for the absurd surprises involving noses, underwear, or, occasionally, heavy petting.

Here at Rangefinders, work is different. Vinnie's three seventy-minute shifts go by so quickly that he would have no idea of the passage of time if it weren't for the achy numbness in the middle of his right palm and the vague nausea that follows so many trips up and down the adrenaline escalator. Vinnie only has one screen now—but what a screen. He can see his Guy and all of the Goodguys on his team, looking buff as always, standing and moving around in the cavernous Main Concourse of Grand Central Terminal, along with the Tourists. His Goodguys call everyone in the vids Tourists, whether they are just that or commuters on the way upstairs for a day of skyscraper work or the cleaning people or cops on the beat—or potential Badguys.

It's a shame the Tourists can't see his Guy (or anyone else on his team), because the flashy fedora he earned in yesterday's action is looking spiffy. Vinnie will never figure out how the geeks managed to merge his teams' avatars into the picture of what is happening in real life and right now on the Tenessee marble floor in the Concourse, but if they could paint that yellow first-down line on the football field without getting it on the players backs, anything's possible. The damn thing is, they can also keep those Badguys popping up often enough to bring on the familiar numbness in his shooting hand. Badguys come in all flavors. The easy ones are goofy evil twins of his Goodguy teammates, with all of the hyped-up color chosen by his less circumspect teammates. Not worth a lot of Numbers when you shoot them, but still fun. Other Badguys look a lot like the Tourists, so you have to think hard before you shoot. But shoot you must, for if a Badguy makes it into the train tunnels or out to the street with so much as a backpack or a box lunch or a fever, you are going to lose some serious Numbers on the big board.

Some of the Badguys are more challenging. Although every figure on the screen is just pixels and polygons, some of them were born in a very fast computer. The digital pictures representing most of the Tourists are from the actual cameras in the wainscots and Sky Ceiling. The most challenging Badguys of all are assholes working for Rangefinders (or its client agency) who try to blend in on the floor in front of those cameras, and whose only mission in life seems to be to cause his team of Goodguys to lose Numbers by giving them the slip. Rumor is that when Vinnie levels up, he'll get to spend time walking that floor and screwing the other teams. Can't wait. In fact, getting Badguys and getting ahead of the other teams is about all Vinnie thinks about when he's not paranoid about his own team's progress.

Vinnie isn't sure how many of the Goodguys on his team are guys at all, because everyone sits somewhere else. In the chat channel on his screen, a couple seem to talk like chicks, and one might even be a bot. Those profiles are exposed mostly in the pre-briefs and after-actions. It's part of the Rangefinders story that you can't trust everyone. On the other hand, if you don't trust anyone, you can't put any Numbers up, because a lot of the action is handing off suspicious characters from Goodguys in one sector to another.

Another reason it's a little hard to be sure everyone is on the same side is because accidents happen. When you screw up and shoot a Goodguy, the wounds look really ugly and it costs you Numbers on the big board. And if you shoot a Tourist, the geeks give you another gory look-see that costs you even more Numbers. Not because Tourists actually get hurt, but because Rangefinder's client has to put boots on the floor and have a little close-up look or a chat with your Tourist. You obviously thought he was a Badguy, so how else would they translate your hard work in the game chaise into making life safe for the real Midtowners? Boot-time on the floor costs real money, so they ding you and your team for crying wolf. But nothing costs Goodguys Numbers as much as letting Badguys out of the house. In the daily pre-brief, Vinnie and the team always talk about fine-tuning the balance between the two kinds of screwups: shooting Tourists versus missing Badguys.

Good Versus Powerful

As far as we know, video surveillance at Grand Central Terminal is still carried out with the conventional technology you can buy at your local electronics supermarket—cameras showing pictures of real people on screens in a security room that has radio links between those watching the screens and officers on the ground. You can't play Vinnie's game yet, but there's nothing technically impossible about the scenario. It would be a game *design* challenge, to be sure, but Vinnie's game already looks a lot like ideas we've sketched out for a large systems integrator in the military and security business. We will come back to Vinnie and his augmented-reality game shortly because it combines our game ingredients in a scenario that is so engaging that it raises important questions about ethical applications of games at work.

By now, you're quite aware of our thesis that the psychological power of games can be applied with the objective of improving productivity for employers and job satisfaction for employees. But it may not always work out that way. Games are not interesting for business because they are inherently good. They're interesting because they're powerful. One of us has spent a good part of his career building and investing in biotechnology companies where the platform technologies were more likely to be useful if they could also be dangerous. Put another way, tools that are powerfully useful, such as fire, nuclear fission, human touch, and, of course, *words*, can also be abused or cause accidental damage. The psychological power of games and the ways it is deployed can have positive and negative consequences for players (and others), and this chapter is about setting the stage to get it right.

Let's start with the impact on employees. The goal may be to design rich environments in which employees experience personal growth as they make meaningful contributions. There are several ways this could go awry. At the highest level, some will be concerned that the powerful potential for work redesign will increase the risk of treating employees as a means to an end and in ways that don't give people sufficient control or autonomy. There is a potential for very successful game environments at work to produce the kind of addictive behaviors that are known to occur with some people using some entertainment games. Stress levels, useful up to a point in creating arousal and attention, can cause diminishing productivity and actual harm at high levels. Games may be designed in ways that depersonalize the workplace and cause isolation rather than connectedness. Physical inactivity and repetitive stress syndromes may also occur as the designs get better. All of these can be mitigated if the issues are kept in mind from the beginning.

We aren't trained in moral philosophy, as professional ethicists often describe their formal discipline. We offer the thoughts in this chapter to stimulate thinking by such experts and by you so that the field we envision can develop with the fewest unpleasant surprises and rare instances of harm. A classic textbook on business ethics offers one pragmatic approach to thinking about choices in business that involve right and wrong.[1] To see if there may be an ethical dimension to a decision, its authors suggest asking the following questions:

- Are any laws likely to be broken?

- Is there a violation of fairness in the action?

- Are anyone's rights being violated?

- Are there any negative consequences from the action?

The answers to these interrelated questions are then examined with respect to who is affected, how serious the effects are, and what exactly is the cause of each effect.

We'll stipulate that in modern enterprises we can rely on the lawyers to be on the lookout for illegal activities in deploying games at work and move on from there. The issue of fairness in games at work is exceedingly interesting because well-designed games with clear rules can be an island of equity in a real-life world that is often tragically and fundamentally unjust. This can be as true for the game of checkers as well as a complex MMO, but the more complex the game, the more likely it is that some players will feel that they have been disadvantaged by objectionable design choices. MMO players have been known to voice such concerns with great energy on collateral websites and blogs, and directly with publishers, who must decide when and how much to adjust to demands.

Poor design of games at work will offer numerous opportunities to violate what are widely regarded as basic employee rights. For example, games represent an extreme example of work design that incorporates electronic monitoring. Every play in the game is via a computer and available for storage and later analysis. Players already make great use of MMO player logs, for example, in high-level raiding parties where second-by-second damage taken and given is recorded, exported to independent websites, and analyzed by guild members to see how each member performed and how he or she can do better. This monitoring is a key enabler of the DKP systems reviewed in chapter 7. This isn't new. There are already a number of occupations where worker behavior and output is measured second by second, such as call center agents and machine operators working in tandem with highly automated processes. Breaks for personal activities, for example, can be charted with exquisite precision.

Electronic monitoring has a clear potential to violate the legitimate privacy rights of employees. Determining what privacy expectations are appropriate for supervisors and coworkers in voluntary compensated employment is complicated. But even after accounting for the right of employers to measure and supervise the work they compensate, the residual privacy expectations of employees could be vulnerable to new and extensive monitoring available in games. In 1987, the Congressional Office of Technology Assessment (OTA) published a detailed analysis of electronic monitoring with lessons relevant to the discussion here, and there was a flurry of literature on the subject in the following decade.[2]

Our focus here is not the stumbles that will come from game efforts that are merely silly or dreadful. Here we consider the potential for real and sometimes subtle harm that may come from the best and most powerful implementations. We will explore ethical issues further by taking a deeper look at Vinnie's game.

Vinnie's Game

We think that jobs such as video surveillance will attract early applications of game technology because they epitomize work that's too easy to do well for extended periods. Jay Walker, the founder of Priceline.com, proposed a distributed game for surveillance of critical infrastructure in 2003 that used a primitive set of game ingredients to encourage participation.[3] Walker's proposal suggests that people are most likely to push the limits of game psychology in settings where much is at stake. Luis van Ahn has proposed something similar for baggage screening.[4] In the case of government efforts against terrorism, the Transportation Security Administration has already decided that it's worth inconveniencing good people millions of times a day in an attempt to make airline travel more secure.

Vinnie's hypothetical security game incorporates all of the ingredients in chapter 4. It would run on a high-end server that integrates actual video camera feeds of the building being watched with computer-generated avatars and objects. The result is a hybrid virtual environment in which surveillance guards carry out real work with a combination of real and virtual information. Some are already calling this a "mixed-reality" or "augmented-reality" game. The only hard technical challenge is the ability to insert life-like human characters into real-time scenes so that the player-guards have difficulty distinguishing real humans carrying out suspicious activity from computer-generated suspicious characters. This is important because it allows the game designer to provide frequent opportunities for the player-guards to react and make decisions.

The quick pace of decisions and related feedback will transform a job that is impossibly boring into an ultra-high-engagement activity. The task of a surveillance guard is to spot potential problems so that additional steps can be taken, usually by an in-person inspection of a suspicious person or object. Actual evildoers are thankfully rare, because it costs serious money to escalate surveillance (e.g., closing an airport or delaying a flight to further examine a bag). Managers must help guards navigate between overlooking danger and crying wolf. By tuning the feedback and reward system in a high-frequency game such as Vinnie's, behavior can be adjusted to the right balance between the two errors. In our estimation, we're barely two generations of computers away from having the graphic chip capacity to do this on high-end consumer machines.

Let's go through the game ingredients one by one and consider some ethical questions that might arise in the design and deployment of Vinnie's game. We think of these as research questions that need to be addressed eventually, or a checklist of issues to be managed, rather than as reasons not to proceed.

1. Avatars

Vinnie plays his game by controlling an avatar he customized himself to look tough and strong, now decorated with insignia that represent his accomplishments in the game. Because the avatar represents design choices that (he hopes) will be seen by other players, the exposure doesn't represent much of a privacy threat to him. But what if he chooses a look for his avatar that is offensive—for example, exaggerated gender or racial motifs? Vinnie has a personal responsibility to make good choices about how he presents himself in the game, but do the developers or the employers who support the game also bear responsibility to set limits? (We mentioned IBM's first draft of avatar guidelines in chapter 5.) Furthermore, might the magic of self-representation in this new media work so well that Vinnie somehow loses some of himself to the virtual guy he spends so much time directing in the game? What does that mean and is it bad for him or others?

2. Three-Dimensional Environments

Highly committed gamers seem to move between their 3D worlds and ours without serious orientation problems. If the designers do a really good job of blending virtual and real video as imagined in this mixed-reality game, there is the potential that Vinnie will transfer some of his highly rehearsed game instincts to the real world. Will he start imagining bad guys around every corner as he walks home from work? A lot of people take their work home in unwelcome ways. A great mixed-reality game may amplify the experience.

3. Narrative Context

For a security guard trying to prevent an actual terrorist attack that could kill or maim, we are comfortable embedding work in a story line that includes violence and aggression, compared with applications in which less mayhem is at stake. A narrative and play action based on shooting realistically simulated bad guys may be very effective in a surveillance context. Even so, there's a possibility that desired behavior inside the game could engender aggressive or violent tendencies outside of it. Possible negative effects can and should be studied as part of early efforts to deploy games such as Vinnie's that are designed around player-versus-player (PVP) competition and combat. Fortunately, games at work can borrow from successful story lines and play action *not* based on violence that are the basis of at least some of the top games. The potential problem of managing aggression among off-duty soldiers or police is certainly not unique to games, and there is a potential for good cross-fertilization on mitigation ideas.

4. Feedback

The designers of Vinnie's game will want to get the positive reinforcement systems just right so that he receives feedback on how he's doing in every relevant time scale: not just frequently, but very frequently, at long intervals, and everything in between. Because the idea is to transform an impossibly boring observation task into a high-frequency twitch game (by giving him lots of simulated bad guys that force lots of choices), the feedback structure could be modeled on highly successful first-person-shooter games. Sports, driving, and chase game genres could also serve as models. There is abundant evidence that this is doable, based on the behavior of players in such games.

We also know that when there is such an exquisite match between the reinforcement structure and a player's response, people sometimes hurt themselves operating the game. Shooting, sports, driving, and chase games have all been associated with repetitive stress injuries of the extremities in conditions termed "Nintindenitis," first described in 1990 (in the *New England Journal of Medicine*, no less), or more recently, "Wiitis."[5] You could argue that keyboard and input design is the culprit in these physical injuries, and there is certainly room for improvement in the physical user interface of games. We think a driving force for the injurious behavior is a well-tuned feedback structure in which designers have failed to provide mitigation in the form of rest periods and other respite in the larger mechanics of the game.

Nonphysical stress is also a side effect of accentuating feedback. Just as there are a host of factors causing conventional job-related emotional stress, so too a broad array of game ingredients could contribute to stress. We are particularly impressed with the power of feedback structures (combined with time pressure) to drive both good and bad consequences. Vinnie's ride "up and down the adrenaline escalator" is the way many gamers describe their experiences. Great media experiences are often roller-coaster rides (or at least undulations) of emotional and physiological stress, so it is unlikely that there will be obvious reference points for what is all right and not all right to design into games. People also differ in their susceptibility to simulated thrills. The problem isn't that the feedback is "too good," it's that powerful feedback must be embedded in a context that is healthy overall.

Rather than looking for limits within games, we will need to focus on the consequences of inviting employees to ride too hard. We already know that reinforcement in games can be cranked up to a point at which some people become addicted. We'll know we have trouble when players start to show the classic signs of any other addiction: loss of quality in personal relationships and health-related problems. But unlike chemical dependency and other classic addictive behavior, work performance may be unimpaired or even exceptional. Evidence of susceptibility to game addiction might somewhere even be the criterion for hiring people for certain jobs in the future. That would be bad.

5. Reputations, Ranks, and Levels

Everyone in Vinnie's game would be able to see his prowess in spotting Badguys, but they'd also know about his amazing screwups. Many employers are careful not to publicize individual performance feedback, especially when it's based on subjective evaluations, because it exposes them to charges of slander or libel if the employee thinks the opinion is unfair. But is it improper to post *objective* performance statistics that are clearly related to productivity or accuracy? On a tour of the USS Forrestal years ago, one of us was impressed with the painfully objective data posted on the "greenie board" in the pilot ready room. It showed the Landing Signal Officer's rating for every landing for every officer on the cruise. The 1987 OTA report raised questions (but doesn't answer) about employee morale, job stress, and performance when the results of electronic monitoring are shared.[6]

Data about individual performance is a mainstay in successful entertainment games, where everyone has opted in and the family income is not at stake. At work, the same powerful systems will need to be deployed thoughtfully. Based on what we have seen in the games, we come down on the side of high transparency when ratings are objective or otherwise fair.

6. Marketplaces and Economies

As with today's best MMOs, Vinnie's game will surely include a vibrant economy where worker-players can exchange virtual goods and currency. As described in chapter 6, when players depend on others and need to trade to advance, games create great interest in collaboration. These systems are "sticky" in that they tend to sustain long-term engagement in the game because value earned in one time period can be stored and enjoyed in the future.

Richly detailed economies with lots of things that can and must be traded are a main reason why players are anxious to create content. People know how to use real money, so they are well equipped to think about play money. Games within games will arise, and there is the possibility that economic speculation and other financial sport might distract from the real work that the game was intended to advance. Employers will be concerned if their game encourages rogue entrepreneurs like Joseph Heller's Milo Minderbinder, whose business interests subverted the Army Air Force's mission in *Catch-22*. The high level of transparency in game economies can discourage such behavior, especially if the right people are watching. On the other hand, transparency raises privacy questions for people playing legitimately. For example, a very good game design might permit players who are weak at one particular game or work skill to nevertheless progress in the game because they can compensate by "buying" credit for those skills in the game marketplace by trading value they have earned with their better skills. This ability to compensate for weakness is potentially very efficient but might be embarrassing if its use is transparent to others.

7. Rules That Are Explicit and Enforced

For Vinnie, the rules provide both boundaries and goals, and they define the pathway by which he achieves his aspirations. Great games offer important insights into how to set goals for employees. As subscription businesses, MMOs have finessed the concept of "how to win" into a desire for sustained winning behavior because they don't want satiated winners to leave the game. If designers of games for work get the other ingredients right, engagement will follow and people will deliver results shaped by the rules.

It's important to get the rules right, but that's easier said than done. In a richly complex game in which players are expected to optimize progress on multiple attributes, this can lead to wildly unanticipated consequences. People will test the limits of game rules, just as they do with office hours, parking places, and expense reports. When they find a loophole in the game, word will spread quickly, and the game owners will need to adjust and maybe even negotiate a solution with the community. Straight-arrow employees who do not exploit defects may feel unfairly treated.

8. Teams

As with many real-world tasks, Vinnie's surveillance work is largely a solo performance that nevertheless requires coordination with others. When suspicious characters leave his zone, he must be able to hand off his observations to guards watching the next sector without wasting their time or dropping the ball. A game design that amplifies the sense of teamwork is smart because it can facilitate mutual encouragement and coaching.

Games offer many new tools to assemble and motivate people to work together. Rules and feedback systems can herd loners and soloists into groups, and the resulting work experience may be unhappy for all. Office politics and the words of unhappy coworkers are sometimes brutal. It will be important that designs for games at work facilitate healthy teams without inappropriate coercion.

A memorable example of how to get this wrong comes from the OTA report cited earlier:

> *A Pacific Western Airlines (PWA) productivity campaign drew*
> *union protests when company posters urged reservation clerks to:*
>
> Compare yourself with your friends.
>
> Compare yourself with ones who aren't your friends.
>
> Are you pulling your weight at the office?

When the monthly statistics are published, ensure you're not dragging down your team and your office.

The union newsletter charged PWA with setting workers against each other and called the campaign a "new low in . . . degradation."[7] We think the core message is fundamentally all right, but there has to be a better way than this clumsy attempt to use data to motivate performance at work.

9. Communication Systems That Can Be Reconfigured by Participants

Vinnie's military-style headset and joystick trigger fits his tough-guy game persona in a real-world security challenge. Other user interfaces will be appropriate for different kinds of work embedded in games. Regardless of the specific user interface, we expect to see games at work exploring the multiple parallel channels of communication seen in MMOs that are customizable by the participants to fit their style and the game mechanics.

Unless these parallel channels are embedded in a thoughtful context where people have tools for focusing and filtering, there is a serious potential for information overload. Successful entertainment games must be getting this right, because we don't hear complaints from gamers about information overload—in fact, usually the reverse. They see this as part of the game, in stark contrast with enterprise workers contending with today's unplanned hodgepodge of e-mail, instant messaging, intranets, news groups, wikis, and the growing web of social media.

10. Time Pressure

During rush hour at Grand Central, Vinnie doesn't have time for a coffee break. As the flood of commuters descends from their offices, so do the simulated bad guys that require his attention. The need to make rapid-fire decisions with the clock ticking is a key tool for generating arousal. Combined with an appropriate feedback structure and embedded in a context with an interesting backstory, video surveillance could be transformed into a highly engaging activity with much higher accuracy. It's also easy to see how employees could be burned out by the stress of this activity unless workflow and attendant breaks were designed thoughtfully.

The Pros and Cons of Stress

Higher engagement drives higher performance, up to a point. There is abundant evidence that many kinds of human performance improve as a person is subjected to increasing levels of psychological stress, up to a critical point beyond where performance rapidly degrades.[8] The shape of this curve varies from one person to another and is dependent on context. A game designer aiming to squeeze the highest level of performance out of a player-worker might use available tools to amp up tension just to that point of peak performance. In a smart design, one could give a player repetitive challenges in order to determine exactly where to set the system to optimize individual performance.

The problem is that optimizing on short-term performance may not be good for the person invited into the experience. This sets up an apparent conflict of interest between the game owner's desire to maximize productivity and the optimal work environment for an employee. One potential win-win solution is to consider a longer time frame for analysis.

Sourcing, evaluating, recruiting, relocating, orienting, and training replacements is a significant part of overall HR expense. Enlightened future employers, no matter how eager to wring minute-to-minute productivity from their workforce, will direct game designers to weigh the cost of excessive stress and burnout and optimize accordingly. Compared with an extreme focus on short-term output, a longer-term view of employee productivity is likely to create healthier workplaces and possibly a win-win situation for those involved.

Outside the context of this discussion, if someone came up with an idea to make call center work "so much fun that we'd have to hold people back," it would probably take a while for anyone to raise ethical concerns. Workflow design is often so impotent that no one would be worried about addiction, at least during the early celebrations about increased productivity. The psychological power of games will change that thinking. There are good examples of high-burnout jobs, and in some of these jobs the real-life stakes are so high that it's easy to see how stress-related health problems would occur. Air traffic control comes to mind, but we don't know how much of that stress is also related to poor design in the human/computer interface that controllers use and the work rules that surround their tasks. We do know that when controllers are on station, they enjoy a high level of flow, and that time seems to disappear. Some even describe themselves as junkies who crave the experience.[9]

Mitigation

When repetitive stress injuries start to show up as a result of ultra-engaging games played at work, we're sure that the Service Employees International

Union will be all over the problem because there are well-developed proto-cols for managing musculoskeletal problems due to work design issues. The management and prevention of work-related *mental* stress is less well devel-oped, and we suspect that games will require fresh thinking on the subject.

The OTA's work cited earlier provides relevant guidance on how to miti-gate the potential harm of electronic monitoring, including monitoring that could occur in games at work. The first suggestion is to involve workers in the design of the systems. Hearing their concerns about privacy and fairness can avoid serious mistrust. Game designers are also game players, and they make extensive use of trials to fine-tune feedback and level design. For pri-vacy concerns, collecting (or saving) only the information needed for a legit-imate business purpose is recommended, as well as letting employees know what is being collected, how it will be used, and why. Game designers also labor to get the transparency of collected data right, so that the benefits of peer pressure occur without undue discouragement for laggards.

To manage the risk of potential addiction to games at work, it will be essential to look for the problem during game development and testing, and to monitor use with addiction in mind. People are already in therapy for entertainment game addiction, and a twelve-step program is being offered via an online community.[10] Reading the posts on the twelve-step website (see endnote) makes it clear that this is not a trivial problem. Planned breaks and cool-down periods should be part of the game. Evaluation and self-evaluation can be designed into the game to help keep people on the healthy side of engagement. These techniques might also help with the potential risks of depersonalization and isolation, but we also envisage the need for ongoing evaluation and monitoring outside the game. A new form of indus-trial hygiene, not yet well developed for the current tools of the information age, will need to be invented to help make sure these powerful technologies are used safely.

In the final chapter, on tactics, we offer a checklist of ways to help keep the power of games at work in play but also in check, and some concrete ways that practitioners can better understand the risks as well as the benefits of this new technology.

Chapter Twelve

Tactics for Change

Feeling all dressed up and wondering where to go? If you're like us, you're excited about the potential to apply the crisp, colorful experience of game play to a workplace that needs more than a fresh coat of business process paint. What's the best first step? Right now, there is no quick answer, but the long answer that follows can start the journey.

As you have seen throughout this book, we're convinced that someday important enterprise tasks will be performed by people in an environment that looks a lot like today's massive multiplayer games. Our forecast is that this will come about in stages in which subsets of game ingredients are introduced into business software currently used by information workers and in which the new features address particular pain points or simply provide refreshing differentiation from competitive offerings. Along the way, experiments with full-blown work-inside-a-game implementations will be tried, sometimes with disappointing results. Just because you invent the idea of movies doesn't mean the first five will be hits. But all it will take is a single major breakthrough in productivity and work satisfaction to send a lot of game, media, and work design talent off to the races.

This chapter outlines some first steps to take—starting today—to move forward in an enterprise revolution that will result in more stimulating, aligned, and productive work. Our experiences suggest a natural flow to the initiatives that will be needed to transform a workforce. The order is probably as important as the action. As you may also notice, the list embodies a feedback loop that resembles other successful approaches to process evolution in complex organizations.

Here's a sequence for how to be an effective change agent regarding games and work:

1. Build your own conceptual map linking games and work.

2. Study what others are doing at the intersection of games and work.

3. Experiment with bite-sized use cases that address real pain points.

4. Commit to a focused application of principles.

5. Measure the impact of what matters to the enterprise and to individuals.

6. Evolve better and more comprehensive systems.

This chapter is organized as a series of exercises designed to stimulate thinking, followed by a smorgasbord of places in the enterprise where you can look for opportunities to apply game sensibilities. Feel free to develop your own way of approaching the problem, especially in collaboration with colleagues who are also intrigued with the concept. Be sure to enjoy the process. Most of our best work has been done in the context of offsite activities organized as games, including scorekeeping, markets, prizes, and good stories that caricature our efforts.

Tactic 1: Build a Conceptual Map Linking Games and Work

It's your turn to map the links between the worlds of games and work. For introspective types, we suggest an inventory of your own interest in the subject to clarify what about the thesis is attractive. However, if you are the type who can't wait to get started, skip right to a set of actions that progress from innocuous work process evaluation (which probably won't get you in trouble) to more radical experimentation (which will definitely get the attention of your colleagues). Whatever your personal player style, it's probably a good idea to consider the style of your colleagues and the self-image of your enterprise before jumping in.

Introspection Anyone? What Here Captures Your Imagination?

Some people like to prepare for action on the basis of first principles. If so, maybe it's worth making notes about why this thesis is interesting enough for you to have read this far. You don't need to be an experienced gamer to think critically about this topic. (We aren't.) That said, those who've achieved advanced levels playing any of the leading MMOs may describe their attraction to this thesis in different terms from us. The dialogue is worthwhile.

Are you one of those gamers with the sense that your highly engaging hours of play ought to be leading to something outwardly productive in addition to the inner satisfaction and escape you experience? If so, you may be feeling some frustration about the challenge of dreaming up a good use case for work in a game because you respect the carefully nuanced design that goes into a fully conceived immersive experience. Perhaps we can side-step some of the hardest challenges by considering the transformation of work one small step at a time. For that task, this chapter turns again to the lessons in chapter 4 learned from experienced gamers.

A Work/Play Mirror Exercise for Gamers

Established gamers can begin by analyzing parallel experiences in their personal worlds of work and play. The point of this exercise is to make sure you have tangible and personal use cases you can readily cite if you tell someone about the thesis of this book. It's good to quickly follow the thesis (which sounds like too much fun) with high-value business cases (which should sound indisputably important). At the end of the exercise, you should be able to give tangible examples of how much better or more interesting your job would be if only your work systems or teams took advantage of a particular piece of game design. Don't worry right now about the need to specify the full deployment path. It's a good first step to be able to articulate clear, simple use cases.

Begin by making a table with two columns: one for play and one for work. Use the rows to see how many personal experiences you can list that are common to both worlds. For example, "meeting new coworkers" might be a match with "meeting new guild members." Listing "events" is a good first start, but the exercise will be even better if, when you name the event, you also focus on how you feel as that moment arises in each setting ("Meeting new people at work makes me uncomfortable"). The first time through, it might be fun to make your list from the first-person perspective so that you're inside your own head looking out rather than at the comfortable distance afforded by an over-the-shoulder game view. In your mind's eye, follow your character from login to logout for a particularly satisfying session in your favorite game to list events in the play column. Then think of the closest analogues in your work.

Populate your list with as many work/play parallels as you can by inverting the exercise and following your real-life character from the beginning to the end of a typical work day. Don't forget the work you do out of the office. (By the way, when you recall your real-life character's path through a day of work, which perspective are you using: first person or over the shoulder?) Once you have a good list of the routine stuff, try including corner cases and oddball moments. Can you think of a frustrating event at work that has a direct parallel in your game life? How about something embarrassing that may have an eerie twin in your parallel universe? Don't forget to list some big upside surprises. Does anything similar to stalking, shooting, grinding, or flirting show up in work? Does anything like office politics, deadlines, procrastination, or a job well done show up on the game side?

Now that you have written proof that you're leading a double life, examine the links between the two worlds. In case you didn't explicitly focus on them as you built the list, take a moment to reflect on the connections between the work event and the game event. How would you explain why the work and play events are analogues or metaphors for each other?

Pick a few of the events for the following thought experiment: which of the game ingredients discussed in chapter 4 might have made life at work more enjoyable or more productive? Don't worry for now about how to get from today's workplace all the way to an ideal future. Simply picture isolated vignettes where you can explore your own ideas. For example, would that endless meeting have been a better use of time if you could magically right-click on each of the attendees and see what they had accomplished recently (transparent reputation system)? What if the boundaries for your last project and the definition of success were as clear as those in your game (explicit rules)?

Work/Play Mirror Exercise for the Rest of Us

If you're not a gamer, perhaps you will be persuaded to give a game or two a try. It wouldn't hurt, and you may be delighted to experience some of the embedded psychology first hand. Even if you don't go there, we urge you to perform your own exercise to reflect on parallels between the game world we've described and the world of work you know well. There are probably juicy examples from your own work experience to add. If you appreciate the importance of fun at work, why not spice up your next few days at work by keeping a log with similar observations? The most boring, frustrating, or embarrassing vignettes can be transformed into your own personal teachable moments with insights about the potential value of game design elements in work.

To help you get started, this section reprises our ingredient list with some features to ponder. Don't be disappointed if you find that some of the ingredients aren't compelling as *stand-alone* additions to today's workplace. Some will probably need to be combined in larger ensembles to deliver optimal value.

1. *Self-representation with avatars.* Can you think of a place in your work life where a "mini-me" might come in handy? We'd all like to clone ourselves from time to time, but instead of an independent duplicate, we're talking about a digital representation that might stand in for you in a meeting in a virtual world, perhaps with people from far-flung locations. Consider the possible value of convening avatars compared with the disembodied voices of a conventional teleconference. How would this compare with one of the expensive new high-end video conferencing systems in which people appear to be sitting across the table from each other? Think about meetings that occur outside conventional office hours. (Admission: our own experience with some of today's popular virtual worlds is that this is highly amusing at first, but that refinement of the user interface and better integration with business data and other game ingredients will be needed for avatars to reach their potential in the workplace.) Look for the names of some specific commercial offerings later in this chapter.

2. *Three-dimensional environments.* A 3D environment gives an avatar a place to call home, allowing these first two ingredients to work hand in hand. Instead of teleporting avatars to a virtual conference room, consider whether there's a way to connect people with the physical environments where your company actually creates value. Think about virtual representations of places such as the design shop, the factory floor, the drilling rig, or the service desk. Wouldn't it be a good idea if the office workers who support these functions were moved (virtually) closer to the action for a better perspective on how the company actually creates value? Maybe then *everyone* could manage by walking around. If this sounds attractive, consider how these "tip of the spear" virtual environments might be used as a context for information worker avatars to meet and conduct business.

3. *Narrative context.* Stories are a key ingredient that differentiates MMOs from virtual worlds. Does your company have a story line? Most good ones do. They go something like this: "Our founder was the first to realize that customers really need [*fill in the blank*] and we've been dedicated to delivering that ever since." Or "We nearly

went out of business but fortunately decided to focus on [*fill in the blank*] and have become a leader in our market." A lot has been written about storytelling as a leadership tool, and we think the principle is sound.[1] Games teach how and why it's important to weave foundational stories into the entire fabric of the workplace. Gamers are quick to spot any disconnect between the play at each level of the game and the fundamental story arc, and designers are quick to mend such tears in the fabric.

Where do people in your company lose track of the motivational and directional value of your company's story, and how could this be remedied? Would your coworkers be quick to point out disconnects between the company story and what's really happening? How can the story be enhanced or clarified (without being dishonest), allowing it to become more useful at every level of the enterprise? Is it time to write a new company story? Can a virtual world or synthetic currency be used as a tool to reinforce the story?

4. *Feedback.* What if your boss gave you timely, accurate, and informative feedback every time you started to wonder if you were on the right track? It might be annoying because it's only human to stray on occasion from consistency or objectivity. We are not just talking about getting complimented more often. In the constrained world of games, designers do a good job of closing the loop between action, result, and adjustment. The stunning impact of such feedback is a prime reason that games are such an advanced form of human/computer interaction. Game play consists of small, short-term activities that combine and build to create larger accomplishments; consequently, gamers receive feedback in multiple and nested time scales. Game feedback is delivered by a myriad of still and animated graphics, as well as sound and text. Pick work tasks that you understand well and see if you can imagine ways that people could receive accurate and useful feedback on all the relevant time scales. How many senses can you involve? Think about the digital analogues of subtle but powerful cues in today's office, such as body language and eye contact. How could the software systems that information workers use provide richer feedback?

5. *Reputations, ranks, and levels.* Enterprise workers are familiar with reputations, ranks, and levels. These organizing principles run far

back through early human tribes and beyond. MMOs extend these primitive cues by combining the perfection of computer record keeping with thoughtful designs that enhance the link between past performance and the expectation of current and future abilities. To the extent that behavior is visible to an automated process, game reputation systems can expose perfectly accurate information about past performance and accomplishment. Can you think of situations in the world of work where people would make better decisions if they had this kind of information? Put aside the annual performance review for a moment and consider small daily decisions about who is best to do what task. How *would* it be in a meeting if you could "right-click" on the face of the new team member and instantly see his or her actual accomplishments in relation to the topic at hand?

Career promotions typically happen at frequencies much longer than one year. Gamers enjoy the challenge and reward of leveling up daily or weekly. Without resorting to trivial markers, can you imagine ways that members of your team could see their personal progress recognized in a series of meaningful steps that are attainable weekly or monthly? It may not be a bad idea to develop more fine-grained descriptions of growth within a particular job level, and then use these distinctions to reward and record progress.

Every player in an MMO has a chance to reach the highest rank. That is not realistic in the organizational chart of a modern enterprise, but perhaps there are analogous ways to preserve an aspiration to greatness. In the U.S. military, dedicated servicemen and women in the noncommissioned ranks can keep adding chevrons to their sleeves, at least up to a point.[2] It shouldn't be surprising that a military institution that retains employees based on commitment to duty and service (rather than economics) would take great care to recognize accomplishments with a rich variety of insignia and rank. Although a rack of ribbons might look out of place while wearing business casual, a well-appointed avatar should be able to pull it off.

6. *Marketplaces and economies.* We are impressed with the range of different applications in which a properly designed synthetic currency could help the enterprise. Economists have argued for years that resource allocation inside companies will benefit when

managers can act as independent economic agents. Enterprises are experimenting with prediction markets, as well as other strategies for aggregating ideas and opinions under the general heading of "crowdsourcing." These have kinship with features in MMOs, and chapter 6 offers several additional ideas. Can you think of routine trading and quid pro quos in your office that suffer from the limitations of barter exchanges? Would these interactions work better if a currency could be used to settle the trades and store value for the future? Are there key resources that are allocated on a first-come, first-served basis that really should be assigned based on which users are willing to give up something scarce in exchange? How could bidding with synthetic currency make the allocation more fair and more efficient at the same time?

7. *Rules that are explicit and enforced.* Break any rules lately? If so, it probably wasn't in an MMO, because most of the rules are encoded in the software and you usually can't get around them. That doesn't mean, of course, that you can't do things that are harmful to yourself or others, but in the games there are usually clear consequences for such behavior. There may be instances in your office where trust suffers because people don't have an unambiguous, shared understanding of the rules of engagement. On the other hand, many offices have way too many rules, and stifle people with process.

    Beyond specifying what you can and can't do, game rules define how you get ahead. Would it help your team if the definition of success for the current project were more clearly stated and the consequences of success and failure more transparent? Maybe you can imagine ways that team members could make up for lack of clarity from the larger organization by taking a strong team point of view about how the group will measure itself. Game guilds often agree on internal standards and rules to fill in the gaps where they think the larger game hasn't provided sufficient clarity.

8. *Teams.* Game teams attract and retain members because fun games require collaboration and they have clear rules, transparent reputations, and a pretty firm sense of what success and failure look like. Teams in MMOs show us new ways to sort out classic issues such as getting individual credit for group accomplishment and the free-rider problem. Of course, there is a degree of volunteerism in entertainment games that may not be the case at the office. In

games, you can easily take your bat and ball and go home but in the big picture, remember that employees are volunteers, too. Think about tools that you could give your teams to approximate some of the nice things we see in games. Clarity regarding mission and boundaries is a good place to start. Think about new score-keeping techniques to support better feedback and leveling up. Fluidity of roles among leaders and followers is a hallmark of gamer teams. Consider whether it is most important to give the business intelligence dashboard to the leader or to those being led who need to know where and how they fit in.

9. *Communication systems that can be reconfigured by participants.* The communication technology available at work is not that far behind what you might see in a popular MMO, but tools are better integrated in the games. That is, the voice and text channels are likely to be layered in terms of broadcasting and narrowcasting, and more easily configured to suit the user and the particular context in the game in which they appear. As a victim of information overload, you may be thinking that the last thing you need is more communication channels. The information overload problem, however, poses at least three different challenges to attention: (1) the absolute amount of new information we're required to view or that may be of interest; (2) the perverse implication of *queued messaging*, where the most recent message (not the most important one) is always on top of the stack; and (3) the impact of interruptions in terms of direct time lost and the substantial secondary impact of the time it takes to get fully back on task.[3] Gamers don't complain about information overload much, and it may have something to do with the more structured experience in a typical play session; that is, there are specific times to catch up, and times to ignore everything not related to the moment. Consider ways an information economy using synthetic currency could give your colleagues more of what they need when they need it and less of what is irrelevant.

10. *Time pressure.* Like you need more time pressure at work! People already don't have enough time now for thoughtful reflection.[4] Instead of thinking about adding time pressure at work, think about rearranging it. Consider structuring the workday with periods of intense focus, free of interruption, alternating with catch-up time. Where are the important tasks that can be uncoupled from

the corporate calendar, and how do you use deadlines for the other stuff to create white space for reflection? For example, a strict allowance for time allotted to e-mail might be healthy because it would lead you to focus on the important messages and set aside non-e-mail time for even more productive work.

Tactic 2: Study What Others Are Doing with Games at Work

A time-honored starting point, especially when it's not entirely clear what to do first, is research. Consider fielding, analyzing, and reporting a survey about who actually plays games in your organization, what kind of games, how much time they spend playing, and what they think they are getting out of it. IBM was surprised when it did such a survey.[5] You might be as well.

On the way to creating disruptive innovation, a survey could turn out to be a practical (and safe) way to begin in an organization threatened by some new ideas. At a minimum, you'll have a chance to discover fellow travelers who either play games or are attracted to this thesis. A well-designed survey might also bring the topic out of the closet. Even if you can't fully legitimize the discussion on the first pass, you might at least engage those most capable of brainstorming in open conversations.

Political campaigns have long used the tactic of clever questions as a way to influence as well as to learn from voters. If you need one, a perfect cover story could be the legitimate need for your organization to be relevant to the up-and-coming gamer generation. Alternatively, a business crisis could motivate a survey to ascertain engagement among the workforce. An innocent survey to find out how many employees (new and old) actually play games might turn up some surprises, especially if respondents feel safe giving honest answers. If necessary, you might construct a credible method to ensure anonymity. If you engage with customers, you can make the case that your company has to be up-to-date on what's going on with early adopters who buy your products. Survey customers, too.

Before you field the survey, think about the role you will take personally in what could easily become a transformative effort in your organization. Authoring this survey could tag you as a leader, especially if you decide to take the initiative to move ideas forward. Alternatively, if you decide that colleagues are not ready, you can use your analysis and conclusions to put the whole thing "into perspective" (i.e, on the back burner) until opportunities ripen. And by the way, what if someone else in your organization is also reading this chapter? Are they friend or foe? It's a bit like a game, isn't it?

Books, Conferences, and Consultants

We have already referenced a number of terrific books on games and game design. If we had to pick three to have in the library, we'd suggest Castronova's *Synthetic Worlds* (Chicago: University of Chicago Press, 2005), Beck and Wade's *Got Game: How the Gamer Generation Is Reshaping Business Forever* (Boston: Harvard Business School Press, 2004), and Koster's *A Theory of Fun for Game Design* (Phoenix, AZ: Paraglyph Press, 2004). There are plenty more as well.[6]

People who write books such as this one are sometimes available to carry out consulting projects to help identify approaches to your pain points or to help implement your own ideas. We urge companies to talk with people who can describe conversations and trials at several different places. There's no need to reinvent wheels or replicate mistakes.

The ideas in this book represent a subset of the applications being considered by many others under the rubric of "serious games"—that is, game technology used for any purpose other than pure entertainment. Training and teaching games, simulation for discovery, and exercise games such as Wii Sports all fall into this broad category. The best single place to learn more about the scope of the field and meet people who are contributing is the Serious Games Initiative, which has a Web presence, organizes workshops, and runs the Serious Games Summit at the massive Game Developers' Conference (GDC), usually held in the spring in San Francisco.[7] Almost everyone associated with the field is represented (or referenced) by the materials associated with one of those meetings. Setting aside a couple of days to attend GDC is a wonderful way to immerse yourself in the technology and to see the future. Hundreds of speakers deal with the challenges for developers, and the most cutting-edge tools are on full display. If you're not a gamer, consider taking a colleague along who can serve as your jungle guide.

Explore!

If you haven't done so already, you might be tempted to spend some time in a virtual online world such as *Second Life*. Just get an account at www.secondlife.com and start exploring. This is almost an essential introduction to avatars and the 3D worlds they inhabit. You'll enjoy (most of) the wild variety of expression and creativity on display. And be sure to try building something yourself. We agree with many gamers who don't consider *Second Life* to be a game, but it is a continuing work in progress, and a spectacular achievement by Linden Lab and the millions of residents who have created the content. The company has responded to corporate interest with a range of tools, programs, and even solutions. You can view them at http://secondlifegrid.net/. If you go very far down this path, you'll likely want to work with one of the vendors who specialize in developing *Second Life* real estate for business use. Before building out a complete island, look also at the virtual online technologies being created by others especially for business.

The field of business-oriented virtual words is moving fast. For example, take a look at Qwaq Forums (www.qwaq.com). This relatively new application has been described as a mash-up of a virtual world and WebEx. It was built expressly for business collaboration, is easier than *Second Life* to get started, and has many office-friendly features, including the ability to share typical office documents in applications appearing inside the virtual environment.

Forterra Systems (www.forterrainc.com/) has been around almost as long as *Second Life* and continues to adapt its solutions for the military and corporate markets. Three virtual online worlds that are bridging entertainment and business applications are Icarus Studios (www.icarusstudios.com), Active Worlds (www.activeworlds.com/overview.asp), and Entropia Universe (www.entropiauniverse.com/index.var). Entropia emphasizes its use of an overt economy convertible into real-world funds, much like *Second Life*'s Linden dollars. Kaneva (www.kaneva.com) is focused on the consumer demographics of social networking sites such as Facebook, but may have the infrastructure for certain types of business applications. Unisfair (www.unisfair.com) provides virtual trade shows and conferences. There are many more, as compiled by the Association of Virtual Worlds (http://associationofvirtualworlds.com/index.php) in its GreenBook (http://associationofvirtualworlds.com/thegreenbook/the_green_book_august_2008_edition.pdf). Finally, take a look a the latest extensions of social media like Facebook and Twitter enabled by increasingly open architecture, and games available as iPhone apps.

You will also want to look at what large enterprises are doing to experiment in the field. An obvious place to start is IBM (http://domino.research.ibm.com/comm/research_projects.nsf/pages/virtualworlds.index.html). We worked with the IBM Global Innovation Outlook team to study leadership in online games, but you will also find a press announcement mentioning an IBM partnership with many of the virtual worlds mentioned here, where Big Blue is either providing computer servers for the virtual world or using the online environment for projects for itself and IBM customers. As we reviewed in chapter 5, IBM has also published its internal guidelines for avatars and behavior in these new environments (http://domino.research.ibm.com/comm/

research_projects.nsf/pages/virtualworlds.IBMVirtualWorldGuidelines.html).
Sun Microsystems is deep into the fray, using its own hardware and software
infrastructure on the way to offering products and services for others
(http://research.sun.com/projects/mc/mpk20.html).

At some point, you might actually want to build a game yourself. We
hope so, because that's where we are heading with these ideas, but don't be
in a hurry to do something on the cheap, because the experience from early
adopters has been mixed. Respectable games for training can be built for
low six figures. Many will meet short-term learning objectives, but the game
experiences often don't compare well with mainstream entertainment titles.
Furthermore, the cheaper games typically don't have the depth of content to
sustain interest over time or for more than a chapter's worth of educational
content. You will undoubtedly learn something from the project, but we are
encouraging experimentation with the building blocks first.

The way the entertainment game industry is structured today, it's possible
to access the hands-on software talent necessary to build all or part of a
game. Many independent game developer shops are trying to feed content to
a handful of publishers who have strong distribution capabilities. Most have
dreams of writing the next *World of Warcraft* or *Grand Theft Auto* but are having to work hard just to keep their heads above water and might welcome
the chance for paid work helping you execute on your vision. Except for the
few who have staked out territory in the serious games space (Virtual Heroes
[www.virtualheroes.com] is one leading player), don't be surprised if a typical game developer has little understanding of your business problem or the
sensibilities needed to execute on a workplace game strategy. In addition to
people who have the development tools and can write code, the good outfits
will have designers with an understanding of the ingredients in chapter 4
who can help you execute designs that integrate them well. They may be
baffled, at first, if you say you want to start with just a few of the ingredients
and that you want to apply them to problems at work.

Tactic 3: Experiment with Bite-Sized Use Cases
That Address Real Pain Points

So where does it hurt? Where is your organization truly being held back from
reaching its potential because of problems with collaboration, innovation,
alignment, or simply the joy of coming to work? Review the ten ingredients

to look for a potential match. The right answer might be to start with only a few of these elements working together in a single solution.

It's fine not to be overly ambitious at first. We like the starting point of using a gamelike virtual currency to help people signal importance in messages, which can then become the basis for trading all kinds of internal resource allocation and crowdsourcing applications. This is a relatively simple first step that is built right into software already available. Badges, leader boards, and other reward structures can easily be built on top of the economic transactions. Avatars and 3D worlds could be added as the technology and business appetite allowed. Others may prefer starting with the 3D worlds so that people can get used to the idea of meeting in digital environments.

You get the idea. There are a lot of ways to mix and match some of the key ingredients on the way to a workplace that is fully embedded in a game. And you already have an incredible resource in your organization to help—the gamers identified in your survey. Enlist them in the cause. Let them help you form a new team to work on this project, where you experiment with game ideas in the way your own team works together, "eating your own dog food" as the expression goes. It will give you confidence and stories to introduce others to the idea.

And, to usefully confuse our thesis with your journey, don't forget to have fun while you are at it.

Notes

Chapter One

1. One recent source about the size of the game audience in the United States is a report titled *Online Gaming 2008*, from the NPD Group (Port Washington, NY). Its study was based on a survey of 5,039 people from a larger consumer survey panel. The group reported that 63 percent of the U.S. population aged fifteen to sixty-five plays some type of online or video game.

2. The most sophisticated games that have inspired this book are known as massive multiplayer online role-playing games (MMORPGs), although many use the letters MMO for short. This note lists references and websites that contain pictures, stories, game current events, industry trends, and bibliographies. We particularly highlight those that have pictures because we decided early in this project that we couldn't do justice to the visual interest of games in a book. General references include the following:

http://www.mmorpg.com (general information about a variety of MMOs)

http://gaming.alltop.com (a comprehensive compilation of game-related news)

http://www.allakhazam.com (general MMO information)

http://terranova.blogs.com (contributions from the best academics, designers, and journalists about trends in MMOs; links in the left-hand column of the home page lead to over fifty of the top titles)

The following are links for playing in the top-selling MMO title, *World of Warcraft*. They describe guild activities, contain pictures and movies of game play, and provide advice about how to organize winning teams. The details on these websites may be daunting to the uninitiated, but you can learn a lot by just exploring:

http://www.worldofraids.com (news site for up-to-the-hour updates of developments in the game)

http://www.wowwiki.com (this site is player updated and contains useful information that can be applied quickly during action)

You can also go to YouTube (www.youtube.com) and type in the name of a popular game. There are usually hundreds of videos available that show play in the top titles (for example, *World of Warcraft, EverQuest II*, or *EVE Online*). All of the games have introduction movies, also usually available at YouTube. Search by the name of the game and "intro movie" (e.g., *World of Warcraft* intro movie).

3. Twelve million people subscribe to *World of Warcraft* by Blizzard Entertainment. This is the most popular current title in the genre of MMORPGs. These are the games, rather than solo games, that are the major inspiration for our thesis.

4. The decline of command and control organizations is treated in detail in Thomas Malone, *The Future of Work: How the New Order of Business Will Shape Your Organization, Your Management Style, and Your Life* (Boston: Harvard Business School Press, 2004).

5. J. L. Read, C. Carlin, I. Greenberg, and G. Blackburn, *The Original Boston Computer Diet* (Boston: Scarborough Systems, 1985).

6. Orson Scott Card, *Ender's Game* (New York: Tor Books, 2006). The book was originally published by Tor in 1985.

7. *The Last Starfighter*, directed by Nick Castle (Universal, 1984).

8. *War Games*, directed by John Badham (United Artists, 1983).

9. Luis von Ahn, "Games with a Purpose," *Computer* 39, no. 6 (2006): 92–94.

10. You can play Ahn's games online at http://www.gwap.com.

11. Julian Birkenshaw and Stuart Crainer, "Theory Y Meets Generation Y," *Labnotes*, Issue 10, December 20, 2008, http://www.managementlab.org/files/LabNotes10.pdf. The Microsoft team website is http://www.42projects.org/8.html.

12. These projects are covered in Byron Reeves and Thomas Malone, "Leadership's Online Labs," *Harvard Business Review*, May 2008, 58–66; and Byron Reeves, Simon Roy, Brian Gorman, and Teresa Morley, "A Marketplace for Attention: Responses to a Synthetic Currency Used to Signal Information Importance in E-mail," *First Monday* 13, no. 5 (2008).

13. Dimitri Williams, Nick Yee, and Scott Caplan, "Who Plays, How Much, and Why? A Behavioral Player Census of a Virtual World," *Journal of Computer Mediated Communication* 13, no. 4 (2008): 993–1018.

14. A new book on games and business that contains many additional examples of how games can be used to relate to customers and to recruit and train employees is *Changing the Game*, by David Edery and Ethan Mollick (Upper Saddle River, NJ: FT Press, 2009).

Chapter Two

1. Data about the number of people who inhabit virtual worlds and games is notoriously unreliable or absent. Christian Renaud, in a presentation at the 2007 Virtual Worlds Conference in San Jose, estimated that the total number of people with avatars exceeded 400 million—that is, if you use only data provided by publishers of the software. He also noted that that figure was likely too high but in any case was into the hundreds of millions. The main focus of his presentation was an argument that much better metrics were needed before these technologies can gain serious attention in business. We agree.

2. Game industry data are from the Entertainment Software Association (www.theese.com/facts/salesandgenre.asp) and was compiled by the NPD Group.

3. Blizzard Entertainment, "*World of Warcraft: Wrath of the Lich King* Shatters Day-1 Sales Record," *Business Wire*, November 20, 2008, http://investor.activision.com/releasedetail.cfm?ReleaseID=349190.

4. Martin Olausson, "Online Games: Global Market Forecast," Strategy Analytics, August 23, 2007, http://www.strategyanalytics.com/default.aspx?mod=ReportAbstract Viewer&a0=3559.

5. Julian Dibbell, "The Life of the Chinese Gold Farmer," *New York Times Magazine*, June 17, 2007.

6. Edward Castronova, "Virtual Worlds: A First-Hand Account of the Market and Society on the Cyberian Frontier," CESifo Working Paper Series no. 618, Ifo Institute for Economic Research, Munich, 2001.

7. See, for example, David Barboza, "Ogre to Slay? Outsource It to Chinese," *New York Times*, December 9, 2005.

8. Dimitri Williams, Nick Yee, and Scott Caplan, "Who Plays, How Much, and Why? A Behavioral Player Census of a Virtual World," *Journal of Computer Mediated Communication* 13, no. 4 (2008): 993–1018.

9. Data from the Entertainment Software Association (www.theesa.com/facts/gameplayer.asp).

10. Gender statistics from various studies, as well as other MMO game demographics, are reviewed in Elaine Chan and Peter Vorderer, "Massively Multiplayer Games," in *Playing Video Games*, eds. Peter Vorderer and Jennings Bryant (Mahwah, NJ: Lawrence Erlbaum Associates, 2006). See also player statistics from the Entertainment Software Association (www.theesa.com/facts/gameplayer.asp), which reports that 44 percent of online game players overall are female.

11. Daniel Terdiman, *The Entrepreneur's Guide to* Second Life: *Making Money in the Metaverse* (Hoboken, NJ: Wiley, 2008).

12. Eric Reuters, "*Second Life* Growth Cools, Women Outnumbered 3-to-1," 2007. This article is written by the journalist (known in-world as Eric Reuters) who writes news stories for Reuters based on experiences in the virtual environment. They are posted at http://secondlife.reuters.com/.

13. The original cartoon was by Peter Steiner and first appeared in *The New Yorker*, July 1993, 61.

14. These statistics about income, education, and race come from D. Williams, N. Yee, and S. Caplan, "Who Plays, How Much, and Why? Debunking the Stereotypical Gamer Profile." *Journal Computer Mediated Communication* 13 (2008): 993–1018.

15. Nick Yee, "The Demographics, Motivations and Derived Experiences of Users of Massively-Multiuser Online Graphical Environments," *Presence: Teleoperators and Virtual Environments* 15 (2006): 309–329.

16. Williams, et al., "Who Plays, How Much, and Why?"

17. Some of the game features discussed here are based on an excellent review of game play, especially first encounters with games, in Edward Castronova, *Synthetic Worlds* (Chicago: University of Chicago Press, 2005), chapter 2.

18. Nicolas Ducheneaut and Nickolas Yee, "Collective Solitude and Social Networks in *World of Warcraft*," in *Social Networking Communities and E-Dating Services: Concepts and Implications*, eds. Celia Romm-Livermore and Kristina Setzekorn (Hershey, PA: IGI Global, 2009), 78–100.

19. There are three good references on the motivations for game play, with good agreement on the categories of motivation among the studies. The categories reviewed here are based on these studies. The links between player motivations and specific game features are based on Yee, "Demographics, Motivations and Derived Experiences." The studies are as follows:

a. Richard Bartle, *Designing Virtual Worlds* (Indianapolis, IN: New Riders, 2003).

b. Nick Yee, "The Demographics, Motivations, and Derived Experiences of Users of Massively Multi-User Online Graphical Environments," *Presence: Teleoperators and Virtual Environments* 15 (2006): 309–329.

c. Thomas Malone, "Toward a Theory of Intrinsically Motivating Instruction," *Cognitive Science* 5, no. 4 (1991): 333–369.

20. Game mechanics are the various actions, behaviors, and control mechanisms afforded to the player within a game context. Together with the game's content (levels,

assets, and so on) the mechanics support overall game play dynamics. See Robin Hunicke, Marc LeBlanc, and Robert Zubek, "MDA: A Formal Approach to Game Design and Game Research" (presented as part of the Game Design and Tuning Workshop at the Game Developers Conference, San Jose, CA, 2004). Available online at http://algorithmancy. 8kindsoffun.com/MDAnwu.ppt.

21. John C. Beck and Mitchell Wade, *Got Game: How the Gamer Generation Is Reshaping Business* (Boston: Harvard Business School Press, 2004).

22. Ron Alsop, *The Trophy Kids Grow Up* (San Francisco: Jossey-Bass, 2008).

23. McKenzie Wark, *Gamer Theory* (Cambridge, MA: Harvard University Press, 2007).

24. Percy Tannenbaum, ed., *The Entertainment Functions of Television* (Hillsdale, NJ: Lawrence Erlbaum, 1980). Chapter 1, "An Unobstructed Introduction to an Amorphous Area," reviews concerns about media effects in general. Also see chapter 9 by Leo Bogart ("Television News as Entertainment") for a discussion of how television news uses entertainment principles.

Chapter Three

1. Michal Smith-Mello and Amy L Watts, *Planning for the Future: Findings from Research on the Commonwealth's Current and Coming Retirees* (Frankfort, KY: Kentucky Long-Term Policy Research Center, 2002). Data from the report cited here is available at http://www. kltprc.net/books/aging/gifs/pg2.htm.

2. Louise Scheiner, Daniel Sichel, and Lawrence Slifman, "A Primer on the Macroeconomic Implications of Population Aging," Finance and Economics Discussion Series 2007-01, Divisions of Research and Statistics and Monetary Affairs, Federal Reserve Board, Washington, DC, 2007. The report is available at http://www.federalreserve.gov/pubs/FEDS/2007/200701/200701pap.pdf.

3. Robert L. Cross, Roger D. Martin, and Leigh M. Weiss, "Mapping the Value of Employee Collaboration," *McKinsey Quarterly*, no. 3, August 2006. Also see Bradford C. Johnson, James M. Manyika, and Lareina A. Yee, "The Next Revolution in Interactions," *McKinsey Quarterly*, no. 4, November 2005, which is described briefly and critiqued by John Hagel at http://edgeperspectives.typepad.com/edge_perspectives/2006/04/the_next_revolu.html.

4. Johnson, Manyika, and Yee, "The Next Revolution in Interactions."

5. Lowell Bryan, McKinsey & Company (presentation at The Management Lab conference Inventing the Future of Management, Half Moon Bay, CA, May 2008). Described in the newsletter *Labnotes* from the London School of Economics, issue no. 9, September 2008, http://www.managementlab.org/files/LabNotes9.pdf.

6. Mihaly Csikszentmihalyi, *Good Business: Leadership, Flow, and the Making of Meaning* (New York: Penguin Books, 2003), 202–203.

7. Cited in a 2001 survey of information work conducted by the Department of Commerce and the National Telecommunications Information Agency. See U.S. Bureau of Labor Statistics press release, August 2, 2005, http://www.bls.gov/news.release/ciuaw.nr0.htm.

8. Torkel Klingberg, *The Overflowing Brain: Information Overload and the Limits of Working Memory* (New York: Oxford University Press, 2008). Also see Kevin A. Miller, *Surviving Information Overload: The Clear, Practical Guide to Help You Stay on Top of What You Need to Know* (Grand Rapids, MI: Zondervan, 2004).

9. Mary Czerwinski, Edward Cutrell, and Eric Horvitz, "Instant Messaging and Interruption: Influence of Task Type on Performance," Microsoft Research, 2000, http://research.microsoft.com/~marycz/ozchi2000.pdf. See also Mary Czerwinski, Eric Horvitz, and Susan Wilhite, "A Diary Study of Task Switching and Interruptions," Microsoft

Research, 2004, http://research.microsoft.com/users/marycz/chi2004diarystudyfinal.pdf; and Gloria Mark, Victor M. Gonzalez, and Justin Harris, "No Task Left Behind? Examining the Nature of Fragmented Work" (paper presented at CHI, Portland, OR, April 2005), http://www.ics.uci.edu/~gmark/CHI2005.pdf.

10. Claudia Wallis and Sonja Steptoe, "Help! I've Lost My Focus," *Time*, January 10, 2006, http://www.time.com/time/magazine/printout/0,8816,1147199,00.html.

11. Ibid.

12. Good proposals for work taxonomies include the following: Robert P. Tett, Hal A. Guterman, Angela Bleier, and Patrick J. Murphy, "Development and Content Validation of a 'Hyperdimensional' Taxonomy of Managerial Competence," *Human Performance* 13, no. 3 (2000): 205–251; and R. J. Harvey, "Empirical Foundations for the Things-Data-People Taxonomy of Work" (paper presented at the annual conference of the Society for Industrial and Organizational Psychology, Things, Data, and People: Fifty Years of a Seminal Theory, Chicago, IL, April 2004).

13. The various O*NET taxonomies and descriptions of methods for updating taxonomies are available at http://www.onetcenter.org/overview.html.

14. The O*NET approach is to identify generalized work activities (GWAs) and detailed work activities (DWAs) to summarize the broad and more specific types of job behaviors and tasks that may be performed within multiple occupations. Using this framework makes it possible to use a single set of descriptors to describe many occupations. For more details see "The O*NET Content Model," http://www.onetcenter.org/dl_files/ContentModel_DetailedDesc.pdf.

15. *Company of Heroes* is a real-time strategy computer game set in World War II developed by Relic Entertainment and released in 2006. A 2007 expansion was *Company of Heroes: Opposing Fronts*.

16. *Diablo II: Lord of Destruction* is a 1997 expansion pack for the action role-playing game *Diablo II* from Blizzard Entertainment.

17. *Guild Wars* is a fantasy-themed multiplayer online role-playing game developed by ArenaNet and published by the Korean publisher NCsoft in various expansions from 2005 to 2007.

18. *Age of Empires III* is a real-time strategy (RTS) game developed by Ensemble Studios and published by Microsoft Game Studios in 2005. It is the third in a series portraying European colonization of the Americas.

19. *Counter-Strike* is a first-person shooter game released commercially by Valve Corporation in 2000.

20. *Star Wars Galaxies* is a multiplayer online game developed by Sony Online Entertainment based on the *Star Wars* franchise themes and published by LucasArts Entertainment in 2003.

21. *Warcraft III: Reign of Chaos* is a strategy game released by Blizzard Entertainment in 2002 as a sequel in the Warcraft Universe series.

22. *EVE Online* is a massively multiplayer online game set in outer space developed by CCP Games and released in 2003 by Simon & Schuster Interactive.

23. *Mount & Blade* is a single-player action role-playing video game developed by TaleWorlds (in Turkey) and published by Paradox Interactive in 2008.

24. Described first in *Labnotes* from the London School of Economics, issue no. 9, September 2008, http://www.managementlab.org/files/LabNotes9.pdf. and subsequently by Gary Hamel, "Moon Shots for Management," *Harvard Business Review*, February, 2009.

25. James C. Collins and Jerry I. Porras, *Built to Last: Successful Habits of Visionary Companies* (New York: HarperBusiness, 1994). An update in the series, a book that directly

addresses the creation of a sense of purpose, is Jerry Porras, Stewart Emery, and Mark Thompson, *Success Built to Last: Creating a Life That Matters* (Upper Saddle River, NJ: Wharton School Publishing, 2007).

Chapter Four

1. The organization of memory and thinking in relation to people and social relationships often goes under the label of "social cognition." A good introduction to this area is Ziva Kunda, *Social Cognition: Making Sense of People* (Cambridge, MA: MIT Press, 1999).

2. Sohye Lim and Byron Reeves, "Being in the Game: Effects of Avatar Choice and Point of View on Arousal Responses During Play" (paper presented to the Information Systems Division of the International Communication Association, San Francisco, CA, 2007).

3. An example study involving arousal and memory is described in M. Bradley, M. Greenwald, M. Petry, and P. Lang, "Remembering Pictures: Pleasure and Arousal in Memory," *Journal of Experimental Psychology: Learning, Memory and Cognition* 18, no. 2 (1992): 379–390. For a theoretical treatment and review of arousal and memory in media research, see A. Lang, "The Limited Capacity Model of Mediated Message Processing," *Journal of Communication* 50, no. 1 (2000): 46–70.

4. For a good discussion of the role of emotions and emotional intelligence in business, see Daniel Goleman, Richard Boyatzis, and Annie McKee, *Primal Leadership: Learning to Lead with Emotional Intelligence* (Boston: Harvard Business School Press, 2004).

5. The theory behind this conclusion is reviewed in chapter 10 of this book. It is discussed extensively in Byron Reeves and Clifford Nass, *The Media Equation: How People Treat Computers, Television and New Media Like Real People and Places* (New York: Cambridge University Press, 1996).

6. The comment from James Gee was made during a presentation to a meeting of Investigators in Health Games Research, a program sponsored by the Robert Woods Johnson Foundation, Baltimore, MD, May 2008.

7. The calculation of the virtual size of *World of Warcraft* is posted at http://www.spaaace.com/cope/?p=111.

8. Derek Clements-Croome, *Creating the Productive Workplace* (London: Taylor & Francis, 1999).

9. For example, the *World of Warcraft* website (www.worldofwarcraft.com) has extensive coverage of the game backstory, character profiles, quests, place descriptions and more.

10. For a basic introduction to the role of narrative in persuasion and psychology, see Annette Simmons, *The Story Factor: Inspiration, Influence, and Persuasion Through the Art of Storytelling* (New York: Basic Books, 2006). For a discussion of the use of stories in business practice, see Joan Margretta, "Why Business Models Matter," *Harvard Business Review*, May 2002.

11. For a wonderful analysis of this topic by a master game designer, see Chris Crawford, *Chris Crawford on Interactive Storytelling* (Berkeley, CA: New Riders, 2005).

12. For a summary of some of the psychological research about narrative, see Linda Alwitt, "Maintaining Attention to a Narrative Event," in *Advances in Psychology Research*, vol. 18, ed. S. Shohov (Huntington, NY: Nova Science Publishers, 2002).

13. Ann Lang, "How Story Impacts Emotional, Motivational and Physiological Responses to First-Person Shooter Video Games," *Human Communication Research* 30, no. 3 (2006): 361–375.

14. Jennings Bryant and Dorina Miron, "Excitation-Transfer Theory and Three-Factor Theory of Emotion," in *Communication and Emotion: Essays in Honor of Dolf Zillmann*, eds.

Jennings Bryant, David Roskos-Ewldsen, and Joanne Cantor (Mahwah, NJ: Lawrence Erlbaum Associates, 2003).

15. For example, better memory for news stories that have a narrative chronology is shown in Annie Lang, "Making News Memorable," *Journal of Broadcasting* 47, no. 1 (2003): 113–123.

16. E. Tulving, "Episodic Memory: From Mind to Brain," *Annual Review of Psychology* 53 (2002): 1–25.

17. Narrative is often discussed as providing a schema (or organized memory) by which new information is evaluated. A schema biases memory in favor of consistent information. For example, see Robert Nemeth and Robert Belli, "The Influence of Schematic Knowledge on Contradictory Versus Additive Misinformation: False Memory for Typical and Atypical Items," *Journal of Applied Psychology* 20, no. 5 (2006): 563–573.

18. There is a large literature on the use of stories and narrative in business and planning. Two good examples are Peter Guber, "The Four Truths of the Storyteller," *Harvard Business Review*, December 2007; and Stephen Dennin, "Telling Tales," *Harvard Business Review*, May 2004. Also see the list of books at http://www.corpstory.com/amazon.htm.

19. The literature on feedback and behavior is extensive and is part of several behavioral theories, including classical and operant conditioning, behavior therapy, and behavior modification. A good review of classic theories and concepts applied to business and human services is Martin Sundel and Sandra Sundel, *Behavior Change in the Human Services: Behavioral and Cognitive Principles and Applications* (Thousand Oaks, CA: Sage Publications, 2005).

20. Behavioral economists are at the forefront of studying primitive responses to reward and punishment. For example, see Andrew Caplin and Mark Dean, "Dopamine, Reward Prediction Error, and Economics," *Quarterly Journal of Economics* 123, no. 2 (2008): 663–701.

21. The necessity of intrinsic rewards in long-term behavior change is a common topic in psychology. An often-cited discussion of the application of that principle in business is Alfie Kohn, "Why Incentive Plans Cannot Work," *Harvard Business Review*, September–October 1993. A review of the classic academic literature in this area can be found in David Kreps, "The Interaction Between Norms and Economic Incentives: Intrinsic Motivation and Extrinsic Incentives," *American Economic Review* 87, no. 2 (1997): 359–364.

22. The leading scholar in research about self-efficacy is Albert Bandura. An example of his writing that applies the concept to business is Albert Bandura, "The Evolution of Social Cognitive Theory," in *Great Minds in Management: The Process of Theory Development*, eds. Ken G. Smith and Michael A. Hitt (New York: Oxford University Press, 2005).

23. I. P. Pavlov, *Conditional Reflexes* (1927; repr., New York: Dover Publications).

24. We suggest one review and one example experiment about reputation systems. For a review, see Paul Resnick, Ko Kuwabara, Richard Zeckhauser, and Eric Friedman, "Reputation Systems," *Communications of the ACM* 43, no. 12 (2000): 45–48. A good example study is Paul Resnick, Richard Zeckhauser, John Swanson, and Kate Lockwood, "The Value of Reputation on eBay: A Controlled Experiment," *Experimental Economics* 9, no. 2 (2006): 79–101.

25. David Barboza, "Ogre to Slay? Outsource It to Chinese," *New York Times*, December 9, 2005.

26. H. Clark and S. Brennan, "Grounding in Communication," in *Perspectives on Socially Shared Cognition*, eds. L. B. Resnick, J. M. Levine, and S. D. Teasley (Washington, DC: American Psychological Association, 1991).

27. Edward Castronova, "A Test of the Law of Demand in a Virtual World: Exploring the Petri Dish Approach to Social Science," CESifo Working Paper Series no. 2355, Ifo Institute for Economic Research, Munich, 2008.

28. The areas of activation for both real and virtual currency are associated with the same brain regions as for general processing of rewards, indicating that the particular signals of reward are not as important as the general concept of reward. For example, see R. Saxe and H. Haushofer, "For Love or Money: A Common Neural Currency for Social and Monetary Reward," *Neuron* 58, no. 2 (2008): 164–165.

29. The influence in business of shared knowledge about rules is discussed in K. Van den Bos and E. A. Lind, "Uncertainty Management by Means of Fairness Judgments," in *Advances in Experimental Social Psychology*, vol. 34, ed. M. P. Zanna (San Diego, CA: Academic Press, 2002), 1–60.

30. H. M. Lefcourt, *Locus of Control: Current Trends in Theory and Research* (Hillsdale, NJ: Lawrence Erlbaum, 1982).

31. T. Hans, "A Meta-analysis of the Effects of Adventure Programming on Locus of Control," *Journal of Contemporary Psychotherapy* 30, no. 1 (2000): 33–60.

32. Nine of the top ten games are multiplayer games rather than solo games. See Seth Schiesel, "In the List of Top-Selling Games, Clear Evidence of a Sea Change," *New York Times*, February 1, 2008.

33. Several articles in an edited volume review studies of social relationships in games. See Peter Vorderer and Jennings Bryant, eds., *Playing Video Games: Motives, Responses, and Consequences* (Mahwah, NJ: Lawrence Erlbaum Associates, 2006).

34. H. Tajfel, ed., *Social Identity and Intergroup Relations* (New York: Cambridge University Press, 1982).

35. Sohye Lim and Byron Reeves, "Computer Agents Versus Avatars: Responses to Interactive Game Characters Controlled by a Computer Versus Other Player" (paper presented at the International Communication Association conference, San Francisco, CA, 2006).

36. T. J. Peters and R. H. Waterman, *In Search of Excellence* (Warner Books, 1982).

37. Bern Elliot, "Magic Quadrant for Unified Communications," Gartner RAS Core Research Note G00160407, September 2008, http://mediaproducts.gartner.com/reprints/microsoft/vol6/article1/article1.html.

38. There is a good discussion of the definition of games in James Gee, *What Video Games Have to Teach Us About Learning and Literacy* (New York: Palgrave Macmillan, 2007).

Chapter Five

1. Gartner, Inc., 2007. Gartner says 80 percent of active Internet users will have a second life in the virtual world by the end of 2011. Gartner Symposium ITxpo, Emerging Trends, April 24, 2007.

2. Among the new companies that are building virtual-world places and businesses are Millions of Us and Electric Sheep.

3. Data about virtual workers and their expected use of virtual worlds is reported in Erica Driver and Paul Jackson, "Getting Real Work Done in Virtual Worlds," Forrester Research, Inc., January 2008.

4. Freda Matchett, *Krsna, Lord or Avatara? The Relationship Between Krsna and Visnu: In the Context of the Avatara Myth as Presented by the Harivamsa, the Visnupurana and the Bhagavatapurana* (London: Routledge, 2000).

5. Edward Castronova, "Theory of the Avatar," http://www.cesifo-group.de/pls/guestci/download/CESifo%20Working%20Papers%202003/CESifo%20Working%20Papers%20February%202003%20/cesifo_wp863.pdf.

6. G. Rizzolatti, L. Fogassi, and V. Gallese, "Neurophysiological Mechanism Underlying the Understanding and Imitation of Action," *Nature Reviews: Neuroscience* 2 (2001): 661–670.

7. Phillip Jackson, Andrew Meltzoff, and Jean Decety, "Neural Circuits Involved in Imitation and Perspective Taking," *Neuroimage* 31, no. 1 (2005): 429–439.

8. An interesting study of social insults is Naomi Eisenberger and Matthew Lieberman, "Why Rejection Hurts: A Common Neural Alarm System for Physical and Social Pain," *Trends in Cognitive Science* 8, no. 7 (2005): 294–300.

9. Yawei Cheng, Andrew Meltzoff, and Jean Decety, "Motivation Modulates the Activity of the Human Mirror-Neuron System," *Cerebral Cortex* 17, no. 8 (2007): 1979–1986.

10. Sohye Lim and Byron Reeves, "Being in the Game: Effects of Avatar Choice and Point of View on Arousal Responses During Play" (paper presented to the Information Systems Division of the International Communication Association, San Francisco, CA, 2007).

11. First-person versus third-person memories are often referred to in psychology as field (third-person) versus observer (first-person) memories. The original treatment of the psychology of these differences is E. Jones and R. Nisbett, "The Actor and the Observer: Divergent Perceptions of the Causes of Behavior," in *Attribution: Perceiving the Causes of Behavior*, E. Jones et al. (Morristown, NJ: General Learning Press, 1971), 79–94.

12. Recent studies have shown that perspective differences can even cause changes in behavior, with third-person imaging more likely to cause people to perform the behavior being imaged; see L. Libby, E. Shaeffer, R. Eibach, and J. Slemmer, "Picture Yourself at the Polls: Visual Perspective in Mental Imagery Affects Self-Perception and Behavior," *Psychological Science* 18, no. 3 (2007): 199–203.

13. R. Friedman and S. Currall, "Conflict Escalation: Dispute Exacerbating Elements of E-mail Communication Conflict," *Human Relations* 56, no. 11 (2003): 1325–1347. See also M. Markus, "Finding a Happy Medium: Explaining the Negative Effects of Electronic Communication on Social Life at Work," *ACM Transactions on Information Systems* 12, no. 2 (2003): 119–149.

14. The project described here, "It Doesn't Matter If You're Black or White," was conducted in a Stanford course (Media Psychology, Prof. Byron Reeves) and was conducted by Phillip Garland, Vanessa Vega, Qian Ying Wang, and Michelle Won in 2004.

15. Several studies about race and interpersonal communication are reviewed in Mark Knapp and John Daly, eds., *Handbook of Interpersonal Communication*, 3rd ed. (Thousand Oaks, CA: Sage Publications, 2002).

16. See http://www.youtube.com/watch?v=obCHKPYHuhA. There is also a great avatar commercial about "making money" as the point of innovation; see http://www.youtube.com/watch?v=v373r0to8Pk.

17. The IBM guidelines for virtual employees can be viewed on the IBM website at http://domino.research.ibm.com/comm/research_projects.nsf/pages/virtualworlds.IBMVirtualWorldGuidelines.html.

18. This is a reference to the classic text by Dale Carnegie, *How to Win Friends and Influence People* (New York: Simon and Schuster, 1936).

19. J. N. Bailenson, J. Blascovich, and R. E. Godagno, "Self-Representations in Immersive Virtual Environments," *Journal of Applied Social Psychology* 38, no. 11 (2008): 2673–2690.

20. R. Guadagno, J. Blascovich, J. N. Bailenson, and C. McCall, "Virtual Humans and Persuasion: The Effects of Agency and Behavioral Realism," *Media Psychology* 10 (2007): 1–22.

21. J. Bailenson and N. Yee, "Virtual Interpersonal Touch: Haptic Interaction and Copresence in Collaborative Virtual Environments," *Multimedia Tools and Applications* 37 (2008): 5–14.

22. J. N. Bailenson, N. Yee, D. Merget, and R. Schroeder, "The Effect of Behavioral Realism and Form Realism of Real-Time Avatar Faces on Verbal Disclosure, Nonverbal Disclosure, Emotion Recognition, and Copresence in Dyadic Interaction," *Presence: Teleoperators and Virtual Environments* 15, no. 4 (2006): 359–372.

23. J. N. Bailenson, K. R. Swinth, C. L. Hoyt, S. Persky, A. Dimov, and J. Blascovich, "The Independent and Interactive Effects of Embodied Agent Appearance and Behavior on Self-Report, Cognitive, and Behavioral Markers of Copresence in Immersive Virtual Environments," *Presence: Teleoperators and Virtual Environments* 14 (2005): 379–393.

24. Joseph Cappella, "The Biological Origins of Automated Patterns of Human Interaction," *Communication Theory* 1, no. 1 (1991): 4–35.

25. J. N. Bailenson, A. C. Beall, and J. Blascovich, "Mutual Gaze and Task Performance in Shared Virtual Environments," *Journal of Visualization and Computer Animation* 13 (2002): 1–8.

26. Edward Hall and Mildred Reed Hall, *Understanding Cultural Differences* (Yarmouth, ME: Intercultural Press, 1990).

27. Nick Yee, Jeremy Bailenson, Mark Urbanek, Francis Chang, and Dan Merget, "The Unbearable Likeness of Being Digital: The Persistence of Nonverbal Social Norms in Online Virtual Environments", *CyberPsychology and Behavior* 10, no. 1 (2007): 115–121.

28. Stewart McCann, "Simple Method for Predicting American Presidential Greatness from Victory Margin in Popular Vote," *Journal of Social Psychology* 145, no. 3 (2005): 287–298.

Chapter Six

1. Attributed by Thomas Friedman to economist Paul Romer (see http://www.nytimes.com/2008/07/20/opinion/20friedman.html) and used by many others http://theenergycollective.com/TheEnergyCollective/30890.

2. Edward Castronova, *Synthetic Worlds* (Chicago: University of Chicago Press, 2005).

3. Julian Dibbell, "MUD Money: A Talk on Virtual Value and, Incidentally, the Value of the Virtual" (paper presented at the Stages of the Virtual conference, Rutgers University Center for the Critical Analysis of Contemporary Culture, April 1995), http://www.juliandibbell.com/texts/mudmoney.html.

4. Castronova, *Synthetic Worlds*, 175.

5. Claude Hermann Walter Johns and T. Clark, *Babylonian and Assyrian Laws, Contracts and Letters* (New York: C. Scribner's Sons, 1904). See also Philip Henry Gosse, *Assyria: Her Manners and Customs, Arts and Arms: Restored from Her Monuments* (London: Society for promoting Christian Knowledge, 1852), 610.

6. Jack Weatherford, *The History of Money: From Sandstone to Cyberspace* (New York: Three Rivers Press, 1997).

7. In addition to Castronova's previously cited book (*Synthetic Worlds*), there are numerous websites and conferences on this topic. One of each that we like are http://terranova.blogs.com and the Virtual Goods Summits held in 2007 and 2008 (see http://vgsummit2008.com).

8. Edward Castronova, "Virtual Worlds: A First-Hand Account of the Market and Society on the Cyberian Frontier," CESifo Working Paper Series no. 618, Ifo Institute for Economic Research, Munich, 2001.

9. Julian Dibbell, *Play Money: Or, How I Quit My Day Job and Made Millions Trading Virtual Loot* (New York: Basic Books, 2006).

10. A good example of a game currency trading service is IGE (www.ige.com). Since 2001, it has been one of the larger networks for trading virtual currencies and game assets. It estimates that by 2009, the market for virtual assets will overcome the primary market for game subscriptions, estimated to become $7 billion.

11. Linden Lab (makers of *Second Life*) now offers a marketplace platform (The LindeX) that facilitates the purchase and sale of Linden dollars. The details are at http://lindenlab.com/pressroom/general/factsheets/economics.

12. Castronova, *Synthetic Worlds*, chapter 8.

13. Thomas Malone, "Bringing the Market Inside," *Harvard Business Review*, April 2004. See also Liisa Välikangas and Gary Hamel, "Internal Markets: Emerging Governance Structures for Innovation" (paper presented at the Strategic Management Society conference, San Francisco, CA, 2001), http://www.strategos.com/articles/internalmkts/markets4.htm.

14. Lowell Bryan, Claudia Joyce, and Leigh M. Weiss, "Making a Market in Talent: A 21st-Century Company Should Put as Much Effort into Developing Its Talented Employees as It Puts into Recruiting Them," *McKinsey Quarterly*, May 2006.

15. Thomas Malone, *The Future of Work: How the New Order of Business Will Shape Your Organization, Your Management Style, and Your Life* (Boston: Harvard Business School Press, 2004).

16. Described briefly in *Labnotes* from the London School of Economics, issue no. 9, September 2008, http://www.managementlab.org/files/LabNotes9.pdf, and and subsequently by Gary Hamel, "Moon Shots for Management," *Harvard Business Review*, February, 2009.

17. James Surowiecki, *The Wisdom of Crowds: Why the Many Are Smarter Than the Few and How* (New York: Doubleday, 2004).

18. Scott Page, *The Difference: How the Power of Diversity Creates Better Groups, Firms, Schools, and Societies* (Princeton, NJ: Princeton University Press, 2007).

19. Jeff Howe, *Crowdsourcing: Why the Power of the Crowd Is Driving the Future of Business* (New York: Crown Business, 2008).

20. Bo Cowgill, Justin Wolfers, and Eric Zitzewitz, "Using Prediction Markets to Track Information Flows: Evidence from Google," January 6, 2008, http://bocowgill.com/GooglePredictionMarketPaper.pdf.

21. The source for the actual comments, which offer a feast of insight into the potential value of prediction markets, is Commodity Futures Trading Commission, Concept Release on the Appropriate Regulatory Treatment of Event Contracts, *Federal Register* 73, no. 89 (May 7, 2008), 25669.

22. The prediction market at Google is described in Cowgill, Wolfers, and Zitzewitz, "Using Prediction Markets to Track Information Flows."

23. Ibid.

24. We designed the currency system (called Attent) with colleagues at Seriosity, Inc. The ideas are described in David Abecassis, Helen Cheng, Mark Phillips, Leighton Read, Byron Reeves, Simon Roy, and Daniel Rubin, "Attention Economy for Attention to Messages, Tasks and Resources," US Patent 7,240,826, issued July 10, 2007.

25. Thomas Davenport and John Beck, *The Attention Economy: Understanding the New Currency of Business* (Boston: Harvard Business Press, 2002).

26. Z. D. Zeldes, D. Sward, and S. Louchheim, "Infomania: Why We Can't Afford to Ignore It Any Longer," *First Monday* 12, no. 8 (August 2007), http://www.firstmonday.org/issues/issue12_8/zeldes/.

27. The synthetic currency software is *Attent*, which is described and available at www.seriosity.com.

28. Byron Reeves, Simon Roy, Brian Gorman, and Teresa Morley, "A Marketplace for Attention: Responses to a Synthetic Currency Used to Signal Information Importance," *First Monday* 13, no. 5 (May 2008).

Chapter Seven

1. For a good review of the economies of DKP systems, see Edward Castronova and Joshua Fairfield, "Dragon Kill Points: A Summary Whitepaper," working paper, Indiana University, January 2007, http://ssrn.com/abstract=958945.

2. The ideas about a group of intimates engaging strangers, cited in Castronova and Fairfield, "Dragon Kill Points," was first proposed in Jacob Strahilevitz , "Social Norms from Close-Knit Groups to Loose-Knit Groups," *University of Chicago Law Review* 70 (2003): 359–360.

3. Jim Murphy and Jennifer Hackbush, "The Knowledge Management Spending Report, 2007–2008: The Market Hits $73B," AMR Research, 2007. Abstract available at http://knowledgemanagement.wordpress.com/2007/09/28/survey-on-knowledge-management-spending-for-2008/.

4. Margaret Neale, "Information Technology as a Jealous Mistress: Competition for Knowledge Between Individuals and Organization," *Management Information System Quarterly* 27 (2003): 265–287.

5. Sirkka L. Jarvenpaa, Kathleen Knoll, and Dorothy E. Leidner, "Is Anyone Out There? Antecedents of Trust in Global Virtual Teams," *Journal of Management Information Systems* 14, no. 4 (1998).

6. Jeremy B. Williams, "Foiling the Free Riders: Early Experience with Compulsory Peer Assessment at an Online Business School," Universitas 21 Global working paper, 2005. Manuscript available at http://www.u21global.edu.sg/PartnerAdmin/ViewContent?module= DOCUMENTLIBRARY&oid=14105. This paper reports on the first twelve months' experience of a compulsory peer assessment system that represents a modest attempt to install such a reporting system, with the goal of calling the free riders to account.

7. Don Tapscott and Anthony Williams, *Wikinomics: How Mass Collaboration Changes Everything* (New York: Portfolio, 2006).

8. The distinctions between tacit and explicit knowledge are widely used in the organizational literature, as reviewed in Neale, "Information Technology as a Jealous Mistress." Several McKinsey & Company publications cited in chapter 6 also deal with this topic.

9. There are several lists of collaboration principles that are similar. This list borrows from Lynda Gratton and Tamara Erickson, "Eight Ways to Build Collaborative Teams," *Harvard Business Review*, November 2007.

10. Byron Reeves and Thomas Malone, with Nick Yee, Helen Cheng, David Abecassis, Thomas Cadwell, Macy Abbey, James Scarborough, Leighton Read, and Simon Roy, "Leadership in Games and at Work: Implications for the Enterprise of Massively Multiplayer Online Role-Playing Games," Seriosity, 2007, http://www.seriosity.com.

11. J. Williams, "Foiling the Free Riders: Early Experience with Compulsory Peer Assessment at an Online Business School," Universitas 21 Global, working paper No. 012/2005.

12. Paul Ingrassa, "How Detroit Drove into a Ditch," *Wall Street Journal*, October 25, 2008, http://online.wsj.com/article/SB122488710556068177.html.

13. L. Gratton and T. J. Erickson, "Eight Ways to Build Collaborative Teams." *Harvard Business Review*, November, 2007.

14. Larry Huston and Nabil Sakkab, "Connect and Develop: Inside Procter and Gamble's New Model for Innovation," *Harvard Business Review*, March 2006.

15. Alph Bingham has speculated on how classifications by nonexperts could be valuable in the medical setting in personal communication and as reported at http://crowdsourcing.typepad.com/cs/2008/09/crowdsourcing-m.html. Our discussion of networks is based on his review.

16. This is a point made by James Surowiecki in *The Wisdom of Crowds: Why the Many Are Smarter Than the Few and How* (New York: Doubleday, 2004).

17. Here is a bibliography not limited to medical diagnosis: http://www.galaxy.gmu.edu/ACAS/ACAS00-02/ACAS00ShortCourse/aggbib.pdf.

18. B. Metcalfe, "Metcalfe's Law: A Network Becomes More Valuable as It Reaches More Users," *Infoworld*, October 2, 1995.

19. D. Reed, "That Sneaky Exponential: Beyond Metcalfe's Law to the Power of Community Building," 2002, http://www.reed.com/papers/gfn/reedslaw.html.

Chapter Eight

1. These player comments were collected by Nick Yee and are part of the Daedalus Project (http://www.nickyee.com/daedalus/archives/001467.php).
2. The discussion of real-world and game leadership in this chapter is taken from a project done for the IBM Global Innovation Summit. The project leaders were Thomas Malone and Byron Reeves. The three sources that were used in chapter 8 are listed below. The comments about similarities and differences are taken from the first unpublished paper listed.

> Byron Reeves and Thomas Malone, with Nick Yee, Helen Cheng, David Abecassis, Thomas Cadwell, Macy Abby, James Scarborough, Leighton Read, and Simon Roy, "Leadership in Games and at Work: Implications for the Enterprise of Massively Multiplay Online Role Playing Games," Seriosity, 2007, http://www.seriosity.com/leadership.html.

> IBM and Seriosity, "Virtual Worlds, Real Leaders: Online Games Put the Future of Business Leadership on Display", a Global Innovation Outlook 2.0 report, 2007, http://www.seriosity.com/leadership.html.

> Byron Reeves, Thomas Malone, and Tony O'Driscoll, "Leadership's Online Labs," *Harvard Business Review*, May 2008.

3. The Sloan leadership model was developed by Deborah Ancona, Thomas Malone, Wanda Orlikowski, and Peter Senge at the MIT Sloan School of Management. The model has been described in several publications, including the following: D. Ancona, "Leadership in an Age of Uncertainty," in *Managing for the Future: Organizational Behavior and Processes*, 2nd ed., eds. Deborah Ancona, Thomas Kochan, Maureen Scully, John Van Maanen, and Eleanor Westney (Cincinnati, OH: South Western College Publishing, 1999); Thomas Malone, *The Future of Work* (Boston: Harvard Business School Press, 2004), 162–167; and D. Ancona, T. W. Malone, W. J. Orlikowski, and P. Senge, "In Praise of the Incomplete Leader," *Harvard Business Review*, February 2007.
4. The concept of sensemaking, as we use it here, was developed by Karl Weick. See K. Weick, *Making Sense of the Organization* (Malden, MA: Blackwell Publishing, 2001).
5. C. Argyris and D. Schon, *Organizational Learning II: Theory, Method, and Practice* (Reading, MA: Addison-Wesley, 1996).
6. A description of the methods used in the research can be found in Reeves and Malone, with Yee, Cheng, Abecassis, Cadwell, Abby, Scarborough, Read, and Roy, "Leadership in Games and at Work."
7. Nick Yee, "The Demographics, Motivations, and Derived Experiences of Users of Massively Multi-User Online Graphical Environments," *Presence: Teleoperators and Virtual Environments* 15 (2006): 309–329.
8. A good summary of the informal learning opportunities is J. Bransford, A. Brown, and J. Pellegrino, eds., *How People Learn* (Washington, DC: National Academy Press, 2000). Also see J. Bransford, B. Barron, R. Pea, A. Meltzoff, P. Kuhl, P. Bell, P. Stevens, D. Shwartz, N. Vye, B. Reeves, J. Roschelle, and N. Sabelli, "Foundations and Opportunities for an Interdisciplinary Science of Learning," in *The Cambridge Handbook of the Learning Sciences*, ed. K. Sawyer (New York: Cambridge University Press, 2006).
9. J. Burton, M. Parker, B. Pleasant, and D. Van Doren, "What Is Unified Communications—And Why Should You Care?" *Business Communication Review*, August 2006. Available at http://www.vanguard.net/DocLib_Docs/UC_why_care_mp_dv_0608.pdf.

10. Michael DeMarco, Eric Lesser, and Tony O'Driscoll, "Leadership in a Distributed World: Lessons from Online Gaming," IBM Institute for Business Value, 2007.

Chapter Nine

1. For a comprehensive review of this literature, see James Harter, Frank Schmidt, and Corey Keyes, "Well-Being in the Workplace and Its Relationship to Business Outcomes," in *Flourishing: The Positive Person and the Good Life*, eds. Corey Keyes and Jonathan Haidt (Washington, DC: American Psychological Association, 2002), 205–224.

2. Brian Sutton-Smith, *The Ambiguity of Play* (Cambridge, MA: Harvard University Press, 1997).

3. The first seven of these concepts of play are taken from Sutton-Smith, *The Ambiguity of Play*.

4. "Solitaire Costs Man His City Job After Bloomberg Sees Computer," *New York Times*, February 10, 2006, http://www.nytimes.com/2006/02/10/nyregion/10solitaire.html.

5. M. Weber, *The Protestant Ethic and the Spirit of Capitalism* (London: Allen and Unwin, 1930).

6. "Games at Work May Be Good for You," BBC News, November 7, 2003, http://news.bbc.co.uk/2/hi/technology/3247595.stm.

7. R. Huizinga, *Homo Ludens: A Study of the Play Element in Culture* (Boston: Beacon Press, 1949).

8. Daniel Oriesek and Jan Oliver Schwarz, *Business Wargaming: Securing Corporate Value* (Burlington, VT: Gower Publishing, 2008).

9. Sun Tzu [Sunzi], *The Art of War*, trans. Thomas Cleary (Boston: Shamhala Publications, 1988).

10. One good example is Aaron Brown, *The Poker Face of Wall Street* (New York: John Wiley and Sons, 2006).

11. Michael Zyda, "From Visual Simulation to Virtual Reality to Games," *Computer* 38, no. 9 (2005): 25–32.

12. For a review of flight simulator effectiveness, see Alfred Lee, "Simulator Fidelity and Training Effectiveness," in *Flight Simulation: Virtual Environments in Aviation* (Burlington, VT: Ashgate Publishing, 2005). For a review of medical simulations, see Lawrence Hettinger and Michael Hass, eds., *Virtual and Adaptive Environments: Applications, Implications and Human Performance Issues* (Mahwah, NJ: Lawrence Erlbaum Associates, 2003).

13. L. Enoshsson, B. Isaksson, R. Tou, A. Kjellin, L. Hedman, T. Wredmak, and L. Tsai-Fellander, "Visuospatial Skills and Computer Game Experience Influence the Performance of Virtual Endoscopy," *Journal of Gastrointestinal Surgery* 8, no. 7 (2004): 876–882.

14. J. Rosser, P. Lynch, L. Cuddihy, D. Gentile, J. Klonsky, and R. Merrell, "The Impact of Video Games on Training Surgeons in the 21st Century," *Archives of Surgery* 142, no. 2 (2007): 181–186.

15. J. Fernandez, ed. *Beyond Metaphor: The Theory of Tropes in Anthropology* (Stanford, CA: Stanford University Press, 1991).

16. Sutton-Smith, *Ambiguity of Play*, 127.

17. Kant's treatment of imagination is described in R. Makkreel, *Imagination and Interpretation in Kant: The Hermeneutical Import of the "Critique of Judgment"* (Chicago: University of Chicago Press, 1994).

18. Andrew Caplin and Mark Dean, "Dopamine, Reward Prediction Error, and Economics," *Quarterly Journal of Economics* 123, no. 2 (2008): 663–701.

19. Mihaly Csikszentmihalyi, *Flow: The Psychology of Optimal Experience* (New York: Harper Collins, 1990).

20. The attributes of flow experiences are taken from Mihaly Csikszentmihalyi, *Creativity: Flow and the Psychology of Discovery and Invention* (New York: HarperCollins, 1996), 110–113.

21. J. L. Sherry, "Flow and Media Enjoyment," *Communication Theory* 14 (2004): 392–410.

22. Michael Sellers, "Designing the Experience of Interactive Play," in *Playing Video Games*, eds. P. Vorderer and J. Bryant (Mahwah, NJ: Lawrence Erlbaum, 2006).

23. Mihaly Csikszentmihalyi, *Good Business: Leadership, Flow, and the Making of Meaning* (New York: Penguin Books, 2003), 202–203.

24. For a discussion of basic emotional categories, see Paul Ekman, "An Argument for Basic Emotions," *Cognition and Emotion* 6 (1992): 169–175.

25. A. Lang, J. Newhagen, and B. Reeves, "Negative Video as Structure: Emotion, Attention, Capacity, and Memory," *Journal of Broadcasting and Electronic Media* 40 (1996). Also see S. Geiger and B. Reeves, "The Effects of Scene Changes and Semantic Relatedness on Attention to Television," *Communication Research* 20 (1993): 155–175.

26. Ann Lang, "How Story Impacts Emotional, Motivational and Physiological Responses to First-Person Shooter Video Games," *Human Communication Research* 30, no. 3 (2006): 361–375.

27. Mary Beth Oliver, "Mood Management and Selective Exposure," in *Communication and Emotion*, eds. Jennings Bryant, David Roskos-Ewoldsen, and Joanne Cantor (Mahwah, NJ: Lawrence Erlbaum Associates, 2003).

28. R. J. Davidson, "Emotion and Affective Style: Affective Substrates," *Psychological Science* 3, no. 1 (1992): 39–43.

29. See chapter 10 ("Negativity") in Byron Reeves and Clifford Nass, *The Media Equation: How People Treat Computers, Television and New Media Like Real People and Places* (New York: Cambridge University Press, 1996).

30. We are currently testing this exact sequence using avatars experienced during brain functional magnetic resonance imaging. The preliminary results have been reported at a neuroscience conference: J. Chen, D. Shohamy, V. Ross, B. Reeves, and A. Wagner, "The Impact of Social Belief on the Neurophysiology of Learning and Memory" (paper presented at the Society for Neuroscience conference, Washington, DC, 2008).

31. For a review of the study of informal learning in the learning sciences, see J. Bransford, B. Barron, R. Pea, A. Meltzoff, P. Kuhl, P. Bell, P. Stevens, D. Shwartz, N. Vye, B. Reeves, J. Roschelle, and N. Sabelli, "Foundations and Opportunities for an Interdisciplinary Science of Learning," in *The Cambridge Handbook of the Learning Sciences*, ed. K. Sawyer (New York: Cambridge University Press, 2006).

32. For examples related to math learning, see K. Himmelberger and D. Schwartz, "It's a Homerun! Using Mathematical Discourse to Support the Learning of Statistics," *Mathematics Teacher* 101, no. 4 (2007): 250–256.

33. D. Schwartz, J. Bransford, and D. Sears, "Efficiency and Innovation in Transfer," in *Transfer of Learning from a Modern Multidisciplinary Perspective*, ed. J. Mestre (Greenwich, CT: Information Age Publishing, 2005), 1–51.

Chapter Ten

1. In addition to following the dot, the actual experiment also asked people to lead and to just watch. Results were similar to those about the instruction to lead that are described here.

2. T. Chaminade, A.N. Meltzoff, and J. Decety, "Brain Mechanisms for Awareness of Interacting with an Intentional Agent: An fMRI Study." Center for Mind, Brain & Learning, University of Washington, 2004.

3. Byron Reeves and Sohye Lim, "Computer Agents Versus Avatars: Responses to Interactive Game Characters Controlled by a Computer or Other Player" (paper presented to the International Communication Association conference, San Francisco, CA, 2006).

4. Heart rate acceleration is only one measure of arousal and can be associated with both higher and lower arousal. In this experiment, we also assessed skin conductance levels (i.e., the amount of moisture in the skin as a result of arousal) and were able to determine that the increased heart rate was attributable to higher physiological arousal.

5. Byron Reeves and Clifford Nass, *The Media Equation: How People Treat Computers, Television and New Media Like Real People and Places* (New York: Cambridge University Press, 1996).

6. These examples are all reviewed in Reeves and Nass, *The Media Equation*.

7. From the 1979 movie *Being There*, adapted from the 1971 novel written by Jerzy Kosinksi.

8. M. Lombard and T. Ditton, "At the Heart of It All: The Concept of Presence," *Journal of Computer-Mediated Communication* 3, no. 2 (1997).

9. For example, *Presence: Teleoperators and Virtual Environments* and the *Journal of Computer-Mediated Communication*, Presence-Research.org (www.presence-research.org), and the International Society for Presence Research.

10. For example, the Instant Messaging and Presence Service (IMPS) of the Open Mobile Alliance (OMA) or the Session initiation protocol for Instant Messaging and Presence Leveraging Extensions (SIMPLE) sponsored by the Internet Engineering Task Force (IETF) (we're not kidding). See http://www.ietf.org/html.charters/simple-charter.html.

11. Jonathan Steuer, "Defining Virtual Reality: Dimensions Determining Telepresence," *Journal of Communication* 42, no. 2 (1992): 73–93.

12. D. Perani, F. Fazio, N. Borghese, M. Tettamanti, S. Ferrari, J. Decety, and M. Gillardi, "Different Brain Correlates for Watching Real and Virtual Hand Actions," *Neuroimage* 14, no. 3 (2001): 749–758.

13. B. Reeves, A. Lang, E. Y. Kim, and D. Tatar, "The Effects of Screen Size and Message Content on Arousal and Attention," *Media Psychology* 1, no. 1 (1999): 49–67.

14. W. R. Neuman, A. Crigler, and V. Bove, "Television Sound and Viewer Perceptions," *Proceedings of the Joint IEEE/Audio Engineering Society*, February 1991.

15. An example study that looks at proprioception is M. Mine, F. Brooks, and C. Sequin, "Moving Objects in Space: Exploiting Proprioception in Virtual-Environment Interaction," *Proceedings of the 24th Annual Conference on Computer Graphics*, 1997, 19–26.

16. See, for example, P. Kenny, A. Hartholt, J. Gratch, W. Swartout, D. Traum, S. Marsella, and D. Piepol, "Building Interactive Virtual Humans for Training Environments," *Proceedings of I/ITSEC*, November 2007.

17. Jonathan Steuer, "Defining Virtual Reality: Dimensions Determining Telepresence," *Journal of Communication* 42, no. 2 (1992): 73–93.

18. K. Wise and B. Reeves, "The Effect of User Control on the Cognitive and Emotional Processing of Pictures," *Media Psychology* 9 (2007): 549–566.

19. Keith Devlin, "Media X: The New Liberal Arts?" *On the Horizon* 10, no. 2 (2002): 15–17.

20. For example descriptions of play in MUDs, see Sherry Turkle, "Constructions and Reconstructions of Self in Virtual Reality: Playing in the MUDs," *Mind, Culture and Activity* 1, no. 3 (1994): 158–167.

21. Paul Messaris, *Visual "Literacy": Image, Mind and Reality* (Boulder, CO: Westview Press, 1994).

22. David Weaver, Randal Beam, Bonnie Brownlee, Paul Voakes, and Cleveland Wilhoit, *The American Journalist in the 21st Century* (Mahwah, NJ: L. Erlbaum Associates, 2007).

23. See, for example, Diana Mutz and Byron Reeves, "The New Videomalaise: Effects of Televised Incivility on Political Trust," *American Political Science Review* 99, no. 1 (2005): 1–15.

24. James Beniger, *The Control Revolution* (Cambridge, MA: Harvard University Press, 1986).

25. Craig Anderson and Brad Bushman, "Effects of Violent Video Games on Aggressive Behavior, Aggressive Cognition, Aggressive Affects, Physiological Arousal, and Prosocial Behavior: A Meta Analytic Review of the Scientific Literature," *Psychological Science* 12, no. 5 (2002): 353–359. An update of this analysis appears in Craig Anderson, "An Update on the Effects of Playing Violent Video Games," *Journal of Adolescence* 27 (2004): 113–122.

26. S. Sherry, "The Effects of Violent Video Games on Aggression: A Meta-analysis," *Human Communication Research* 27, no. 3 (2001): 409–431.

27. Ann Lang, "How Story Impacts Emotional, Motivational and Physiological Responses to First-Person Shooter Video Games," *Human Communication Research* 30, no. 3 (2006): 361–375.

28. M. D. Griffiths and I. Dancaster, "The Effect of Type A Personality on Physiological Arousal While Playing Computer Games," *Addictive Behaviors* 20, no. 4 (1995): 543–548.

29. Michelle Fleming and Debra Rick Wood, "Effects of Violent Versus Nonviolent Video Games on Children's Arousal, Aggressive Mood and Positive Mood," *Journal of Applied Social Psychology* 31, no. 10 (2006): 2047–2071.

30. Richard Davidson, "Dysfunction in the Neural Circuitry of Emotion Regulation: A Possible Prelude to Violence," *Science* 289, no. 5479 (2000): 591–594.

31. Rene Weber, Ute Ritterfeld, and Klaus Mathlak, "Does Playing Violent Video Games Induce Aggression? Empirical Evidence of a Functional Magnetic Resonance Imaging Study," *Media Psychology* 8, no. 1 (2006): 39–60.

32. The survey by Nick Yee regarding addiction to games is reported http://www.cbc.ca/consumers/market/files/health/everquest/study1.pdf.

33. American Psychiatric Association, *Diagnostic and Statistical Manual of Mental Disorders*, 4th ed., text revision (Washington, DC: American Psychiatric Association, 2000).

34. Ibid.

35. Robert Kubey, "Television Addiction Is No Mere Metaphor," *Scientific American*, February 22, 2002.

36. For an excellent treatment of gender portrayals in early computer games, see Justine Cassell and Henry Jenkins, eds., *From Barbie to Mortal Kombat: Gender in Computer Games* (Cambridge, MA: MIT Press, 1998).

37. Children Now, *Fair Play: Violence, Gender, and Race in Video Games* (Oakland, CA: Children Now, 2001), http://publications.childrennow.org/assets/pdf/cmp/fairplay/fairplay-video-01.pdf.

38. Karen Dill and Kathryn Thill, "Video Game Characters and the Socialization of Gender Roles: Young People's Perceptions Mirror Sexist Media Depictions," *Sex Roles* 57, no. 11–12 (2006): 851–864.

39. Gender balance in *Second Life*, for example, is reported at the *Metaverse Journal* at http://www.metaversejournal.com/2007/03/31/the-sl-gender-balance-change-continues/.

40. Kwan Lee and Wei Peng, "What Do We Know About Social and Psychological Effects of Computer Games? A Comprehensive Review of the Current Literature," in *Playing Video Games*, eds. Peter Vodoror and Jennings Bryant (Mahwah, NJ: Lawrence Erlbaum Associates, 2006).

41. This evidence is reviewed in Lee and Peng, "What Do We Know?"

42. Edward Castronova, "The Price of 'Man' and 'Woman': A Hedonic Pricing Model of Avatar Attributes in a Synthetic World," *CESifo Working Paper Series* no. 957, Ifo Institute for Economic Research, Munich, June 2003. Available at http://ssrn.com/abstract=415043.

43. Leonard Epstein, James Roemmich, Jodie Bobinson, Rocco Paluch, Dana Winiewicz, and Janene Fuerch, "A Randomized Trial of the Effects of Reducing Television Viewing and Computer Use on Body Mass Index in Young Children," *Archives of Pediatrics and Adolescent Medicine* 162, no. 3 (2008): 239–245.

44. D. Kasteleijn-Nolst, A. da Silva, S. Ricci, C. Binnie, G. Rubboli, C. Tassinari, and J. Segers, "Video Game Epilepsy: A European Study," *Epilepsia* 40 (1999): 70–74.

45. Eugenia Kolasinski, "Simulator Sickness in Virtual Environments," technical report 1027, U.S. Army Research Institute, May 1995.

46. Deborah Lieberman, "Management of Chronic Pediatric Diseases with Interactive Health Games: Theory and Research Findings," *Journal of Ambulatory Care Management* 24, no. 1 (2001): 26–38.

47. For example, the Robert Wood Johnson Foundation has recently funded several new studies in its program on health games research.

48. L. Read, C. Carlin, I. Greenberg, and G. Blackburn, *The Original Boston Computer Diet* (Boston: Scarborough Systems, 1985).

49. For uses in chemotherapy and psychotherapy, see M. Griffiths, "The Therapeutic Use of Videogames in Childhood and Adolescents," *Clinical Child Psychology and Psychiatry* 8, no. 4 (2003): 547–554. For biofeedback training, see A. Pope and E. Bogart, "Extended Attention Span Training System: Video Game Neurotherapy for Attention Deficit Disorder," *Children Study Journal* 26, no. 1 (1996): 39–50. For the treatment of phobias, see B. Wiederhold, "The Impact of the Internet, Multimedia and Virtual Reality on Behavior and Society," *CyberPsychology and Behavior* 6, no. 3 (2003): 225–227. For memory training, see B. Drew and J. Walters, "Video Games: Utilization of a Novel Strategy to Improve Perceptual Motor Skills and Cognitive Functioning in the Non-institutionalized Elderly," *Cognitive Rehabilitation* 4 (1986): 31–36.

50. C. Green and D. Bavelier, "Action Video Game Modifies Visual Selective Attention," *Nature* 423 (2003): 534–537.

51. For examples of military games, see D. Coleman, "PC Gaming and Simulation Supports Training," *Proceedings of United States Naval Institute* 127 (2001), 73–75.

52. P. McClurg and C. Chaille, "Computer Games: Environments for Developing Spatial Cognition?" *Journal of Educational Computing Research* 3 (1987): 95–111. Also see K. Subrahmanyam and P. Greenfield, "Becoming a Better Student with Computer Games," *Journal of Communication* 42 (1987): 73–93.

53. P. Greenfield, G. Brannon, and D. Lohr, "Two-Dimensional Representation of Movement Through Three-Dimensional Space: The Role of Video Game Expertise," *Journal of Applied Developmental Psychology* 1 (1994): 87–103.

54. D. Walsh, "Interactive Violence and Children: Testimony Submitted to the Committee on Commerce, Science and Transportation, United States," March 21, 2000.

55. Brigid Barron, "Interest and Self-Sustained Learning as Catalysts of Development: A Learning Ecology Perspective," *Human Development* 49 (2006): 193–224.

56. Kurt Squire and Henry Jenkins, "Harnessing the Power of Games in Education," *Insight* 3 (2003): 7–33.

57. Steve Jones, *Let the Games Begin: Gaming Technology and Entertainment Among College Students* (Washington, DC: Pew Internet and American Life Project, 2003). Also available at http://www.pewinternet.org/pdfs/PIP_College_Gaming_Reporta.pdf.

58. For lack of relation with popularity, see A. Sakamoto, "Video Game Use and the Development of Socio-Cognitive Abilities in Children: Three Surveys of Elementary-School Students," *Journal of Applied Social Psychology* 24 (1994): 21–42. For relation with the other social aspects discussed here, see K. Durkin and B. Barber, "Not So Doomed: Computer

Game Play and Positive Adolescent Development," *Journal of Applied Developmental Psychology* 23 (2002): 373–392.

59. Reed Stevens, Tom Satwicz, and Laurie McCarthy, "In-Game, In-Room, In-World: Reconnecting Video Game Play to the Rest of Kids' Lives," in *The Ecology of Games: Connecting Youth, Games, and Learning*, ed. Katie Salen (Cambridge, MA: MIT Press, 2008).

60. Data collected by Nick Yee and reported under the rubric of the Daedalus Project (http://www.nickyee.com/daedalus).

Chapter Eleven

1. Milton Snoeyenbos, Robert Almeder, and James Humber, *Business Ethics* (Amherst, NY: Prometheus Books, 2001).

2. The report from the Congressional Office of Technology Assessment (OTA) was titled *The Electronic Supervisor: New Technology, New Tensions* (Washington, DC: U.S. Government Printing Office, 1987). A review of issues related to the report can be found in E. Kallman, "Electronic Monitoring of Employees: Issues and Guidelines," *Journal of Systems Management* 44, no. 6 (1993): 17–21.

3. The details of Walker's proposal can be found in "Webcam Homeland," *USA Today*, May 26, 2003, http://www.usatoday.com/tech/news/internetprivacy/2003-05-23-webcam-homeland_x.htm.

4. Sharon Weinberger, "TSA Screening: The Video Game," Wired Blog Network, 2007, http://blog.wired.com/defense/2007/08/tsa-screening-t.html.

5. R. Brasington, "Nintendinitis," *New England Journal of Medicine* 322 (1990): 1473–1474; J. Bonis, "Acute Wiiitis," *New England Journal of Medicine* 356 (2007): 2431–2432.

6. Office of Technology Assessment, *The Electronic Supervisor.*

7. Lawrence Archer, "I Saw What You Did and I Know Who You Are," *Canadian Business*, November 1995 cited in OTA, *The Electronic Supervisor.*

8. For a review of the relationship between stress and performance, see Anthony Gaillard, "Concentration, Stress and Performance," in *Performance Under Stress*, eds. Peter Hancock and James Szalma (Burlington, VT: Ashgate Publishing, 2008).

9. T. Egan, "Air Traffic Controllers Fight Stress and Savor It," *New York Times*, February 10, 1991.

10. Information about the twelve-step program for possible game addiction can be found at http://www.olganon.org.

Chapter Twelve

1. See the list of books at http://www.corpstory.com/amazon.htm.

2. See United States Department of Defense, "The United States Military Enlisted Rank Insignia," http://www.defenselink.mil/specials/insignias/enlisted.html.

3. Z. D. Zeldes, D. Sward, and S. Louchheim, "Infomania: Why We Can't Afford to Ignore It Any Longer," *First Monday* 12, no. 8 (2007), http://www.firstmonday.org/issues/issue12_8/zeldes/.

4. See references compiled by David Levy at http://portal.acm.org/citation.cfm?id=1065385.1065450#abstract.

5. Michael DeMarco, Eric Lesser, and Tony O'Driscoll, "Leadership in a Distributed World: Lessons from Online Gaming," IBM Institute for Business Value, 2007.

6. Raf Koster has an extensive bibliography on his personal website: http://www.raphkoster.com/gaming/links.shtml. Several reading lists from those most active in game design are available at http://terranova.blogs.com/. Especially see the section entitled "Research Report Rolodex." A new book on games and business that contains many

additional examples of how games can be used to relate to customers and to recruit and train employees is *Changing the Game*, by David Edery and Ethan Mollick (Upper Saddle River, NJ: FT Press, 2009).

7. Information about the Serious Games Initiative is available at http://www.serious-games.org/index2.html. For a comprehensive taxonomy of serious games, see a slide deck by Ben Sawyer at http://www.managementlab.org/files/LabNotes10.pdf.

Index

About the Authors

Byron Reeves is the Paul C. Edwards Professor in Stanford University's Department of Communication, and currently serves as Codirector of the Stanford H-STAR Institute (Human Sciences and Technologies Advanced Research). He is also founder and faculty director of the Stanford Media X Program that organizes research and knowledge transfer between industry and Stanford IT researchers.

An expert on the psychological processing of media in the areas of attention, emotions, and physiological responses, Byron is coauthor of *The Media Equation*. He has published over one hundred research papers and his research has been the basis for products of companies such as Microsoft, IBM, and Hewlett-Packard, in the areas of voice interfaces, automated dialogue systems, conversational agents, enterprise software, and interaction design. He is currently working on applications of multiplayer game technology to the conduct of work and is cofounder, with Leighton Read, of Seriosity, Inc.

Byron received his PhD in communication from Michigan State University, and his BFA in graphic design and journalism from Southern Methodist University. Prior to joining the faculty at Stanford in 1986, Byron was a professor at the School of Journalism and Mass Communication and Associate Director of the Mass Communication Research Center at the University of Wisconsin-Madison. He is an elected fellow of the International Communication Association and holds research and career awards from Michigan State University and the University of Wisconsin.

J. Leighton Read is a successful entrepreneur, CEO, and high-tech investor. Some of the companies he has founded or cofounded include Affymax NV, acquired by Glaxo; Aviron, the biotechnology company acquired by MedImmune that developed FluMist™; and Avidia, acquired by Amgen. He is a general partner in four funds at Alloy Ventures in Palo Alto, California.

He has a long-standing interest in the psychological principles that under-
lie successful electronic games and is Chairman of Seriosity, Inc. (www.
seriosity.com).

Leighton received a BS from Rice University in psychology and biology,
an MD from the University of Texas Health Science Center at San Antonio,
and internal medicine training at Duke and the Peter Bent Brigham Hospital,
where he held appointments at the Harvard Medical School and School
of Public Health. His publications cover decision theory in medicine, cost-
effectiveness analysis, and medical innovation policy. He produced a successful interactive PC game in 1984 to promote healthy lifestyles based on
text-based adventure games and behavior modification.

He is a frequent public speaker and serves as a director of six young companies in the fields of biotechnology, nanotechnology, cleantech, and software and serves as a trustee or director of BeneTech, BioVentures for Global
Health, The UC Berkeley Foundation and School of Public Health Council,
and the Santa Fe Institute. His awards include several as coinventor of technology underlying the Affymetrix GeneChip™ and Ernst & Young's California
Life Science Entrepreneur of the Year.